TESTIMONIALS

Lana Lamkin's story reads like a modern-day Job as her serene, idyllic life careens into sudden tragedy. Yet, even as she endures all the heartbreaking struggles and constant setbacks, Lana refuses to blame God. Her story is a touching celebration of love, perseverance, and the healing power of faith. And although only the Lord knows how her tale will finally end, one thing is for certain— All things will work together for good, and through it all, God will continue to be glorified.

— NATHAN CROCKER,
Best-Selling Author of "The Loyal Angel" series

Breathing in the Unexpected captivates you from the very beginning and you will remain that way until you finish. Through my work with the Lung Transplant Foundation, I have had the great pleasure to meet a multitude of amazing individuals who have received the gift of life through lung transplant. However, Lana's unique perspective as a fitness coach and enduring the unthinkable during COVID gives the reader a unique insight. Lana's faith throughout her health journey will challenge you to, trust in the Lord with all your heart and lean not on your own understanding (Proverbs 3:5) when you are faced with life's storms.

— NICOLE WILLS,
Double Lung Transplant Recipient

In *Breathing In The Unexpected*, Lana shows us what it looks like to trust God's sovereignty through the uncertainties of life. As her friend and pastor, I've watched Lana fight for her life. While she is an incredibly strong woman, her greatest strength is found in the depth of her relationship with God. As you will discover from her story, it's possible to trust God's heart when you can't trace His hand.

— SHANE FREEMAN,
Lead Pastor, Southbrook Church

Through Lana Lamkin's memoir, *Breathing in the Unexpected*, readers are taken on a remarkable journey of faith, resilience, and the life-saving power of organ transplantation. As Lana's transplant nurse coordinator and a witness to one of my own loved-one's transplant, I am inspired by her sheer determination. This memoir is a beautiful testament to the power of the human spirit, complete faith in God, and a strong foundation of personal wellbeing. Lana offers a valued beacon of light to the individuals and families navigating the complexities of life during and after transplant.

> — ALI PEARSON, BSN, RN, Transplant Coordinator
> Duke Tranplant Center | Lung Transplant Program

Breathing in the Unexpected is a MUST READ for anyone in the healthcare profession and for any student pursuing such a profession. On the really hard days and during the tough times, it helps for us to be reminded that our compassion and kindness to patients matter AND that God is always at work performing miracles!

> — SUSAN M SMITH, BSPh, PharmD, BCPS,
> Associate Professor of Pharmacy & Director of
> Interprofessional Education, Wingate University

What a beautifully written masterpiece! I was both heartbroken and uplifted. I laughed, and I cried. I felt disappointment and fear and hope and gratitude. I was reminded of the beauty of friendships and the gift of family. And most of all, I was INSPIRED by the faith in our Heavenly Father and unwavering dependence on him. Our God is SO faithful.

> — JENNY STONER,
> DC Coaching & Founder of Shine Teens

BREATHING IN THE UNEXPECTED

A STORY OF COURAGE, FAITH, & THE MIRACLE OF NEW LUNGS

LANA LAMKIN

ISBN:
979-8-218-23265-8
979-8-9888349-0-8
979-8-9888349-1-5

Cover Design by Sublmnl Creates

Content and Copy Edits by Lauren Sims

First edition: August 2023

To my loving husband, John.

This memoir is dedicated to you, the love of my life.
This story is a testament to our faith in the Lord, unshakeable resilience, incredible love, and extraordinary life together.

TABLE OF CONTENTS

THE FINALE

ACKNOWLEDGEMENTS

I would like to express my heartfelt gratitude to the following individuals and groups who have played an integral role in my life and the writing of this memoir:

To my beloved husband, John. Thank you for being my rock through every triumph and tribulation, providing unwavering comfort and encouragement when I needed it most. Whether tending to countless bandages, supporting me as I regained my ability to walk, or simply holding me in moments of overwhelming vulnerability, you have been my anchor. Your constant presence, fervent prayers, and enduring love have been the driving force behind my unwavering perseverance. I am forever grateful and incredibly blessed to have you by my side as my companion, confidant, and pillar of strength. Throughout this extraordinary journey, your presence has been a resounding reminder that together, we can conquer any trial that comes our way.

To my cherished family, your love and encouragement have sustained me throughout the challenges I've faced. Thank you for your steadfast support, for standing by me during the darkest moments, and celebrating every milestone. Your presence in my life has been an incredible blessing. To my sweet Mackenzie, your willingness to step in and invest your time learning to be my secondary caregiver means more to me than you could know. Your commitment to supporting me and John cannot be understated or undervalued.

To The Tribe, my soul sisters, and confidants. You have been pillars of strength in my life. I cannot imagine facing my trials without you. You have not only been there to pray for me but also to uplift me during the most challenging times and keep me laughing as I face them. Your genuine care has been a source of endless comfort and inspiration. You, my Tribe, hold a special place in my heart, for you have shown me the true meaning of friendship and the power of a united spirit.

To my dear friends, your friendship has been a constant source of joy and strength. Thank you for your consistent encouragement and for always believing in me. Your friendship has enriched my life in countless ways, and I am grateful to have you in my corner.

To my prayer warriors, thank you for your faithfulness and for lifting me in your prayers. Your spiritual support has been a source of immense comfort and strength. Your positive energy and encouragement have carried me through even the most challenging times. I am forever grateful for your love and intercessions.

To my esteemed physicians, Dr. Haney and Dr. Reynolds, and my entire dedicated medical teams at Duke Hospital and Novant Hospital, you are the heroes who saved my life and continue to do so. Your expertise, care, and commitment to my well-being have been nothing short of extraordinary. I owe my second chance at life to each one of you. And to my coordinator, Ali, your exceptional skill and compassion guide me in navigating the ever-changing life of a transplant recipient. Thank you all for your tireless efforts, compassion, and always going above and beyond to ensure my health and happiness.

To my daughter, Lauren. I want to extend my wholehearted appreciation. As my dedicated editor, your meticulous attention to detail, insightful feedback, and unwavering commitment to refining every word have elevated this book beyond my wildest expectations. Your invaluable contribution has breathed life into the pages, and I am forever grateful for your tireless efforts. Additionally, I would like to express my sincerest thanks to Justin, my son-in-law and creative designer. Your artistic vision, innovative ideas, and guidance have transformed this manuscript into a visually captivating masterpiece. You have both left an indelible mark on this work with your contributions.

To all those who have touched my life in ways big and small, who have offered a helping hand, a listening ear, or a word of encouragement, thank you. Your presence has made a profound impact on my journey, and I am grateful for all of you.

Lastly, I would like to express my gratitude to the readers of this memoir. Your support and interest in my story mean the world to me. It is my sincerest hope that my experiences can inspire, uplift, or offer solace to those who may be facing similar challenges.

With deepest appreciation,
Lana

BREATHING IN THE UNEXPECTED

PROLOGUE

It was April 20, 2020, when my life took an unexpected turn. I found myself in the hospital, a place I had only visited twice before for the deliveries of my daughters. Little did I know that this stay would be unlike anything I had ever experienced. I believed I would go home soon, but that couldn't have been further from reality. Instead of a wheelchair to the exit door as I had hoped, ten days later I traveled by gurney to the intensive care unit.

The world was in the grip of the COVID-19 pandemic, and hospitals had imposed strict visitor restrictions. Unfortunately, this meant my family couldn't be by my side during this challenging time. Surrounded by unfamiliar faces, strange smells, and unsettling sounds, I grappled with symptoms that defied reason. Despite being in the best shape of my life, I was struggling to breathe and losing muscle mass faster than I thought possible.

In my desperation, I pleaded with God to restore the healthy body I had known just weeks earlier. Instead, He answered my pleas with a promise that left me wondering what lay ahead, "No matter what happens, We are with you."

Shortly after arriving in the ICU on April 30, the attending physician entered my room and bluntly announced that I needed to be on a ventilator and that there was no time for discussion. However, I was granted a brief phone call to my husband, John.

Our conversation was quick and to the point. I blurted out the few words I could find, "I'm terrified. I don't want to do this."

"I know, baby, but you have to. It's the only option you have. I love you so much."

Through tears, I choked out my response, "I love you, too."

This conversation would be the last I'd have with my husband for several weeks.

I had been on the ventilator for only a few hours when the doctor encouraged John to call the family, gather our children, and prepare for the worst.

"Our concern is that she might not make it through the night."

As morning broke, relief washed over my family and friends when they learned I had defied the odds and was still clinging to life. I remained in critical condition, but I'm a fighter. Twelve days later, I was life-flighted to a renowned hospital, where I would receive the best care available and ultimately receive the gift of life from an organ donor in the form of two lungs.

Having accepted Jesus as my Savior at the age of fourteen, I had experienced His guiding presence throughout my Christian journey. His voice was one I easily recognized. And although I knew His familiar voice, I didn't completely understand what He meant by the reassuring words that He shared with me in the CT scan until months later. However, when I found myself in an unfamiliar hospital with a feeding tube in my nose, a tracheostomy in my neck, various tubes in my torso, and seventy-two staples across my chest, it began to sink in.

"No matter what happens, We are with you."

Throughout this grueling journey, His presence was undeniable. In the midst of the storm, I couldn't help but recognize Him, not only in Spirit but also in the faces of those around me. He had intricately woven together the people and circumstances of my life, preparing me for a battle unlike any other.

God had led me to develop a deep passion for fitness, unknowingly equipping my body to withstand the demands of a sudden double-lung transplant. The knowledge and education He had allowed me to acquire had instilled in me a zealous desire to maintain optimal health. The athletic drive He nurtured within me provided the determination to persevere as my body recovered from the devastation caused by autoimmune diseases that had ravaged my lungs and muscles.

By His grace, health and fitness ultimately saved my life. I am compelled to share my story to inspire others, to show them that they, too, can conquer seemingly insurmountable challenges if they hold onto faith and refuse to surrender hope.

Now, let me bring you up to speed on the unexpected turn my life took in 2020 and how it changed me forever.

PART I

THE FALL

CHAPTER ONE

BEGINNINGS

My name is Lana Lamkin. At age 50, while in a coma and on life support, I was diagnosed with dermatomyositis, a rare autoimmune disease characterized by muscle weakness primarily in the skeletal muscles, and the presence of a skin rash. But that wasn't all. I was also diagnosed with an extremely rare antisynthetase syndrome (anti-PL7), which specifically attacks the lungs. The estimated incidence of dermatomyositis is 9.63 cases per million people. And as close as my husband, John, and I can predict, of those 9.63 cases, as few as 5% of myositis patients are also diagnosed with anti-PL7. So, I guess you could say I'm as rare as a unicorn.

I don't know how long I've had these diseases. But, looking back, I now recognize that their symptoms had manifested throughout my life–fatigued muscles, minor joint pain, inflammation, and recurring rashes. However, since these symptoms never became significant issues and didn't persist for long, I didn't give them much thought. But in January 2020, myositis and anti-PL7 began to rear their ugly heads, and they were monsters!

It all began in mid-January with what I called "the crud." It was merely a dry cough, and I didn't feel sick at all–no sniffles, no fever, just a cough. But in February, I started feeling an unusual level of fatigue. By March, my body felt weak and overworked. Despite it all, I continued my daily routine, which included running our business, Snap Fitness Waxhaw. That is until I landed in the hospital in April.

Before we delve deeper into my story, let me take you back to how I became a gym owner and how it played a significant role in my health crisis.

If someone had told me six years earlier that I would own a gym, I would have laughed and said, "Not a chance because I don't like to sweat." But truth be told, I knew I was far from being at the physical fitness level I should be.

However, in March 2014, John had major shoulder surgery. His physical therapy included both total immobilization and movement, which was not a simple task. He wasn't allowed to move his arm alone; he had to rely on his physical therapist and me to keep his shoulder mobile. John and I spent between three to four hours each day doing his assigned exercises. It wasn't until then that I realized how heavy a human arm could feel.

During his recovery, John and I came to a mutual realization—we had both allowed our bodies to decline over the years. His desk job required hours of sitting, while I, no longer having an office job, had neglected prioritizing physical activity.

John and I were both athletes in our younger years. John played several sports, including basketball and football, where he was an outstanding placekicker. But baseball was his true passion. He began playing on a little league team and continued through American Legion. His team won back-to-back state championships, and as a result, he was inducted into his hometown Sports Hall of Fame.

As for me, in middle school, I made the track team as a sprinter and even secured a position on the basketball team. But unfortunately, I spent most of my basketball career on the bench. Honestly, I still don't know why the coach allowed me on the team, given my lack of basketball skills. Despite my nearly nonexistent talent in basketball, I discovered I made a pretty good cheerleader from the sidelines. So, in addition to continuing track, I added football and basketball cheerleading to my high school years.

After high school, I landed a job as a gate agent with American Eagle Airlines, which involved a significant amount of walking, which kept me physically active. But the airline industry depleted me emotionally. I spent eighteen months there before the stress from being on the receiving end of passengers' "trips gone wrong" was more than I could handle. Finally, after an evening laced with death threats from a group of drunk golfers who missed their flight to their beautiful beach destination, I determined I was better suited for office work. So, I transitioned to the agency side of travel and sat down at a desk for the long haul. Eighteen years as a travel agent passed, along with my desire to stay active.

Even after John and I agreed that I would quit my job to plan our wedding in 2006, I struggled to tap into the athlete within me. With two young daughters, Mackenzie (9) and Lauren (6), from my previous marriage, I wanted to devote all my time to them and John, making it difficult to consider adding a fitness routine to my already busy schedule.

Now, you may be curious how John and I met. Well, it's quite an interesting story, one that seemed to be orchestrated by God.

It was Valentine's Day, February 14, 2005. I was still working at a travel agency on the operations team when Wendy, one of our on-site agents, needed a new printer installed in her office. Though I didn't always tag along with the IT guy on installations, I volunteered to lend a hand this time because her office was near my home in Charlotte.

Wendy and I had known each other for several years, and she was well aware of my recent separation. She also knew about her single co-worker, John.

When I say "recent separation," I mean it had been three weeks since my struggling marriage finally crumbled. My two little girls were still trying to process their parents' inability to stay together. Needless to say, I wasn't looking for a date. And I was certainly not interested in another relationship. My life was a bit of a mess, and I was an emotional wreck. However, Wendy was undeterred in her divine mission to play Cupid.

She set up a scenario where John would "accidentally" bump into me while I was in her office. It didn't cross my mind that Wendy was trying to matchmake. I was too overwhelmed to think clearly. After all, it had only been three weeks! Although John was charming, funny, and handsome, those qualities appeared hazy through the fog in my mind.

After successfully installing the printer, I wrapped up my time in Wendy's office and returned to my home office. It was around 4:00 pm when my phone rang.

"Hello, this is Lana. How may I help you?" I answered.

"Hey, girl. Thanks for setting up my new printer today," Wendy's voice came through the line.

"Sure. It was nice hanging out with you for a while," I replied.

Then, with as much subtlety as she could muster, Wendy revealed her true motive for calling. "So, I talked to John after you left. He was wondering if he were to call you and ask you to go for a motorcycle ride, would you be interested?"

"What? Are you kidding? Wendy, you know where I am right now," I exclaimed.

"I do, but he's a great guy. It would just be a short ride. No commitment. Come on; you deserve to have a little fun. It would be good for you," she persisted.

I could almost envision the mischievous grin on her face as I contemplated her words. It had been ages since I had done something enjoyable. Maybe a motorcycle ride would be a good break for me.

Taking a deep breath, I replied, "Okay. If he calls, I'll go."

"Great! I'll give him your number."

Barely five minutes passed before my phone rang again. I looked down to see the number of the incoming call. It wasn't one I recognized. Could it be?

"Hi, this is John; we met earlier today. Wendy gave me your number. I hope you don't mind me calling," he said.

And with that phone call, our relationship began. We made plans for a motorcycle ride and lunch the following weekend.

When Saturday morning arrived, the weather was chilly–too cold for a motorcycle ride, in my opinion. But I was determined not to back out.

Nervous and excited, I rummaged through my closet, trying to decide what to wear. I didn't have suitable attire for a motorcycle ride in 50-degree weather. What was I even doing? And what if I ended up liking him? What then?

Luckily, Wendy had leathers she offered me to borrow, so we decided to meet at her house. As I heard the sound of John's pearl-white Harley Davidson approaching, I tried to steady my racing heart. He pulled into Wendy's driveway, and we said our hellos before strapping on our helmets and hopping on his bike, setting off on our first date.

During a relaxed lunch, our conversation flowed effortlessly. John made me feel comfortable and secure, even though I had just met him. There was something different about him. However, I couldn't let my guard down. I hadn't yet told him about my current, shall we call it, situation.

"Do you have kids?" he asked.

"Yes, I have two girls. Mackenzie is nine, and Lauren is six. How about you?" I noticed a hint of concern in his eyes, but we continued our conversation.

"I have two girls, as well. They're both grown. Ali is 23. Jessica is 20." Then came the inevitable question. "Wendy told me you're separated. How long ago was that?"

The moment had come for me to drop the bombshell. I knew it would catch him off guard, and I wasn't sure I was ready to say it aloud.

After a brief pause, I glanced away slightly and uttered, "Three weeks ago."

"Oh," he responded.

"I know. It was a tough marriage. It probably wouldn't have lasted as long as it did if it weren't for the girls."

I assumed this revelation would send him running, but it didn't. Instead, as our bitterly cold date came to an end, we both felt a heavenly spark that neither of us could explain. We knew it wouldn't be long before we saw each other again.

John later confirmed that the hint of concern I thought I saw in his eyes on that first date was genuine. He had made a promise to himself not to enter a relationship with someone who had young children. He had raised his kids and was determined not to do it again. But as our relationship progressed, so did his relationship with my girls. He grew to love all three of us, and we loved him in return.

Fast forward nine years later, we found ourselves lacking the ability to do basic exercises. As John's shoulder healed, we made a pact to regain our fitness as soon as he was able. And that's precisely what we did.

We started by taking walks around our neighborhood. Eventually, we incorporated some jogging into my walks. Gradually, we increased the distance we jogged until we found myself running more than walking.

During this time, I made two significant discoveries. Firstly, I realized I hadn't stopped enjoying physical activity; I merely stopped doing it. Secondly, I still despised running long distances. I'm definitely more of a sprinter. I preferred short bursts of intense effort. So, due to my lack of enthusiasm for running farther than a few yards, I decided to leave 5Ks and marathons to those who actually enjoyed them.

Once I acknowledged that long-distance running wasn't my forte, I set out to find an exercise regimen that I genuinely enjoyed and could commit to long-term. That's when I stumbled upon shorter, high-intensity workouts and quickly fell in love. Weightlifting, burpees, push-ups, and jumping became part of my daily routine. After years of searching, I had finally discovered my passion, and high-intensity interval training became my signature workout style.

As the Lord grew my enthusiasm for exercise, I began sharing with others about how great it was to be fit again. It felt like the natural progression to become a personal trainer. I was on fire, eager to teach others how to improve their well-being and relish the journey.

In April 2016, I earned my personal training certification, then I completed my health coach certification in 2017, and became a nutrition coach and corrective exercise specialist along the way. These achievements paved the way for what was to come–buying our own gym, a culmination of my passion and dedication to helping others achieve their fitness goals.

CHAPTER TWO

THE TRIBE

In the summer of 2017, John and I became the proud owners of a gym nestled in a small town just twenty minutes south of Charlotte, NC. It was a place called Snap Fitness Waxhaw, where I devoted myself to the day-to-day operations, serving as a personal trainer and nutrition coach. This gym quickly became my sanctuary, my second home—a space where I felt not only welcomed and needed but genuinely loved.

Surrounded by like-minded individuals who shared my passion for fitness, I was blessed with the opportunity to pour my heart into them. I invested every ounce of effort in crafting an atmosphere that I believed fostered incredible workouts, new connections, and a sense of camaraderie. Through the small group classes I led, I discovered the beauty of building friendships. Some of these connections have naturally faded as life took us on different paths, as often happens, while others have blossomed into lifelong bonds.

Within the walls of this humble gym, something truly remarkable happened—God brought together my tribe, affectionately known as The Tribe. These extraordinary women have become my closest confidantes, my pillars of support. I cannot fathom my life without their unwavering presence.

The Tribe initially started as an advanced workout group designed for those courageous souls who weren't afraid to push their limits, break a sweat

(I can honestly say I enjoy a good sweat sesh now), and take on a challenge. As you can imagine, convincing people to join took a bit of coaxing. Some tried it and chose to move on, but eventually, I found four women willing to do these crazy, intense workouts with me.

The first courageous soul to embrace the challenge wholeheartedly was Donna, our beloved Go-Getter and a constant source of comic relief.

Donna's a five-foot-tall, blonde Italian spitfire with a heart of gold. She is a dedicated wife and a mother of two children. When we met, both her son and daughter were in high school, so I shouldn't call them children. But in fairness, they're still kids to us.

To begin, Donna signed up for a few personal training sessions. She put in the effort, but it was evident that the experience didn't exactly ignite her passion. And she didn't shy away from letting me know. That's what I truly admire about her—she fearlessly speaks her mind, always conveying her thoughts with genuine honesty and heartfelt sincerity.

It became a familiar refrain to hear Donna exclaim, "I hate this! I hate this place. See you tomorrow!" Yet, what made it all the more endearing was that she never failed to pair those words with a warm wave and a playful smile.

That's Donna for you—honest, straightforward, kind, funny, and beneath that no-nonsense exterior, incredibly compassionate.

Donna worked alongside me for a considerable period until, out of the blue, she abruptly stopped coming to the gym. I can't say I was entirely surprised when it happened. It's a common pattern to witness people commit wholeheartedly for a short period, pouring their everything into their workouts, only to eventually lose motivation. I understand—working out is hard, and it can be disheartening until you find the approach you enjoy and yields the results you've been seeking.

And then, to my surprise, Donna made her triumphant return. She looked fantastic, clearly having achieved her weight loss goals.

Seizing the opportunity, I hopped onto the treadmill next to her and struck up a conversation. "I'm thrilled to see you back, and you look incredible. What did you do?"

With a mischievous grin, Donna exclaimed, "I got shingles!"

"Oh my! That's not what I expected to hear."

After some shameless begging on my part, I finally managed to convince Donna to give the Tribe classes a try. It turned out to be a perfect fit for her, and she quickly became hooked. In every group training session, she showed up with unwavering determination, ready to give her all until the very end.

Pointing a finger directly at me, she playfully threatened, "There better not be any cardio." Deep down, though, she knew all too well that there would indeed be plenty of cardio involved.

Donna enjoyed the Tribe workouts so much that she took it upon herself to recruit others. She enthusiastically spoke to fellow gym members and even brought along friends who were not yet part of our gym community.

And that's when I was introduced to Dawn, The Conversationalist.

Dawn grew up in California. Armed with a Master's degree in Journalism and a flourishing career as a freelance writer, she keeps us on our toes with her whirlwind of activities. I remember texting with her once, and somewhere within our quick conversation, she casually mentioned she was in Germany. Oh, the stories this woman shares. There's no wonder she chose journalism as her career.

While Dawn is an avid runner, she had a particular desire to tone and sculpt her arms when we first crossed paths. As luck would have it, she and Donna were acquainted through their sons attending the same school. Observing Donna's noticeable increase in muscle mass, Dawn became intrigued and accepted Donna's invitation to join a few classes. Seeking to achieve her own muscle-building goals, she soon became a regular in our sessions.

Dawn's presence brought an incredible dynamic to our group. She's endlessly talkative and entertaining, always ready to engage in a lively conversation. Now, I do enjoy a good chat, but I must admit that it occasionally posed a challenge for me to stay focused. Nonetheless, we all relished hearing about her thrilling life adventures, all while trying to keep her on track with our exercises.

The circuit work, in particular, provided moments of amusement. As the others dutifully moved from one designated station to another, Dawn would often meander towards whichever station piqued her interest at the time.

"Dawn, what are you doing over there?" we'd inquire with a hint of laughter in our voices.

"Oh dear, is this not the right one? I honestly have no clue," she'd respond, promptly followed by an infectious giggle.

Rosy would kindly redirect her to the correct station, and we'd resume our workout from where we left off, all the while cherishing the joy that Dawn's unpredictable antics brought to our workout.

Let me introduce you to our sweet Rosy, The Encourager.

In Rosy's presence, it's nearly impossible to stay downcast. She possesses an innate ability to uplift spirits with her words of wisdom and support. But that's not all—she's also incredibly courageous.

Rosy's love story began at a wedding in her hometown of Monterrey, Mexico when she met her husband. In her thirties, with limited knowledge of the English language and knowing nobody outside her own country, she took a leap of faith and tied the knot, embarking on a new life in the United States.

Rosy was a member at Snap Fitness before I began working there. Upon receiving an email offering a complimentary fitness assessment, she seized the opportunity to learn more about the gym equipment and booked a session with me. Subsequently, her husband purchased a personal training package for her. As our training sessions progressed, I introduced Rosy to the concept of our Tribe group. Although initially hesitant, she eventually agreed to give it a shot.

She tells us that joining the group intimidated her at first, doubting her own capabilities. However, the truth is that Rosy possesses remarkable strength and unwavering determination. Nothing can stand in her way.

When it comes to workouts, Rosy is the voice of reason. She encouraged us to push ourselves but also emphasized the importance of setting realistic expectations and finding enjoyment in the process. That's how she approaches life as well. Beneath her cheerful demeanor, she's a master motivator, often without uttering a single word. Like a stealthy force, when the rest of us would be on the verge of giving up, Rosy would keep going, silently leading by example. So naturally, we found ourselves following suit.

Diana, in particular, frequently remarked on Rosy's unwavering determination and uncanny ability to inspire others.

Let's talk about Diana, The Fighter.

The day Diana walked through the gym doors, I was sitting at the front desk. It was evident that she felt a bit uneasy. With her head wrapped in a turban and her gaze fixated on her favorite treadmill tucked away beside the leg press machine, she sought solace in a safe corner, away from prying eyes.

It didn't take long for us to strike up a conversation. This radiant young Asian woman, whose smile could light up the world, shared with me that she had recently completed her breast cancer treatment. My heart sank, but I could sense her fighting spirit and knew she had come to the right place to continue her battle. With a husband and two young boys awaiting her at home, she longed to rediscover her health and fitness.

As Diana stuck to her regular treadmill routine, she couldn't help but notice a group of women working out together, their camaraderie evident in the mirror before her. Assuming they were close friends due to their easy banter and shared lives, Diana desperately wanted to regain her strength and confidence and become part of this workout group. So, she turned to Tammy, one of our staff members, to inquire about this intriguing group. Tammy, well aware of Diana's keen observation, directed her to me to join The Tribe.

Diana seamlessly integrated herself into the group and swiftly proved in our Wednesday boxing classes that she hadn't lost as much strength as she had thought. I must admit, standing behind the mitts waiting for her punches was a tad intimidating. She strikes with speed and power, demonstrating her unwavering determination with each blow. I'm not entirely sure why either of us would find ourselves in a situation where a random brawl might break out, but I often joked with her that she's the person I'd want by my side if such a fight should happen.

The five of us formed a tightly knit crew, meeting every Monday through Thursday at 10:00 am. I looked forward to our time together each day. The Tribe had evolved into something far beyond my initial expectations. Of course, I aimed to assist these remarkable women in discovering their healthiest selves. But little did I know, they would end up helping me far more than I could ever repay. Their prayers, unwavering encouragement, and support, coupled with my family's steadfast love, would become the very backbone of my survival.

Now that you've met The Tribe, you most likely understand that these women get me. They know my strengths, my weaknesses, and my hurts and hang-ups. They love me deeply and aren't afraid to call me out when I'm not handling things to the best of my ability. I must admit, though, that it's not always easy for me to listen when I should.

Shortly after I had "the crud" in January, Donna pointed out that something seemed off several times in the weeks that followed. During our workouts, my heart rate was increasing faster than it typically did, pushing me to my anaerobic peak sooner and causing me to need more frequent rests.

In a nudging tone, Donna asked, "What's up with you? Are you sure you're okay?"

"I'm fine. I think I'm just overtraining and need some rest," I replied.

"Please don't ignore it. You should stop doing the workouts with your other groups and just guide them through the exercises. Give your body a break."

Rosy chimed in, saying, "Yes. We don't want anything bad to happen to you."

"I'll take a break as soon as I can. But I'm fine. I promise."

"Really? You've had to decrease the amount of weight you're lifting too. That's not typical for you," Donna urged me to pay attention.

"Listen to your body," Dawn added.

Diana spoke up as well, saying, "Please take care of yourself."

I assured them again, "I won't let it get out of hand. If things worsen, I'll get some rest and go to the doctor."

Regrettably, I didn't heed the advice of my dear friends. Instead, I continued to push my body to its limits. After all, if it doesn't challenge you, it doesn't change you, right? That turned out to be the worst kind of encouragement I could have given myself. I know that now, yet, strangely enough, I still struggle to silence my inner competitor and remember that sometimes everything is not fine.

CHAPTER THREE

EVERYTHING'S FINE

Mid-westerners are tough. They have a knack for keeping emotions close to their chest and a tendency to perceive everything as "fine." Perhaps it's their way of sparing themselves and those around them from unnecessary worry; I can't say for sure. But when you ask about their well-being or the weather, their customary response is a simple "Fine." That was certainly the case with my family.

I grew up in Southern Illinois in the 1970s and 80s, a stone's throw away from the small town of Vandalia. Three country miles are a lot different than three within a city. This short distance takes you away from buildings and businesses, leading you straight into the vast farmlands.

Our house stood unintrusively on fourteen acres of land. A one-lane oiled road separated us from a sprawling field that extended as far as the eye could see. To the north, another. Depending on the year, those fields would come alive with the vibrant hues from corn, wheat, or soybeans, painting the landscape with nature's ever-changing palette. The closest neighbors were a quarter mile to the south, residing just beyond our modest pasture.

It was a peaceful place to grow up. As the evening descended, the chorus of frogs and the calls of whip-poor-wills would serenade us from a distance. The moon and stars would cast their ethereal glow upon the open space surrounding us, their radiance only slightly dimmed by the gentle hum of a pole light illuminating our backyard.

Our home was cozy and filled with love. I shared a small bedroom with my older sister, Cindy, and we shared the home's only bathroom with our parents. Like many others in our area, we didn't have the luxury of air conditioning. Instead, we relied on an attic fan to draw in and circulate fresh air during the hot summer months. Countless nights were spent lying in our beds, each of us leaning close to our respective window, longing for a cooler breeze to sweep through.

Our mother, Lualice (affectionately known as Lu), held the position of head cook in one of Vandalia's three grade schools. Her job was perfect for our family. It allowed her to be with us during the summer months, school breaks, and teacher workdays. She was always waiting for us when the school bus dropped us off, and her loving presence remained constant during those blissful school-free days.

Even in the heart of our predominantly farming community, our father, John, devoted three decades to the grader line at the Caterpillar plant. Dad was a man of few words, so the intricacies of his work remained a bit elusive. All I can tell you is that he played a role in "putting together graders." The Caterpillar plant was located about 45 minutes away, which meant Dad relied on a daily carpool with a group of fellow workers. He left our house sharply at 5:00 am, meeting the van in a parking lot across from the high school. And like clockwork, at 5:10 pm, he would step back through our front door. Mom awaited his return, a warm meal prepared and on the table. He'd offer her a gentle peck on the cheek, hang his cap on the back of his chair, and settle down to savor his dinner.

Without fail, every weekend, we would visit my grandparents. But it wasn't just our grandparents we would see during those cherished moments. Our aunts, uncles, and cousins were all there, too. We played, went fishing, climbed the bales of hay in the barns, indulged in bags of penny candy from the corner country store, and shared meals with our loved ones.

If you'll indulge me for a brief detour, my cousin Lisa has persistently reminded me to include her in this book. I couldn't bear the thought of her living a lifetime of profound disappointment, so this special shout-out is dedicated to her. Love you, cuz!

Thank you for joining us in this momentary aside. Now, let's return to the story at hand.

As you can see, I had a wonderful childhood. But emotions weren't something we often discussed, and as I observed those around me, I grew up assuming it was best to tuck them away and adopt the "I'm fine" attitude.

That attitude got me through many trials and tribulations over the years. However, it proved less helpful when my body began exhibiting more symptoms at the onset of my illness.

As February came and went, I continued to over-exert myself. Engrossed in training and assisting other women on their health and fitness journeys, I, like many coaches, ignored the subtle messages my body was desperately trying to convey. It was engaged in a silent battle with itself, pleading for my attention.

"I sure am cleaning up a lot of hair in here. Do you think your hair is getting thinner?" John had already noticed my thinning hair, and one morning as I got ready for work, he nudged me to acknowledge the change.

While I had indeed noticed an increased amount of hair in the shower drain and on the bathroom floor, I attributed it to my hair's length. "No, I don't think I'm losing more hair than before. It has always fallen out like this, but it's more noticeable now that it's longer. I'm fine," I reassured him.

Similar conversations with John and numerous discussions with The Tribe took place over the following weeks. Still, I stubbornly brushed aside their concerns, chalking everything up to excessive training.

Little did I realize that the cough, accelerated heart rate, hair loss, and weakened muscles were all symptoms of something more significant brewing within me. However, I refused to entertain the notion that it could be anything beyond the effects of overtraining. Besides, I was confident that I would be just fine.

CHAPTER FOUR

ALL MY SYMPTOMS

By March 25, 2020, COVID-19 had become a worldwide pandemic, leading to a government mandate to shut down all non-essential businesses, including our gym. I can honestly say I wasn't entirely disappointed by this. Initially, everyone anticipated a temporary closure lasting just a few weeks. I couldn't help but feel a sense of relief, knowing I would finally have some time to rest and recuperate. Determined to adapt, I created a plan to continue training my clients virtually, offering online small-group sessions and personal training. In between these sessions, I made it a priority to recharge while eagerly awaiting the day we would receive the green light to reopen.

It didn't take long to get in the groove of virtual training. Granted, it wasn't the same as being physically present with my clients, but it allowed me to step out of the frame when I struggled to find my breath, which seemed to be happening more frequently.

In April, it became undeniable that what I was experiencing was more than overtraining, and it was clear that I was not "fine." On April 2, my ankles started to swell, and an unexpected rash appeared on my arms. The following day, the rash spread to my legs, and my knees became noticeably swollen. The swelling made it difficult for me to walk very far, but John and I managed to take short neighborhood walks to keep me moderately active.

Since John had previously undergone shoulder surgery, we had an ice machine at home, and I decided to give it a try on my knees. Unfortunately, despite my efforts, the swelling persisted, and the ice had only minimal effects. Amazingly, the inflammation caused my weight to increase by four pounds in four days. It was then that I came to terms with the fact that it was time to call the doctor.

John and I explained everything that had happened since January to our family physician, Dr. Missick, on April 6. He promptly ordered a comprehensive blood panel, which included tests for rheumatoid arthritis, and prescribed a six-day course of prednisone. Reflecting on our conversation, I now realize that I downplayed the severity of my condition. Once again, my tough "I'm fine" exterior wouldn't allow me to admit the seriousness of my situation.

I saw the effects the steroids had on my body, and although I still couldn't bend my knees past 90 degrees, I noticed a slight improvement and found myself able to move a bit more freely.

Encouraged by this progress, I decided to do a light workout on the day following my initial dose of prednisone. But after that workout, I experienced swelling and discomfort in my hands, wrists, shoulders, and right elbow.

On April 9, I woke up with a pounding headache after a restless night of sleep. Unfortunately, the following day greeted me with another headache accompanied by a wave of nausea. Despite that, I managed to take my medication and some Tylenol and went for a long walk. Then the swelling improved significantly early that afternoon, and I could bend my knees fully again. Suddenly, I was confident I was on the mend.

Later, Dr. Missick contacted me with the test results. The labs looked good overall, but my iron was a little low. So he recommended incorporating an iron supplement into my regimen. While the test results for rheumatoid arthritis were negative, the antinuclear antibodies (ANA) and ribonucleoproteins (RNP) results indicated a slight elevation, suggesting potential markers of an autoimmune disease. Recognizing the need for deeper investigation, Dr. Missick offered a referral.

"I'd like to refer you to a rheumatologist. They'll do more research into the possible causes of all your symptoms. Keep in mind, they may take a little longer than usual to contact you due to the Covid restraints, but I'm hopeful it won't take too long."

"Okay. I'll wait for the call," I responded, relieved to learn that rheumatoid arthritis had been ruled out. It hadn't occurred to me at that point that there could be something more concerning lurking within me.

April 11 was my last day on prednisone. My shoulders, wrists, and hands remained stiff, and my body ached from head to toe. To make matters worse, my appetite vanished, and finding a comfortable position seemed impossible. On top of it all, I developed a low-grade fever that further added to my misery.

Despite exhaustion, I dragged myself out of bed a few hours later to prepare for Easter brunch. As with all gatherings during the quarantine, our family met virtually. Although John and I have a relatively large family, this virtual call included only my two girls, John's two daughters, their husbands, and our granddaughter.

Mackenzie and Lauren have both grown up now. Mackenzie graduated from the University of North Carolina Wilmington in 2018 and has a job in Charlotte. She bought a townhouse just ten minutes from John and me and went on to complete her Master of Science degree in instructional technology at UNCW. Lauren graduated from North Carolina State University in 2020 and temporarily moved in with her dad five minutes from us. She then decided to continue her education at Appalachian State University in Boone, NC. She will complete her Master of Science in speech-language pathology at the end of 2023. She will also marry her fiancé, Matt, around the same time.

As for John's girls, Ali is a highly respected high-school teacher, adored by her students. Her husband, Dillon, is an engineer for a company that specializes in advanced finishing machinery. Jessica spent several years working as a director for Make-A-Wish in Charlotte while also using her remarkable talent as a singer on the weekends. She then made a career change and now thrives in the high-end real estate arena. Jessica's husband, Justin, is a successful entrepreneur, runs his own graphic design company, and has invested as a partner in a local brewery.

Ali and Dillon's daughter, Inara, is our only grandchild to date. She's twelve years old and very witty. She gives her love away freely and is always making us laugh.

When she was around five or six, she and her parents prepared to leave our house. She was buckled in the back seat in her booster, ready for the ride home. As Dillon put the car in drive, Inara's window came down. She placed two fingers on her cheeks just below her eyes and quickly pointed them straight at me. Then, in a mysterious little voice, she boldly stated, "I'm watching you like a two-headed monkey."

Her window went up, and their car drove away, leaving G-pa and me laughing in the driveway. It was as if she had planned the whole thing, perfectly timing her theatrical role.

Spending quality time with our family is undeniably one of my favorite things in life. But whatever this illness was, it was taking a toll. While I ached all over, I fought the urge to end our brunch short. My shoulders, wrists, and hands were stiff, and I still had a low-grade fever. Discomfort and a low appetite remained. I went directly to the couch when brunch was complete, and I stayed there for the rest of the day, tossing and turning, exhausted through and through.

To my relief, the next day, the swelling in my knees and ankles subsided, and there was a noticeable easing of stiffness in my shoulders, wrists, and hands. Although I was still stiff, the pain had diminished. My appetite returned for a short time, and my fever even broke for a few hours.

Could I be on the mend? Was I really going to be fine, like I hoped?

Unfortunately, not yet. My fever made an unwelcome return around 3:00 pm.

On Tuesday, April 14, my weight was back to normal, but my hands and wrists were swollen and painful again, and I continued to have a fever, but that wasn't all. In addition to the symptoms, I developed a dry cough and was finding it challenging to take deep breaths. Nevertheless, I somehow managed to push through a short cardio workout.

I contacted Dr. Missick the following day to discuss my new symptoms and explain that the swelling was back in my feet and ankles. But once again, I gave little weight to how I felt overall. He prescribed another round of steroid treatments.

By the afternoon, my body had hit a wall. I landed on the couch at 1:30 pm and lay there until 7:00 pm. Every movement triggered bouts of coughing, and I struggled to catch my breath. While I started feeling slightly better after taking a dose of steroids, having a shower, hydrating, and eating, the challenge of breathing persisted. The possibility of COVID-19 was becoming an increasingly pressing concern.

Thursday, April 16, was a day of ups and downs. Despite desperately needing rest, any sleep I managed to find was fleeting at best. The swelling seemed to improve slightly, yet my joints were still somewhat achy. The frequency of my coughing episodes diminished, and I could take deeper breaths, which gave me some relief.

However, as evening came, the familiar pattern returned. I've never understood why my symptoms seem to worsen at night. My fever had resurfaced, and every movement triggered a fit of coughing. The only reprieve I could find was by remaining absolutely still. So I rested quietly, being as motionless as possible.

The following three days were not unlike the previous. My fever came and went with the help of acetaminophen, and coughing episodes continued. To accommodate my shortness of breath, John thoughtfully placed a chair in the shower as standing for any duration became increasingly challenging. The swelling in my hands and wrists showed no signs of waning, plus the severe headache returned. Every day, breathing became harder and harder, leaving me increasingly concerned about what was unfolding.

I was miserable and growing very tired of all of this. Something had to give! But it didn't, and little did I know, this was just the beginning.

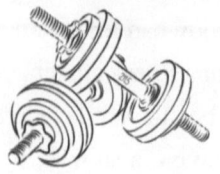

CHAPTER FIVE

I CAN'T BREATHE

Monday, April 20, is a day I'll never forget. I woke up with an intense headache and severe shortness of breath. I could not walk from our couch to the bathroom without resting in the kitchen, which was the halfway point. Our home is a nice size, but we don't live in a mansion. It's really not that far from the living room to the bathroom.

While sitting on a stool at our kitchen island, trying to catch my breath, John expressed his concern in a kind yet assertive manner, "I want you to call Dr. Missick and tell him the truth. Stop trying to be a superhero. You have to stop downplaying this. I think it's time for you to be tested for Covid and to find out what's going on."

"You're probably right. I'll call this afternoon if things don't improve."

"I want you to call now. And if you don't, I will."

"John, I don't think it's Covid. What will they do if it's not? Give me more steroids and send me home? They can do that over the phone."

"At least you'll be sure it's not Covid; then we can stop assuming. You need to talk to Dr. Missick."

Allow me to explain why we were considering COVID-19 as a possibility. COVID-19 was a new virus, and no one knew how each individual would be affected. The prominent symptoms of COVID-19 included:

- Fever and cough
- Shortness of breath
- Fatigue
- Muscle and body aches
- Headache
- Sore throat
- Congestion and runny nose
- Nausea and vomiting

I had been experiencing several of these symptoms, and we had to take them into account.

Furthermore, this virus was very aggressive; I most certainly needed treatment if I had it. This was why John wouldn't allow me to minimize my condition any longer.

A few sentences into my conversation with Dr. Missick, John interjected, "Dr. Missick, I don't think you understand Lana's actual condition. She's pretty good at making things seem better than they really are. She can't walk across the room because she can't breathe. It's time to do something else."

The sudden concern in Dr. Missick's voice was evident through the speaker on my phone. "There's a drive-up respiratory clinic in Matthews. I know the doctor on staff there. I'll call over to let him know you're coming. Someone will meet you at your car when you arrive."

"Thank you. We'll head that way. It will take us between twenty to thirty minutes to get there," John said as he grabbed his car key.

We said goodbye to Dr. Missick and set off to the respiratory clinic.

John and I arrived at the respiratory clinic around 10:30 am. The clinic was set up in a small medical office, and we spotted the nurses waiting outside, ready to assist patients who arrived in their cars. A nurse met us at our car in the drive-through lane, and John explained that Dr. Missick had called ahead and the doctor on staff should be expecting us. The nurse quickly listened to my lungs from her position outside the passenger window. She then directed us to pull into a parking spot close to the building while she went in to get the physician.

Within minutes, the nurse returned accompanied by a doctor. Extending his stethoscope through the car window, he carefully listened to my lungs.

"I'd like for you to come inside with me. We'll get a wheelchair for you," the doctor stated. As the strong, stubborn woman I am, I replied, "No need for a wheelchair. I can walk."

"Are you certain?"

"Of course," I casually said.

As we stepped through the clinic's doors, it was evident that bringing patients inside the building was not the usual protocol during this stage of the pandemic. All eyes were on me. And although I couldn't see the expressions of concern behind their masked-covered faces, I'm sure the entire medical staff knew something was more serious than I even realized.

The doctor guided me into an examination room, which resembled any other typical medical office. I used the pull-out step and scooted onto the exam table covered with disposable paper. The doctor proceeded to check my vital signs and posed several questions about my symptoms. Then, he attached a small monitor to the tip of my finger to measure my oxygen (O_2) saturation. When he looked at the reading, he seemed very surprised. After a brief moment, he excused himself and returned with another physician.

Without hesitation, the doctor explained the situation. "Mrs. Lamkin, your oxygen saturation level is at sixty-nine percent. That is extremely low; you shouldn't have been able to walk in here with it being that low. We've called an ambulance to take you to the hospital. They'll be taking you to Novant Main in uptown Charlotte."

Doubt lingered in my mind as I thought, "Surely I don't need an ambulance."

I gazed at the doctor and suggested, "My husband is waiting in the parking lot. Can he take me?"

"No, that's not an option. You're in a very dangerous situation. You need someone attending to you as you go, and you absolutely cannot be left alone from this point forward. We're going to do a swab to test for COVID-19 and get chest X-rays before you leave," the doctor responded firmly.

The Covid swab test is far from pleasant. A long swab is placed up the nostril and twisted around for about 10 seconds, ensuring ample fluid is collected from the back of the nose. However, as uncomfortable as a Covid test is, having chest X-rays when you're struggling to breathe is far worse.

After being escorted from the exam room and down the hall to the X-ray room, I met a technician who didn't seem particularly empathetic to my current condition.

"Mrs. Lamkin, I'm your X-ray technician. I need you to stand tall while facing this board. Good. Roll your shoulders forward a bit. Now, take a deep breath and hold it," she said as she slipped into the small room that protected her from the radiation.

I wanted to shout, "Hold it! Are you kidding me? Did I mention I can hardly take a deep breath, and you need me to hold it?"

The side X-ray is no better. It's basically the same process, except you have to raise your hands over your head. Try doing that when you can't breathe. It felt like my lungs were being crushed. But despite the severe discomfort, I somehow managed.

When my X-rays were complete, the doctor walked with me to the ambulance where John was waiting. We had about a minute to say our goodbyes. John handed me the few personal belongings I had brought: my purse and phone. Following a quick peck on the cheek in the parking lot of a makeshift emergency respiratory clinic, I stepped into the ambulance, where I received the gift of a hose that delivered direct oxygen into my nostrils. I closed my eyes and took in all the air I could. It was a blessing I hadn't had for a few weeks and was ever so refreshing.

Twenty-five minutes later, we arrived at the hospital's emergency department, where I would spend the next twelve hours confined to a small, dim, sterile room with a sliding glass door veiled by a privacy curtain. Doctors, nurses, and respiratory technicians came and went trying to improve my oxygen levels and unravel the mysteries within my body.

Normal oxygen saturation is ninety-five percent or above. Even with treatments, mine was only reaching the low eighties at best. It was becoming evident I would be spending the night in the hospital. Other than the births of my daughters, I had never stayed in a hospital, and I certainly wasn't planning an extended stay this time.

CHAPTER SIX

COVID, COVID, COVID

For quite a few years now, our family has relied on GroupMe to share important information. They were all aware I hadn't been feeling well, and John decided that messaging the group would be the most efficient way to provide updates on my situation. It helped me stay connected since I couldn't hold lengthy phone conversations due to my breathlessness. So my lifeline to the outside world quickly became centered in these GroupMe and text messages.

April 20, Around 1 PM, Our Family GroupMe

John: I just wanted to keep you guys in the loop regarding Lana. I have just returned from a respiratory testing center, and they took her by ambulance to Novant Main. She is extremely sick with COVID-19, including extremely low oxygen levels and pneumonia. I will ask all of you to keep her in your prayers. I will let you know her status as I get updates.

Kathy: Of course, we'll pray. Let us know if there's anything we can do. Love both of you.

Ali: Oh no!!!!!! We love you guys! Please let us know if there is anything we can do.

Jessica: Dad, please let me know if you run low on anything. We'll be happy to bring groceries and/or whatever you need and leave it on the porch. We love you both very much and will pray hard for healing and comfort.

John: I appreciate all the offers, but I think I'm OK for now. We had groceries delivered last week, and I'm pretty sure she'll be in the hospital for several days.

Meanwhile, back at the hospital, the attending physician ordered another COVID-19 test. The results from both tests returned negative, which was good news. At least, that's what I thought. However, because this virus was so new, no one understood what to expect exactly, and hospital protocols were changing rapidly.

Although both Covid tests I had taken were negative, the doctors weren't convinced that the tests were accurate. Then, roughly twenty minutes later, a different diagnosis was presented to me. Rheumatoid arthritis resurfaced as a potential explanation, despite my earlier April lab results indicating otherwise.

2:40 PM Our Family GroupMe

John: I just received a text from Lana:

Bilateral pneumonia. Probably because of RA. He can't think of any other reason I'd have it. He said the pictures don't look at all like what they're seeing with Covid, and with the test being negative, he's pretty certain it's a bad case of pneumonia. PS I'm hungry.

Frank (our nephew): That's good news. Still, don't hesitate to let us know if you guys need anything.

Jeanne: I'm glad she has tested negative. Still praying for a speedy recovery.

Linda (who has a nursing background): That sounds very encouraging! Pneumonia sucks, but COVID-19 is not on anyone's bucket list, to the best of my knowledge! Will they keep her in the hospital?

John: Yeah. They still have her there and will probably keep her for a few days. I think she currently has three IVs and is on some pretty strong antibiotics.

Linda: Gotcha. Also, from what I understand, the lungs have very distinctive images with the Covid patients. So the chest X-rays sound very positive! Of course, it's still no fun being in the hospital, even in the best of times!

John was part of the first generation of his family to grow up in the foothills of North Carolina. His parents came from a long line of descendants who had lived in the Appalachian Mountains on Shooting (or Shootin' to the locals) Creek, North Carolina, for over 300 years. In 1950, they moved to Gastonia, NC.

Regrettably, John's dad, Frank, passed away before John and I met, so I didn't have the pleasure of knowing him. However, I've heard many stories of what a good man he was. He dedicated several years of his life serving as a Navy Seabee and went on to pursue a fifty-year career as a barber.

His mother, Dale, had a spirit unlike any other I've ever witnessed. I'll go as far as to say she reflected the image of Jesus as much as a human can. Her love for every person she met was truly genuine. Her soul was gentle, and that gentleness flowed out of every pore on her body. She was a quiet, reserved woman, but it was easy to become entangled in her presence. Dale's smile was contagious, and her hugs had unexplainable powers.

Dale passed away in September 2016 at the age of ninety-four after suffering a stroke.

Frank and Dale left their legacies within their seven children. In their family line, John is next to the youngest. He had two older brothers, Bob and Jim, who are both deceased, and four sisters. Kathy, Linda, and Julia are older than John, and Jeanne is the baby. They care for one another deeply, which makes it easy to stay close. I was thankful God had placed me and my girls in such a loving family, never more so than at this very moment.

A steady stream of medical personnel entered my room through the sliding glass door covered by a curtain hanging from a track on the ceiling. Some came in fully suited in hazmat gear, while others arrived at my bedside in routine scrubs with simple surgical masks covering their faces. Everyone was learning how to handle this pandemic on the fly, doing their very best to keep their patients and themselves safe with the small amount of knowledge they had at the time.

One of the key uncertainties surrounding my condition was whether I should be assigned to a regular room or placed on the Covid floor. This confusion made it clear that the doctors didn't know if they should trust the test or not. One physician told me that even though my X-rays didn't look like what they had been seeing in patients with confirmed cases of COVID-19 and I had multiple negative Covid test results, there was still a possibility I had the virus.

While the staff was determining my room location, I took a moment to text John, providing him with an explanation of the ongoing developments.

4:33 PM

Me: Hey there!

John: How are you feeling?

Me: Tired and hungry, but I like the oxygen because now I can breathe.

John: Hopefully, they will feed you and let you get some rest.

Me: I'm still in the ER. They have a bed ordered for me now. The nurse went to try to find a turkey sandwich.

John: Do you have any indication of how long you might have to stay?

Me: Not yet.

John: It says online that the average stay is 4 to 6 days.

More doctors, nurses, and respiratory therapists came and went, diligently monitoring my vital signs, closely observing my oxygen levels, and kindly inquiring if there was anything I needed. They were working very hard to take care of my needs and reassure me. However, the overwhelming workload in the emergency department meant they were stretched thin and could only do so much.

5:04 PM

Me: Swabbed again. Heading for CT.

John: CT, is that Covid test?

Me: CAT scan and they did the Covid test again.

John: Is the CT for your lungs? Another Covid test.

Me: Yes, I think I've confused them. No results from this Covid test yet.

The evening dragged on ever so slowly. The room I was in wasn't designed for an extended stay. There was no television to pass the time, the bed was uncomfortable, and the temperature seemed to be set at an arctic level. I was cold, bored, and still hungry. But I had my phone, which allowed me to stay connected to my family and friends. And that's exactly what I did for the next several hours.

I compiled a list of items I believed would need to get through the next several days in the hospital and sent it to John, who assured me he would gather everything and bring it to me as soon as possible. While he was taking care of that, I had a text conversation with The Tribe.

6:33 PM

Donna: Lana, are you still in the ER/admitted/home?

Me: Still in the ER. We're waiting for the results of another Covid test before they will move me to a room. I haven't been told how long I'll have to stay, but I expect up to a week.

Donna: Oh, gosh. You poor thing. We're all going to keep asking for updates, so get ready for a crap-ton of caring.

Rosy: A week. Oh my gosh, that's a long time. I hope you are wrong. Anyway, I'm sure you are going to be a good girl and follow what your doctor tells you. Please keep us updated. We will be praying for you a speedy recovery.

Me: I'll take a crap-ton of caring and love it!! Thanks, girls!

Another hour passed. Still, nothing changed.

7:55 PM

John: In a room yet?

Me: Nope. But I got the Covid test result. Negative!

John: Yeah!! I just dropped your stuff off in the lobby, and they called the emergency department to have someone come pick it up.

And another hour.

8:36 PM - The Tribe

Me: Still not in a room, but it's confirmed (twice now) that I will be in a Covid-free suite. Thanks for loving on me today.

Diana: Hurray for Covid-free!!!

Dawn: Yes! That is good news.

Rosy: Yes. Hurray!! You will be out in no time. Thinking of you, wish you a good night's sleep.

Donna: You're too tough for Corona.

And yet another hour.

I was still waiting for a room and a turkey sandwich. Another one of the very kind nurses realized I still hadn't had anything to eat all day. The cafeteria was already closed, but she was finally able to find a very dry turkey sandwich from a vending machine for me.

9:47 PM

John: How are you?

Me: Had to pee, had a breathing episode, and now I'm no longer allowed to move. Still in the ER, but I have more blankets, so I'm warmer.

John: A breathing episode?

Me: Yes, same breathing issues I've had at home. The oxygen wasn't helping.

John: Grabbing something to eat. Can I call you when I'm done?

Me: Yes

Before John could even finish his late dinner, my oxygen needs surpassed what the small nasal cannula could provide. There was no need for him to call me because I couldn't carry a conversation through the oxygen mask now covering my face.

I assured him by text that I would let him know when I was finally in a room. It was around 11:15 that evening when the decision to move me to the Covid floor was made.

11:27 PM

Me: In a room.

John: *smiley* What number?

Me: 6310

John: I can't even begin to tell you how much I love you and how much I miss you. Get some rest, sweetie.

Me: I love you, too. Goodnight.

John: Sleep well and let them take care of you.

Me: I will. You sleep well, too. Try not to worry. I'm in good hands.

I was beyond ready for sleep, but it didn't take long to realize sleep would often be interrupted by the comings and goings of medical and hospital staff during my stay. However, I was glad to receive the treatment I needed to restore my health completely.

As I settled in for my hospital stay, I convinced myself again that everything was going to be just fine.

CHAPTER SEVEN

SETTLING IN

Tuesday, April 21

My room was larger than I expected. If visitors had been allowed, they would've been comfortable sitting beside my bed on the sofa or in the recliner. A large HEPA filtration system hummed steadily in one corner of the room, providing clean air. I was restricted to a small area of the room by the lines, cables, and cords of the monitors and oxygen machine on my right at the head of the bed. Although these lines didn't reach the bathroom near the end of the bed, I could catch a glimpse of it from where I sat, and it seemed to be a decent size.

I knew John would be worried, leading me to text him a good morning message at 7:14 AM. He's such a strong man, displaying remarkable strength in handling complex situations and circumstances. His love for his family knows no bounds, and I was confident he would be researching and studying everything he could find to get some answers and clarity about what we might be facing. I also knew he would be spending a lot of time in prayer.

I became acutely aware of and very thankful for today's technology. It allowed me to talk with Mackenzie and Lauren on FaceTime, text with The Tribe, and stay connected with family and my gym staff through GroupMe.

These digital platforms not only occupied my time but also helped me organize my thoughts. They provided solace by reminding me that numerous people were offering prayers and keeping me in their thoughts.

My symptoms remained the same, with the exception of a returning headache reminiscent of a few days ago. I hadn't slept well, and the oxygen therapy had little effect on my saturation levels. Furthermore, I had officially been put on bed rest, prohibiting me from leaving my bed unassisted. Even with the assistance of a nurse, I was restricted from going any further than the bedside commode.

Breakfast was delivered around 7:45 AM. Since becoming a nutrition coach, I'd become relatively particular about my nutrition, so I focused on the quality of the food in front of me–scrambled eggs, turkey sausage patty, and a low-fat blueberry muffin. I rarely allowed myself to indulge, but I felt it was okay to give myself a little grace under the circumstances and have the muffin. Besides, it was low fat.

The morning nurse brought me an incentive spirometer: a hand-held medical device used to exercise the lungs and force deep breaths. My competitive nature led me to use the spirometer as a challenge. Why not? At this point, my lungs needed all the help they could get.

8:04 AM - The Tribe

Donna: Good morning, lovely ladies! Lana, are you settled into a comfy room and feeling better?

Me: Settled and oxygenated.

Diana: We are cheering you on, Lana.

Me: *I attached a picture of my incentive spirometer.

I have a great game to play now. I have to suck on this hose and try to get the white thing to the top. It's like trying to ring a carnival bell. I'm losing so far, but I'm determined to win a giant stuffed animal. LOL

Dawn: Love your attitude, Lana! Ahh, the little things in life. Like breathing fully!!! Sheesh. Ugh! We're rooting for you to win that gigantic stuffed panda.

Me: Don't take one breath for granted, ladies. Stay strong!

Rosy: Lana, you are so strong. An inspiration for everyone who has the pleasure to know you, so this is going to be one more of your accomplishments. You get this.

You've likely heard the expression "find your tribe and love them hard" and perhaps wondered how that would truly feel. Let me tell you, no friendship could be a better example of that saying than our Tribe. As I read their messages, I could hear their voices in my head, especially Rosy's, with her sweet Spanish accent. I cannot emphasize enough how uplifting it is to have friends like these incredible ladies. They make me feel like it's possible to conquer the toughest of situations, even when I find myself confined to a hospital bed with an oxygen hose strapped to my nose

Mid-morning, John had a conversation with the doctor on duty. After sharing their discussion with me, he relayed an update to our family. While John was bringing everyone up to speed, another Covid test was ordered, aiming to confirm the doctor's suspicion that I did indeed have Covid.

10:15 AM Our Family GroupMe

John: I thought I would send an update. I spoke with the doctor a few minutes ago, and despite the two negative tests, she is confident that Lana has COVID-19. Lana is currently in the acute phase but stable. They have taken her off antibiotics and will start treating her with hydroxychloroquine in hopes that it will help. The doctor also thinks that Lana has probably had COVID-19 for a few weeks, and the issues that were suspected to be RA could very well, in fact, be Covid.

Jessica: Wow. That's a lot to process. Thank you for keeping us posted, Dad. My prayers continue for you both. Is there anything we can do for Lana or send to make her more comfortable in the hospital? And are you feeling okay today? Need anything?

John: Thanks for asking, Jess, but I feel okay. I just spoke with Lana, and at this point, she is not in ICU, but they are watching her closely. They are going to change her oxygen and hope it will keep her from being on a respirator. With that being said, they have brought one to her room.

Kathy: Our prayers will keep going for both of you. Please let us know if you need anything. Love you and Lana. Thanks for keeping us posted.

Julia: John, I am working, so I am not responding, but I am definitely keeping up with the reports. I love you both and am keeping you in my prayers.

A few hours later, the results of the third Covid test came back negative. And yet the doctor was still not convinced I didn't have the virus. The treatment for pneumonia and COVID-19 continued. Additionally, because my oxygen levels were dropping to the 80s when I got up, the medical team decided to move me to the more aggressive oxygen machine.

The dietitian called shortly after lunch to discuss my appetite, and our conversation revolved around nutrition. The nurses were concerned that I wasn't eating and my BMI was low. I told her I was a personal trainer and wasn't eating what was brought from the cafeteria because the food didn't meet my standards. I reassured her that John had brought me fruit and meal bars, so I wasn't going hungry. She was relieved to know starvation wouldn't be my cause of death while I was under her supervision. We both acknowledged that my expectations were a bit over the top and shared a good laugh about it.

Nevertheless, she empathized with my perspective and made a few adjustments to the meals I received. However, even with those changes, it still wasn't enough for me. No matter how many times I requested it, I couldn't seem to get mustard, only mayonnaise. That's when I decided to ask John to start bringing me a daily salad for lunch.

Part of being a successful fitness professional is understanding proper nutrition. I researched and studied the components of a healthy diet for several years. I know how to balance macronutrients to get the best results for each specific body type. I know the process of determining proper caloric intake. And I can create nutrition plans to help my clients reach their personal health goals. I used these skills for my benefit, as well, including figuring out how to maintain my low body fat.

While having low body fat sounds desirable, I allowed mine to stay low for too long, and my body was suffering in ways I didn't realize. Ways that potentially added to my health crisis.

And I had other problems I didn't realize. It wasn't until I decided to take an extensive nutrition course that I discovered I had developed an eating disorder called orthorexia nervosa. It's a disordered eating pattern characterized by the need to eat "clean" and "pure" foods to the point that the individual becomes obsessed with this way of life.

I completed this advanced course in November 2019 and worked to improve my relationship with food. But based on my persistent need for homemade salads and mustard instead of mayonnaise, I clearly hadn't succeeded yet.

I spent the rest of the afternoon scrolling through social media, watching random videos, and taking short naps. It was mindless, but I was doing my best to keep myself occupied. It didn't seem to matter how still I was, my lungs continued to struggle, and I was becoming restless.

4:44 PM

> **Me**: I'm starting to worry about this new oxygen. It keeps beeping, and I do NOT want to go to ICU. I don't feel any worse.
>
> **John**: Do you think it is the monitor or your oxygen?
>
> **Me**: I have no idea. I feel tied down!
>
> **John**: What do you mean?
>
> **Me**: I want to move around. Tubes and wires everywhere.
>
> **John**: Do you have any flexibility to move, or are you too restricted?
>
> **Me**: None. I can wiggle in the bed, but I want to sit somewhere else.
>
> **John**: Have you asked the nurse if you could stretch for a minute or change the bed's position?
>
> **Me**: I've moved around a lot in the bed, but they won't let me out of bed other than to use the commode.

My days were typically filled with movement starting from morning training sessions all the way through group workouts in the evenings. Therefore, being confined to complete bed rest was not an easy assignment.

Earlier in the day, I received a phone call from a courier attempting to deliver a package to me at the hospital. He insisted he couldn't leave it with anyone other than me. I couldn't help but wonder who had imposed that particular directive. With Covid restrictions keeping visitors from the hospital, did they honestly think patients could leave their rooms to meet their couriers in the lobby? Anyway, I digress. After a brief phone conversation, he left, taking the package with him.

6:11 PM

Donna: Getting some rest?

Me: Yes, a little. I'm not allowed out of bed for anything. I really have nothing else to do besides nap and text.

Donna: I'm here for whatever you need, even middle-of-the-night entertainment. The Tribe sent you something to-day, but not sure they've brought it up to you yet. Once you get it, you'll have something else to do. I'm so sorry this is happening to you. Thank GOD you are physically and mentally strong.

Me: Thank you, my sweet friend. You're so thoughtful! I couldn't get what you sent me because the guy couldn't leave it with anyone. He said I had to come down to get it. Um, that couldn't happen. I'm sorry! He said they would refund the charge. I thought it might have been from you, but I wasn't sure.

I've lost it a few times in the past few days, but I have so many praying for me I was able to gather up the tears and move to the next step. I'm fighting like hell to stay out of ICU.

Donna: Oh, I'm so sorry! He was instructed to leave it at the desk like all hospital deliveries. I will do my best to make different arrangements. Take good care of yourself, and text or call me anytime. I'm always awake!!! XOXOXOXO

Me: Maybe you should take a nap. *laugh* I haven't told Roger, but I'm certainly not keeping this from him for any specific reason. It's okay if it happens to come up. Thanks again!

Donna: I didn't want to tell anyone without your permission. I'll let him know. You could use the extra prayers.

Roger was the one brave soul in the gym who would fearlessly join The Tribe for our workouts. Cardio seemed effortless for him, and his prowess with the jump rope was truly awe-inspiring. His speed and flawless technique left us amazed. He faithfully joined us every Monday morning, motivating us to push through our challenging cardio exercises. He often reminded us, "We can do anything for thirty seconds."

Because Roger had become a good friend, I wanted him to be aware of my situation. I knew Donna would be sure to get the message to him because she was correct; I could use all the prayers I could get.

John knew it was difficult for me to breathe if I talked a lot, so we continued taking advantage of text messaging to stay in contact with one another.

7:35 PM

John: How's your oxygen?

Me: Around 93. The nurse seems satisfied with that. Rosy and Donna both texted me, and Mackenzie called, too.

John: Have you heard from Lauren?

Me: A little, but she has finals this week.

John: Well, I know everyone's thinking about you.

Me: No doubt.

John: You seem tired.

Me: This headache! I'm sorry.

John: Try to rest now, and I'll talk to you later. One last thing. I love you!

Me: I love you, too.

I didn't expect to hear from Lauren often, considering her demanding schedule of double majoring in Psychology and English at NC State, with graduation just around the corner in May. Her schedule was packed as she completed her capstone project and prepared for final exams. I did love it when she could squeeze in a few moments during the day to send a text or call to check on me, though.

John and I spoke on the phone around 9:30 PM to wrap up our day and say good night. I wanted him with me more than I could explain. Covid was causing so much chaos and confusion. And although I could feel the presence of the Lord and had peace, I was worried that things might get worse before they got better.

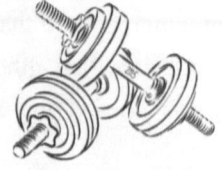

CHAPTER EIGHT

THE HEALTHIEST PERSON I KNOW

Wednesday, April 22

The day began the same as the day before. Nurses arrived early to assess my vitals and administer medications. Shortly after their rounds, breakfast came. Despite the persistent struggle to breathe and anxiety about being in the hospital, I had a good night's rest and woke up without a fever. For the most part, the day was quieter than previous days, so I spent much of my time talking and texting with my loved ones.

Feeling a deep sense of gratitude and the need to convey my thoughts before any interruptions, I decided it was the perfect time to express to my family how much they meant to me and how appreciative I was for their continuous prayers and unwavering concern.

7:27 AM Our Family GroupMe

Me: Hi, all. I just wanted to tell you I love and appreciate each of you so much! I'm reading every word here, and it helps me stay encouraged.

Jeanne: Are you feeling any better, and is there anything we can do?

Lana: I wish I could give a confident yes to that question, but it's more like a solid maybe. I have good moments, but I still struggle to catch my breath when I stand up, which is very limited. Prayerful that I'll turn a corner today so I can get out of this dang bed. The thing I need most is for the prayers to keep going up. God hears each one, and I feel them.

Kathy: It's great to hear from you. Prayers have been going steady and will continue. If there's anything I can do, let me know. Love you and wish you a speedy recovery!

I had every confidence my loved ones would continue praying for me. They knew I was under the care of very competent physicians, and there was little else that could be done at this point.

Without hesitation, I called John immediately after messaging our family. Speaking with him brings me joy and a sense of grounding. Our conversations have always been a source of comfort for me. When we were dating, we spent hours talking on the phone daily. He would call me on his way to work to say good morning and randomly throughout his workday, including his lunch hour. I could expect my phone to ring as soon as he got in his car after work, even though his destination was typically my house. Even after spending the evening together, we would continue chatting as he drove home. Seventeen years later, it's still not uncommon for us to call one another when we're in our cars or have been apart for more than a few hours. Our phone conversations are among my favorite things about our relationship.

"Were you able to eat anything this morning?" he asked.

"I was. I had eggs, a blueberry muffin, and an orange. And my oxygen is at 93," I replied.

"Can you feel the increased oxygen?"

A little. It doesn't take much movement for it to drop, though. The game today is not to make the machine beep because of low oxygen. So far, I'm losing. But, as you know, everything's a competition," I chuckled.

He laughed at this running joke. We both enjoy good competitions and often find ourselves playfully racing to complete everyday tasks to claim the title of winner. Our challenges include everything from who can get in bed first each evening to who loves the other more. It may seem silly, but it's fun for us.

Because I struggled to talk, we ended our conversation much sooner than we wanted, but we continued communicating throughout the day. I did my best to convey what was happening at the hospital. I knew how much he longed to be with me and how hard it was to receive information through short conversations and text messages—especially knowing how John likes to receive many details to process situations. He operates best when armed with a lot of information. It allows him the opportunity to analyze so he can fully understand why decisions are being made and decide if he agrees with those decisions. In short, he values being well-informed. However, the abbreviated version was all I could manage. Thankfully, with the help of my doctors, we made it work.

The Tribe checked in around 9:30 am, and, as always, their words of encouragement lifted my spirits. As our text conversation ended, it was time for another round of visits from physicians, the nurse, and the respiratory therapist.

The respiratory therapist on duty this day was Willis. I don't recall the exact day I met him, but he will hold a special place in my heart for the rest of my life. For some reason, Willis took a particular interest in my well-being. Even when I wasn't on his list of patients, he would come to my room to check on me.

Willis and I formed an instant connection. To begin with, my maiden name is Willis, which sparked a great conversation about how easy it was for me to remember his name even though I had just met him (along with the lack of oxygen reaching my brain). This initial conversation somehow led us to discuss our faith, and we quickly realized that we were brother and sister in Christ. So, not only could I count on Willis to provide me with the life-saving oxygen I needed, but I could also trust that he would be praying for me. And that is precisely what he did, plus so much more in the days to come.

After some light-hearted conversation, he made the necessary adjustments to my oxygen supply. As he left to continue his workday, he assured me he'd see me again soon.

Mid-morning, the nurse helped me clean up as best as possible, but unfortunately, my hair wasn't on her cleaning checklist. It had only been a few days, but I was used to washing my hair daily. Now, I began to notice how gross it felt. A girl can only go so long with dirty hair, so I texted John to request a delivery of a bottle of dry shampoo and a brush. It wouldn't be the same as sticking my head under warm water and lathering up, but it would be better than nothing. I know these items don't seem like a big deal, but they helped me feel human again. Something I desperately needed.

John passed my delivery request to Mackenzie, who gladly made the drop-off shortly after lunch.

2:03 PM

Me: Thanks again for bringing my stuff! My hair is a little cleaner now.

Mackenzie: You're very welcome. Hope it helps you feel better by being a little cleaner.

Me: It does.

Mackenzie: Good. I'm glad I could help in some way. Did you try Disney+ today?

Me: I just started a movie. I've been on the phone basically all day.

Mackenzie: Oh, man. I bet that was exhausting.

Me: Not too bad. My oxygen levels are up, so it's much easier to breathe. I actually stood up and didn't make the alarm go off until I was back in bed. That's a huge thing! It has been sounding as soon as I stand up.

Mackenzie: Wow, that's very good. Could you imagine how it would be if you weren't the healthiest person I know? That would be super rough.

Me: I have to think my fitness level has helped.

Mackenzie: I can only imagine that it has.

I had been called "the healthiest person I know" by several people, and I admit I liked the title. I was proud that others noticed how hard I worked to care for my body. I also enjoyed looking the part. Women value feeling beautiful, and although I still had flaws, I felt good about how my fit body looked. But honestly, it went deeper than any of that. Being fit at 50 helped me enjoy life. I could take on physical tasks and challenges without fear, knowing I had the strength and stamina to succeed.

I remember creating challenges for the members of our gym. Typically, these challenges would require the members who chose to take part to complete as many repetitions of one exercise as possible in one minute. The exercises ranged from squats to push-ups to burpees (the most torturous of all moves but one of my favorites). I did my best to ensure options were available for everyone. In addition to asking our members to participate, I also encouraged our staff to take part; then, we would post their results under a "beat the staff" section. I never included a challenge that I wouldn't do. As I mentioned earlier, I enjoy competition. And the competition at the gym was strong: men and women of all ages, and many of them were very fit. I didn't always win, but I'm proud to say I never lost.

Little did I know that as I was playing games with my fitness abilities, the Lord was preparing me for the most difficult challenge of my life and that it was silently headed straight toward me at full speed.

By early evening, I welcomed random chit-chat. And that task was perfect for my mom.

One thing I love most about my mom is that she likes conversation. It doesn't matter what is talked about; she is never short on words. When going through a major medical crisis, most messages require you to talk about how you're feeling and what your doctors have said. But Mom's text messages made things seem somewhat normal before we got to all the medical stuff. And as a bonus, she'll pray for everything.

I got a little chuckle from the start of this evening's message.

5:20 PM

Mom: You tried artichoke. Did you like it?

Me: Um, I like artichoke dip.

Mom: I've never tasted it. I got a new Mediterranean cookbook that I've had ordered for a while, and it uses artichokes in several recipes.

Me: Give it a try. It's not bad.

Mom: I will when I can get out to the store. Are you bored, or do they keep bothering you so you can't rest?

Me: I watched most of a movie and then took a nap. I'm currently trying to get the oxygen monitor to stop beeping. I get so flipping hot when I lay down on all this plastic: the pillows and the mattress. Of course, they have sheets over them but no circulation under there.

Mom: Oh, I know. I hate plastic covering. I wonder if they would let Mackenzie bring in one of those foam mattress things. That way, it could be destroyed when you leave. Why is the monitor beeping?

Me: They can't move me to put it on. They did a speed sheet change this morning while I was out of bed. It's beeping because my oxygen saturation is too low. It's been in the high 90s today, but I'm below 90 right now for some reason.

Mom: Darn. Lord God, we ask you to please raise Lana's oxygen saturation. You know what is blocking it, and we know you can remove the problem. Bless the medicine in her body now and all that is entering. With your blessing, it has to do what it is intended to do. Place a coolness between her and the plastic. Let her be comfortable so she can rest and heal. Amen.

Me: Thanks, Mom!

I followed our text conversation with a prayer of my own. Once again, I shared my confusion with the Lord. How could I, "the healthiest person I know," be struggling to breathe? I told Him I didn't understand the purpose of this life detour or how He could use it to further His Kingdom on earth. I didn't try to hide my irritation and displeasure with my illness. After all, He already knew, and I find that it's always best to share my honest feelings with Him. He didn't need to hear them, but I needed to express them.

Then I reminded myself that wallowing in self-pity would do no good. It wouldn't get me out of the hospital, and it certainly wouldn't help me stay strong to push through whatever was happening to my body. I've found that that kind of mindset is rooted in moments of little faith and unbelief. But the Lord didn't create me to be a person who gives up. So, I asked Him to forgive me for my lack of faith and to give me the strength to walk whatever path He would lead me down.

As I was pondering artichokes with my mom and talking to God, the doctor called John. Shortly after their conversation, he shared with me what they had discussed.

Amidst the flood of information being presented to me, my current state made it challenging to grasp and comprehend everything. It became clear that

John would need to be the one to decipher the doctors' messages. Keeping up with the details seemed like an impossible task for me in my condition.

Along with oxygen saturation, another number closely monitored was my C-Reactive Protein (CRP) level. CRP is a protein made in the liver and sent into the bloodstream in response to inflammation. Inflammation is the body's way of protecting its tissues if it's been injured or has an infection. Normal CRP levels are less than 10 mg/L. At the beginning of April, when all of this began, my CRP was elevated. But now, even though visible swelling had lessened, my level was very high.

5:53 PM

Me: So, the number that is still rising for me is the CRP? Is that right?

John: Yes, it was your CRP number. When you were tested on April 1, it was 59. As of today, it was around 170. Dr. Jervis said that it was rising slowly now. I think he hopes you're about as high as you will get in that area.

Me: Would you mind putting out a specific prayer request that it stops rising and actually starts to drop? I think it would be good for prayers to be more specific now. Also, my oxygen saturation has been around 95-96 most of the afternoon. I took a nap and got hot again, so I struggled a bit, but it's creeping back up and is currently 93.

John: I'll be glad to do that. I'll text Pastor Kevin and let him know. Are there others you would like me to contact?

Me: The family.

After calling our care pastor, John sent a message to our family, as I had requested. They quickly replied with promises of prayers and concern for me and John. He reassured them he was taking care of himself and would let them know if he needed anything. It relieved me that the family knew what was happening and that they would take care of John as he cared for me.

CHAPTER NINE

IN THE RIGHT DIRECTION

Thursday, April 23

My oxygen saturation level had dramatically improved. In the early part of the day, it had reached a promising 96 percent. However, even the slightest movement would cause that number to drop drastically into the low 70s. While my CRP had stopped climbing, it still remained at a high level.

Dr. M. (I called her that because I never fully caught her last name) didn't want me to get excited about any improvements. She said, "Your numbers are still fluctuating, and you are requiring a significant amount of oxygen. You're in a stable condition, and perhaps in a few days, we'll begin to see more noticeable improvements."

Because blood clots are common in bedridden patients, Dr. Jervis decided to increase my anti-clotting medicine. Given the known issue of clotting with the Covid virus, he wanted to be sure clotting didn't happen.

Both doctors still assumed I was dealing with COVID-19, a virus that didn't typically subside quickly. John was tasked with telling me that I would be in the hospital longer than I anticipated. He informed me I should expect at least eight to ten days or perhaps even more. It had already been four days with very little change, so even though the news stung a little, I knew in my heart a quick recovery wasn't likely. Unless a miracle occurred, the reality was that eight days was wishful thinking. But as my mom often reminded me, "Our God is a God of miracles."

Despite everything that was happening, I couldn't seem to keep my mind off the Tribe and how I felt that I was letting them down. I sent them a text, letting them know that it was doubtful I would be back to lead our group workouts for at least another week. I encouraged them to meet without me, acknowledging that while they preferred having a leader, they were all capable and knowledgeable. Even so, it wasn't easy to accept that I wouldn't be with them. We were a team, and I wanted to be in the game. Sitting on the sidelines was never easy for me.

I laid my head back to rest and did my best to process the whirlwind of emotions swirling within me.

I was excited to receive a text message from Mackenzie a few hours later. Unfortunately, our conversations were limited due to her full-time work and graduate classes. She was swamped, but she made an effort to check in whenever possible.

10:56 AM

Mackenzie: How are you feeling today, Mom?

Me: I'm feeling pretty good. The respiratory therapist gave me a new challenge today by lowering the oxygen flow. Still a high amount (30 lpm) but less forced air. Trying to keep my oxygen saturation number at or above 92. Before they changed it, I was at 96 this morning. I'm at 93 right now, but any exertion sends it down in the low 80s pretty quickly. If you would, please pray there is no blood clotting. That's a major concern with this virus, and my numbers are up a bit. They are upping the amount of medicine they are giving for that. Blood clots are not at all what I need.

Mackenzie: So, the medicine is helping clear your lungs and breathe better? Obviously not the anti-clotting medicine, but the other stuff.

Me: Well, not big improvements as far as numbers go. Baby steps. The doctors are even saying, "every case is different, and we just don't know what will work from one person to the next." I thought I was breathing better until they dropped the flow. Now, not so much. No one should have to sit this still.

Mackenzie: Ugh. So is it just trouble breathing, like someone is sitting on your chest, or are you congested, too, and coughing up a lung?

Me: It's weird. It doesn't feel like that. I just can't take deep breaths. My lungs will not fill up. Not really any congestion or coughing to speak of. Coughing would probably be a good thing. It might mean my lungs were clearing.

As the day unfolded, I found myself engrossed in reading about the situation beyond the confines of the hospital. It was disheartening to learn that the temporary closures of businesses had been extended. Like many others, I couldn't help but feel frustrated. None of us had ever experienced a global pandemic before, and it was challenging to comprehend the rationale behind the initial decision to shut everything down. The North Carolina government introduced phased reopening plans, which left us even unsure of what the future would hold.

3:56 PM

Me: Did I hear gyms and salons won't be in phase 1?

Donna: I'm trying to find confirmation of that. All I'm seeing is not much will change in Phase 1; very little will change in Phase 2, and I may never see my mother-in-law again because of the nursing home restrictions that will continue rigorously. I don't see gyms and salons mentioned in any of the articles I've checked. Does anyone else have any different info?

Me: I can't imagine how lonely the elderly are. It's been four days for me, and it's driving me mad—that and the fact that I need a shower.

Donna: I agree with you 100%. I wish I lived in Georgia or Tennessee right about now. I'm about ready to run out and lick everything I see. I'm sorry you're so alone in this.

Me: If they would let me out, I'd promise not to lick anything. I'd even wear a mask.

Diana: Gosh, Lana, I hate that for you so much!! Masks and extra sanitizers for everyone. Nobody has time for any of that is right. As someone who has spent time in the hospital, I can vouch for loneliness and boredom. There is only so much hospital food and daytime television that you can watch! When in doubt, wear one of those messy buns on top of your head. That will hide a few extra days for you.

Me: Dry shampoo can only do so much. Diana, thank you for your words. I know it wasn't the purpose of your statement, but I heard a gentle reminder to be grateful. I realize things could be so much worse, and this battle will be short compared to what so many others face. I'm so blessed!

While I was irritated by the gym's closure, John was taking advantage of it and had spent the day cleaning its floors. We chatted some throughout the day, but not as much as we had the past few days. When his day was complete, and he had a few minutes to spare, he sent our family a summary of the day's news.

7:13 PM Family GroupMe

John: Sorry for the delay in responding and giving the update, but I was at the gym cleaning. I spoke to Lana's doctor earlier, and her CRP has stabilized and is no longer going up. That indicates that the inflammation in her body is not getting worse. There is another marker they are watching that is also consistently present with Covid. It measures the clotting of her blood. One of the issues with COVID-19 is excessive blood clotting. They have given her a higher dose of anti-clotting medicine. According to the doctor, they see a very small blood clot. He said she's not in danger of having a stroke, but it inhibits the ability to uptake oxygen. Her fever has been back for the last couple of days and has been typically around 100 or a little higher.

The good news is she has stabilized. Hopefully, we will start to see some improvements over the next couple of days. I asked the doctor how long we should anticipate her being in the hospital, and he said a reasonable guess would be 10 to 14 days.

They have reduced the flow of oxygen today, and as a result, she has to be very careful about moving around. She remains in good spirits but wishes she could get to the shower and wash her hair! I can promise you that she and I both appreciate all of your prayers and your concerns.

Jessica: Oh my. So glad she has stabilized, but man. I'm sure the long hospital stay isn't what either of you was hoping for.

Julia: It's really good to hear that she has stabilized. Keeping you in our prayers. Thanks for the update. Love you guys.

Jeanne: So glad to hear she is going in the right direction. Continued prayers coming in your direction. Love you guys.

Kathy: Glad to hear the situation appears to be going in the right direction. Continue to keep both of you in my prayers. Love you both.

We all felt the same as Kathy. It did appear I was headed in "the right direction." But being stable didn't mean I would fully recover or that life would return to normal. As we know, no one can see into the future. And as much as we longed to know how this situation would end, we didn't have that luxury. Our only choice was to approach each day as it came and confront whatever challenges lay ahead. Thankfully, our family is very good at living life as it happens. We're a tough bunch, and we knew that in the end, everything would be, as they say in Illinois, fine.

CHAPTER TEN

MAYBE IT'S NOT COVID

Friday, April 24

I was trying not to let it show, but discouragement was setting in. As much as I hated to admit it, I realized my situation was more serious than I thought and continued to head in the wrong direction. Even though we were all trying to keep our spirits up, I was in the trenches, and frankly, that's a hard place to be hopeful. I spent a lot of time praying, and my prayers rapidly became desperate pleas for healing.

Dr. Walls, a doctor I hadn't met before, made his rounds. His face was covered by a mask, like everyone else's, making it impossible for me to know what he actually looked like. But I remember he seemed tall from where I sat. And there was something about his demeanor that appealed to me. I couldn't put my finger on it until life began returning to normal in late 2020. It was then that John told me Dr. Walls is from the St. Louis, Missouri area, and his family lives in a small town about 25 miles from my hometown. That was the link! God knew I needed a little of the Midwest in my room.

Dr. Walls' take on my illness differed slightly from Dr. Jervis'. Since my body wasn't responding to the Covid-specific treatment, he told me he wanted to take a step back.

He explained, "I want to evaluate you as if Covid doesn't exist and consider what our diagnosis would be if that were the case."

That made all the sense in the world to me. I'd had countless negative Covid tests, yet all the treatment I had received so far was for Covid. I was relieved that someone was willing to look beyond this one virus.

Meanwhile, a new concern emerged–rising ferritin levels. Ferritin is a blood protein that contains iron. If a ferritin test shows higher than normal levels, it could indicate various conditions, including excessive iron storage, liver disease, rheumatoid arthritis, other inflammatory conditions, or hyperthyroidism.

Time and medication were the only things that would improve my ferritin level. I would have to be patient and let my body heal, which isn't in my nature. I had to come to terms with the fact that I would be in the hospital until I was able to get out of bed and actually breathe at the same time.

After informing John about the latest unexpected development in our ever-evolving journey, I reached out to the Tribe.

I brought them up to speed on all my medical news, and we chatted about how the quarantine was affecting our family members. We all have kids, and their ages range from elementary schoolers to married adults. Taking classes and tests online and working from home wasn't an entirely new concept, but it wasn't a regular occurrence until now. They were all struggling to adjust. Then we lightened the conversation by sharing our most recent, unusual for us, dietary choices.

10:19 AM

Donna: There are so many unintended consequences of the virus and the quarantine! We can't help but learn a lot about ourselves during this time; the good and the bad. I'm eating like crazy, but I know I can pull it back once the stress lets up. If anybody else has a confession, pop in! Drinking too much? Not drinking enough? Too much social media? Checking out completely? 'Fess up. It feels good!

Me: I'm not breathing enough. Hahaha. Oh, and I ordered a brownie with dinner tonight.

Donna: Now THAT'S a huge confession!

Rosy: I have the same confessions as you, Donna; you know that I love my sweets and having Sara baking delicious things. It makes it even easier to sin. We are together, my friend. You will see that the "normal" will be back. By the way, I love brownies. Good choice, Lana.

Dawn: A friend delivered cupcakes yesterday that was sent to her son by his boss. Her son really doesn't eat them, so instead, she dumped them on several friends. Ha! We didn't mind. There were five yesterday!

Donna: We'll all be fine after this. I promise—brownies, cupcakes, wine, comfort food. Whatever gets you through the night is alright.

This chat was exactly what I needed to brighten my day. But our light-hearted conversation was another glimpse of my eating disorder. Even though I casually mentioned ordering a brownie, it was very difficult to allow myself to indulge. I was afraid I would slip into bad habits that would take me back to an unhealthy lifestyle. Before I learned to like nutritional food, I was a junk food junkie. Bacon cheeseburgers, french fries, and Diet Coke made up many of my lunches in the past. Training my palate to enjoy salads had taken a lot of effort. I was scared that I was about to sabotage all my hard work. And if I recall correctly, I didn't eat the entire brownie that evening. Right then, I knew this was a problem I would need to address as soon as I was back on my feet.

Shortly after my chat with the Tribe, I created a list of additional items I would need for an extended stay in the hospital and sent it to John. After lunch, he picked up the final necessities from the drugstore and delivered them to my nurse. Little did I know at the time that this trip would be the first of many for him as he continued to make drop-offs for various miscellaneous items, some of which I later realized I didn't truly need.

Around 12:30 pm

John: Mission accomplished. Your nurse is pretty awesome.

Me: They have all been amazing and kind. Why do you say she's awesome?

John: Just kind. You can tell that she cares about her patients. I told her you really would like to get in the shower somehow.

Me: And she probably said something like, "I bet she would."

John: Pretty much exactly that.

Me: That's the nice way of saying, "Not a chance. Let's see if she can sit in a chair first."

Once John delivered the latest batch of requested necessities, I wanted to put them to use as soon as they were in my hands. Sadly, I still couldn't take that shower I had longed for, and I had to settle for another bed bath. The hygiene process wasn't easy. So, when I managed to complete the task, I needed a considerable amount of time to recuperate before moving again. Nevertheless, my determination pushed me to make the move and finally settle into the chair a little before 3:30 pm. I remained there for approximately two hours, during which time my oxygen saturation level stabilized around 93. All things considered, I deemed it a successful endeavor.

Returning to the bed made my oxygen saturation drop to the high eighties. Although it quickly rebounded once I settled back into position, I couldn't shake off the overwhelming sense of helplessness that washed over me, and my frustration and irritation were evident.

5:37 PM

Me: It takes everything in me to move from a freaking chair literally three feet away. And that's with oxygen shoved up my nose.

John: Don't get frustrated, sweetheart. Think about where you are now compared to Monday or even last week. Being still for so long, you know it's going to take some time once you start moving around.

Me: But I can't move around, and that's what's killing me!

In addition to my physical immobility, there were other aspects of this journey that infuriated me. I discovered numerous things on this journey that aren't in the least bit glamorous. Topping that list were bedside commodes. They tend to challenge your dignity, but they're a necessary evil when you can't walk to the bathroom. And, as I learned later, there are worse options.

6:24 PM

Me: Peed without making the machine beep! *high five* Only a mom can truly appreciate that text! Also, why do you see more nurses between midnight-7 am than you do from noon-7 pm? It's messed up!

Mom: Hallelujah! LOL Day shift must be busier, and at nighttime, everybody's sleeping, so they have to make sure they're okay.

True to form, the day continued to unveil unexpected twists and turns. Dr. Walls was now entertaining the possibility of cryptogenic organizing pneumonia (COP), a form of interstitial lung disease where the bronchioles (small airways) and alveoli (tiny air sacs) become inflamed, leading to difficulty breathing. The only way to determine if that was the case was to do a lung biopsy, which I was in no condition to undergo. If COP were indeed the case, the prescribed treatment would involve a prolonged course of steroids spanning several months.

In addition, Dr. Walls ordered another blood draw (the third for the day) to perform an antibody test and determine whether I had previously contracted Covid-19. Adding to the complexity, rheumatoid arthritis resurfaced as a potential consideration.

The Lord sent a wonderful traveling nurse my way that evening. Her name was Khadijah, and she was from Florida. Recognizing my exhaustion and frustration resulting from disrupted sleep throughout the night, she took swift action. Khadijah placed an order stipulating that no one should enter the room between midnight and 6:00 am, allowing me the precious gift of a solid six hours of uninterrupted sleep—a truly magical prospect.

I called John to share the news and catch up on his day's events. When we ended our call, I settled in for the evening, hoping that tomorrow I'd be one step closer to going home.

As it had become his evening routine, John provided our family with another update, informing them of the ongoing situation.

9:22 PM

John: Time for a daily update. I didn't have any information until I spoke to the doctor just a little while ago, so I didn't really have anything to report earlier today.

The good news is that Lana was able to sit in a chair for a while today and maintain reasonably good vitals. On the other side of the coin, she is still struggling to breathe. Due to shift changes, she had a new doctor today. He does not think she has COVID-19 based on all of her symptoms. What he suspects is a disease called cryptogenic organizing pneumonia. It's a rare lung disease that only affects about one or two people for every hundred thousand admitted to the hospital for her symptoms. The treatment for this disease is corticosteroids. The only way to confirm the diagnosis is by doing a lung biopsy. At this point, there is zero chance that they will do that because of her current condition. He is not confident she would survive that relatively simple operation.

He will see her again in the morning, and I think he will start her on corticosteroids tomorrow. Depending on how she responds, we could see improvement as quickly as 72 hours. Unfortunately, the course of treatment can last for up to a year. I don't have a lot more information than that without getting into too much detail that is rather mundane. I will say that based on the timeline of Lana's medical events, along with what he has said and what I have read after speaking with him, my gut says he is correct. I will let you know more tomorrow as I learn more.

Jessica: Wow. Just wow. Not much else to say than that, but praying hard. I love you and wish it were possible to come to visit and give you a giant hug.

Jeanne: Wow! I'll be looking for tomorrow's update. Meanwhile, the prayers will continue. Love you guys!

Julia: Oh, man. Thank you for taking the time to give such detailed updates. Just know that you are all in our thoughts and prayers. Let me know if there is anything we can do to help.

John: Well, if he's accurate, I'm pretty sure I don't have COVID-19. I could probably use a hug right now.

Following a call to Mackenzie and Lauren, hopeful we would both find rest, John made his way to the bedroom. Weary from the whirlwind of thoughts swirling within his mind, he longed for the thoughts bouncing around in his head to settle enough for him to rest.

DID YOU KNOW YOU COULD EAT HOSTA?

Saturday, April 25

Even with fewer disruptions, I had a restless night of sleep because I couldn't get comfortable. My breathing was labored and even painful at times.

7:12 AM

Me: Good morning.

John: Good morning, sweetheart. How did you sleep?

Me: Not well. I struggled to get comfortable.

John: Did the nurses leave you alone?

Me: Mostly. Vitals at 3 AM, but no blood was drawn until 6:00.

John: How is your breathing this morning?

Me: Up and down. I think that's what was happening last night, too. It's like my lungs decide to gasp for air every once in a while—it kind of hurts.

John: Let's pray they figure this out and get you started on the right medication today.

Me: It's hard not knowing.

John: Yes, it is.

About an hour later, my mom shared a video about naturally protecting your immune system. The video told the story of a man's dad who was hospitalized with heart issues. Until his hospitalization, he didn't realize he was sick. Then, only a few months after being released from the hospital, he lost his hearing from an inflammatory issue. He searched for two years before finding answers.

There was much more to the story, but ultimately the gentleman, a doctor, stated he learned viruses and diseases prey on a weakened host. A disease cannot exist in a body with an immune system functioning 100%. He encouraged those watching to use natural methods such as eating nutritiously and exercising regularly to stay healthy.

I pondered what he said. I knew my immune system wasn't functioning correctly, but I still had no confirmed diagnosis. As a personal trainer, I did everything this man mentioned and educated many others about the benefits of a healthy lifestyle. I was led back to the question I had from the beginning, what had caused my immune system to get so out of whack?

Mom texted to be sure I had received the link for the video and asked if I had watched it. I confirmed that I had and shared my concerns that maybe I had contributed to my illness. I wondered if maintaining such low body fat for a long time, along with the stress of overtraining, had done more harm than good.

To this day, I still wonder if my desire to be exceptionally fit pushed my body beyond its limits. This question may never be answered, but I firmly believe it's a strong possibility.

As they often do, the conversation with my mom took an unexpected turn. Thankfully the shift lightened my mood a little.

8:41 AM

Mom: Did you know you could eat hosta plants? I didn't.

Me: Why would you?

Mom: They can be used like spinach or asparagus in a lot of recipes, apparently. I guess they are healthy as well as look nice. We ate wilted dandelions in the spring when I was a kid. Of course, Mom made us go down along the road ditches to get them and only young new ones. The dogs were in the yard, so those weren't good to get. Your dad hadn't ever eaten them till he married me.

My mom always has a way of making me feel better. I remember many times growing up when I would sit on my bed with her by my side, wiping my tears. She was the one I would turn to when I needed a reassuring word, guidance, and prayer. She knew exactly how to comfort me. The way she encouraged me was extremely loving but always honest. She never told me I was right when I wasn't. She wasn't afraid to share the truth, even if it hurt. She allowed me to express my feelings as long as I needed. And then, once all the emotions were out, she'd do just what she did on this day; she'd change the subject. I believe it was her way of saying, "Okay, we've dealt with that one. Now let's move on."

She's still who I call when I need some extra love. We'll talk about whatever is weighing heavy and then chat about things like eating hosta plants. I couldn't ask for a better mother-daughter relationship.

My sister, Cindy, five years my senior, deals with her feelings much differently than I do. I'm an open book; I wear my heart on my sleeve. She, on the other hand, is much more reserved. So, when I received a message from her later that day, I knew she must be concerned about me.

1:34 PM

Cindy: How are you doing today, Sis?

Me: Very emotional today.

Cindy: I love you, Sis! I wish I could give you a hug! A big sister hug!

Me: I really need one.

Cindy: Me, too!

The text was brief, but even the shortest conversations with her were incredibly precious.

Respiratory therapists and nurses flitted in and out throughout the afternoon, making minor adjustments to my oxygen and taking my vitals. It was nice to have the one-on-one interaction, but I could do without all the poking and prodding.

As the day continued, John and I spoke on the phone several times. We discussed everything the doctors were doing to solve this mystery.

Dr. Walls informed us that if the COVID-19 antibody test returned negative and the steroids worked, I would need to quarantine for a few months after completing my steroid regimen. That meant we might be looking at as long as eight months. My heart crumbled. I never wanted a positive test for a disease so much in my life.

I missed John terribly. And the reality of how bad things were becoming was starting to set in. To say I was ready for all this to be over is an understatement.

3:25 PM

John: Are you okay?

Me: I will be.

John: I love you.

Me: I love you, too. Are you okay?

John: I'll be better when you are.

Me: I feel like I lost a life in my game. Gotta start over.

John: At least the game isn't over.

Me: It got a whole lot harder—too many levels.

John: A lot of levels, that's for sure. It's the only way the game can challenge a great player.

Me: I'm not that good.

John: Yes, you are that good.

Me: *disappointed face*

John: I think God has been preparing you for this by teaching you to be a coach. Consider applying the principles of lifestyle change that you teach—one step at a time.

Me: I'll try

John: I absolutely, 100% believe in you.

Me: I just need to wrap my head around it all. And I need a shower!!!

John: A shower and a real meal would probably help! At any point, I will bring you a good meal. But, unfortunately, I can't do much about the shower.

Me: And time with you!!

John: No doubt about that! I would just like to hold your hand and let you snuggle over against me. I'm looking forward to it!

Me: Me, too. So, so much!

John: Just don't forget that you are the baddest ass I know. I'm not the only one who says that. It's what everyone who knows you thinks.

Me: I wish I felt like a badass right now. I'm sorry. I'm trying to get past this, but it hit me really hard.

John: It's perfectly normal to take a little time to feel bad about it. And then, we will start figuring out how to normalize our quarantine period.

Me: I need to not even think about it until the antibodies test comes back.

John: And you should do that.

Me: One step at a time.

John: Precisely.

Based on the messages I received once this news got out, I could tell I wasn't the only one worried. I sensed the concern in each one.

4:25 PM

Mom: Heavenly Father, words are hard right now because our thoughts are all over the place. This doesn't make sense. Something feels wrong. I know I can't go by my feelings, but how does this fit into your plan? Why would there be a need to quarantine after treatment?

God, help us sort this out so we can understand the meaning of this.

Lord, I have no doubt that you have all the answers, and they may be different than I think, Lana thinks, or different than the doctors think. Lana needs to be given an answer and not taken from one thing to another.

There is no doubt you want her to trust you and to lean on you, but at the same time, you understand why she is shaken to the core.

God, I am boldly asking for this to be misinformation. I am humbly but boldly asking for her health to be fully restored and for that not to be too long from now. She will be your witness as she has been in the past.

Forgive my rambling and searching for words to bring into your presence; I am confused. If I am this confused, she has to be much more so.

Please make things clear to her. Hold her close and bring her peace. Please overwhelm her with your peace.

As always, all glory goes to you.

Amen

4:36 PM

Donna: Let us know if you want us to storm the hospital and kidnap you. Yes, I'm that eager to go somewhere.

Me: So much!!!

4:48 PM

Mackenzie: I love you.

Me: I love you, too!!!

Mackenzie: How are you?

Me: I'm okay. Very emotional.

Mackenzie: I'm so sorry. I wish there were something I could do.

Me: Me too, sweetheart. I wish I could be with my people!

Mackenzie: Me, too. You can call me whenever you want to. I don't know when to call you because I don't know how you feel. But feel free to call me whenever. My schedule is a lot more flexible than your ability to breathe.

As the early evening arrived, John and I talked more about how Covid-19 contributed to us possibly having to quarantine once I could leave the hospital. It remained a difficult conversation. I couldn't bear the thought of being away from people for so long. But we again determined that we would figure everything out when the time came.

John then sent me pictures of the "Get Well Soon" cards that had started arriving at the house. Each one touched my heart because they were evidence of the people God had placed in my life for this very moment.

Following a little more small talk, he sent the daily update to our family, and I made this journal entry:

My Journal

Did not sleep well, still struggled to breathe, and couldn't get comfortable. Dr. suspects organizing pneumonia instead of Covid. Waiting for antibodies test to try to confirm or rule out Covid. Began steroids to try to help my lungs repair. CRP dropped from 169 to 41. Ferritin is also starting to drop. Had to change oxygen back to 60 to help recover. No fever for two full days. My blood pressure is good. My heart rate is still hovering between 90 and 100.

I was tired–physically and mentally. But even so, I wouldn't end my day without saying goodnight to John.

9:30 PM

Me: One more chat?

John: Heck yeah!

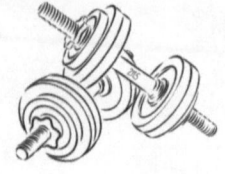

CHAPTER TWELVE

SCARY LANA

Sunday, April 26

I've enjoyed being in church since I was in junior high when my friend, Maryna, asked me to join her. I didn't immediately agree to go, but after numerous invitations, I finally said yes and realized how much fun it was. From that point on through my school years, I spent my Wednesday evenings and Sunday mornings at First Baptist Church of Vandalia learning about Jesus. It was during that time that I accepted Him as my Savior.

Over the years, Sunday became my favorite day of the week. John and I usually have a casual lunch, and then I might squeeze in a nap while he watches sports. Of course, that all comes after Sunday services at Southbrook Church, which we have been attending since the summer of 2007.

This Sunday would be different than usual, though. As with all other events and gatherings, church services were streaming online. Fortunately, that was to my benefit. The new format meant I could watch services from any church I'd like, not just Southbrook. I was thrilled to have the opportunity to visit LifeChurch Reno.

In 2017, my friend and colleague, Mia, moved to Nevada with her family. Her husband, Greg, had been the worship pastor at Southbrook before accepting a new position at a church in Reno. Mia's voice is beautiful, and she often leads worship alongside Greg. I missed hearing both of them sing praises to the Lord. So after watching services streamed by my church, I hopped over to their church's Facebook page to worship with them, as well. The mix of both services filled my longing to worship God and be in His Word. And although our congregations couldn't gather in person, there was a sense of being together through online comments during the live streaming, which filled my heart with joy.

Before streaming the services, I took advantage of the window of privacy I was getting and washed up. That's when I realized how quickly losing muscle mass can happen. Due to the atrophy, my legs were almost unrecognizable. I was shocked. Even if I could return home soon, I knew I had a long way to go before I would be strong enough to work out with the Tribe again. My hope had been deflated again. As I began to cry, a prayer arrived in the form of a text message from my mom.

9:59 AM

Mom: Heavenly Holy God, I come this morning with praise in my heart and on my lips. I'm asking the Holy Spirit to give me the words to approach you this morning. As I sit here, my heart is full. Full of love for you, full of praise for you, and thankfulness for your love and mercy. My eyes are on you and all I know you are doing for Lana. I am looking at her situation through worship this morning. I know what the doctors say. I know what the numbers say. I know what the X-rays say. I know that she struggles to breathe, but I also know you. I know your goodness. I know your mercy. I know your power. I know if you choose to open her lungs and fill them with health, it will be done immediately. Your word tells me and shows me that is true many times over. You rescue your people in times of trouble and distress. I'm still boldly asking for a miracle on her behalf. I'm boldly but humbly asking you to clear every speck of disease from her body. I'm not asking because she or I deserve it. After all, we are sinners simply saved by the sacrifice of Jesus. I'm asking because I know you and your power. I will proclaim your greatness no matter what, but I desire to share this miracle with all who will listen—Exodus 23:25. Worship the Lord your God, and His blessing will be on your food and water. I will take away sickness from among you. Thank you, God, for your faithfulness in keeping your promises. If it were not so, you would have told us. All glory is yours. Amen.

As I read Mom's text, I reflected on how wonderful she is. She certainly knows how to praise God through the tough stuff. I took a few minutes to express my gratitude to the Lord for allowing me to be her daughter.

My moment of reflection was interrupted by the doctor. Thank goodness live streams can be played later because church services would have to wait this morning.

"How are you doing this morning, Lana," he asked with a look of concern.

I replied, "I'm doing okay, I guess. I still have some discomfort in my chest."

"Let's get another chest X-ray to ensure it's a skeletal issue. I don't want to risk it being a blood clot."

"Another chest X-ray sounds great," I answered in the cheeriest voice possible and accompanied it with a forced grin.

We briefly discussed cryptogenic organizing pneumonia again, and when he left, I thought it would be wise to research it a bit further. In my search for answers, I found that I wasn't experiencing any of the symptoms of COP, so I began to question the validity of the diagnosis.

I thought, "If it's not COP, what in the world could be happening?"

I gave my mind a little time to absorb what I had studied before I finally settled in to watch both church services. I wouldn't let myself slip away from God during this crisis. I needed Him more now than ever.

It wasn't much later that the liquid in the oxygen machine ran out. I quickly discovered the benefits of moist air and learned dry air is very uncomfortable. I was uncomfortable enough. I certainly didn't need anything else added to this situation.

However, getting the nurse's attention wasn't easy. I could feel what my gym staff called "scary Lana" surfacing. "Scary Lana" isn't mean; she just knows what she wants and can be stern when ensuring she gets it. And right now, "scary Lana" needed moist air.

I never enjoy being pushy, but I got my moist air back even though it took longer than I liked.

As evening approached, John texted to check on me again. We had already spoken several times throughout the day, so he knew how my day went. But I also wanted to be sure he was doing okay. He had sent messages bringing a few of our friends, including my staff, up to speed before playing guitar, watching TV, and reading. At the end of our text conversation, I shared that my oxygen saturation was staying around 92, and it had done so even during calls to my mom and my daughter, Lauren. He was pleased to hear some positive news.

After I spoke with John around 8:30 pm, he communicated with our family. I even jumped into the conversation this time. As always, they had great questions and offered much support.

8:49 PM - Our Family GroupMe

Julia: John, how is Lana today, AND how are you today?

John: Hey Julia, thanks for asking. I'll take the easy one first; I'm OK. I just wish she would get better. Lana is about the same as far as her breathing goes, but she is eating better, and some of her markers are in a much better place now. Her CRP, an indication of inflammation, has decreased dramatically.

On the other hand, she has developed a second issue. She has what is called spontaneous subcutaneous emphysema caused by a partially collapsed lung. It's not life-threatening, but it is uncomfortable. All those big words mean that she has air that has somehow gotten out of her lung and is under the skin on her chest and neck. They will have to monitor it to make sure it doesn't get out of control.

I took some things to her today, and part of it was a good healthy meal. Then I came home, and we had lunch together via video conference. I think she liked it, so we may make that a daily event.

Speaking with the doctor, he seems pretty sure she'll be there for at least another week. She's lost quite a bit of weight, and her muscles have atrophied some. As hard as she has worked to get fit, it's frustrating her.

Julia: Will her body gradually absorb the air that has gotten outside of her lungs?

John: The steroids that she is taking are causing her to sleep restlessly and tend to affect her mood. When I spoke with her early this morning, she was rather emotional, but as the day went on, she felt much better. With all that is going on, I couldn't possibly be prouder about how she is fighting.

Yes, her body will absorb the air. It just takes some time.

Frank: I'd be emotional too if I'd gone through what she has so far. Based on the few times I've spoken to her and on your updates, I'd say she's handling this like a champ. Also, as far as building muscle back, take it from me, it can be done. So she shouldn't be too worried about that right now. Just focus on getting better, and then she can get her muscles back.

John: Yeah, Frank, we've talked about how quickly she should be able to recover her muscles once she can start exercising again. But it may take her a while to get to that point.

Julia, her fitness has undoubtedly been to her advantage as far as being able to operate on such a low oxygen level. She probably should have been unconscious when they admitted her to the hospital, but she walked to the ambulance. One of the downsides to her fitness level was that we didn't know just how sick she was.

Julia: Please let her know she's got lots of prayers going up for her. The entire finance department of Gaston county schools has added her to lots of prayer chains. I will tell everyone to keep it up.

Me: Thanks for all the love and support!! I'm reading every word but letting John send the updates. So much info! Love you all!

Julia: You try to rest tonight and focus on getting better. Love you!

Jessica: Love you bunches!

Kathy: You keep doing what you're doing to improve, and we'll keep asking God to give you a hand. We both know that He has you in His hands and is working with you. Lots of prayers and lots of love!

Jeanne: Lana, get some rest and keep healing! Prayers for a speedy recovery and lots of love coming your way!

When the texting settled, my heart was full, yet my mind was racing. It had been a day of ups and downs. Making sense of all the doctors were telling us remained difficult. Evidently, they were searching for answers to a condition they had never seen before. Sure, they had dealt with many of the symptoms I was experiencing, but never in the form that was present in me.

I turned to God and asked for healing again as I tried to accept that recovery may not come in the manner I hoped it would.

The final message of the day was short but precisely what I needed.

10:04 PM

Me: Good night. *heart*

John: Good night. I love you!

CHAPTER THIRTEEN

A CHAIR AND A HAZMAT SUIT

Monday, April 27

I felt like nothing was changing. I'd been in the hospital for seven days and was no better than when I arrived. The air trapped in my chest was uncomfortable, to say the least. I was restless and desperately wanted to be with John and my friends.

I told the Tribe about my partially collapsed lung and expressed how much I needed time with them. I was accustomed to being with them four times every week. I suppose that was causing me to miss them as much as I did. After some discussion, we made a virtual date for Thursday at 2:00 pm, and I was already looking forward to it.

When the nurse arrived to administer one of the two shots I received each day in my belly to avoid blood clots, she commented on how little body fat I had on my abdomen. To which I replied, "It's all about the food."

God opened the door for a 10-minute conversation about her desire to create healthier eating habits. Then she told me that I most likely wouldn't have survived if I weren't as fit as I was when all this happened. That was the first of many times I would hear that said over the coming months and the first of many thanks I would whisper to the Lord.

Later in the morning, around 10:45, a hospital attendee came to move the lounge chair in my room. She was dressed in a full hazmat suit. I should have felt sorry for her, but for some reason, I got a kick out of it instead (so much so that I have a little video clip of the action). She struggled to move around as the suit slipped off her shoulder and the head covering dropped in front of her eyes. She couldn't hear anything I said between her suit and my partially collapsed lung. I chuckled as I envisioned a small crowd laughing at our comedy scene. Then finally, after ten minutes or so, she found success, and my chair was back in position for me to sit in it. I still occasionally watch that video for sheer entertainment. The event mirrors the calamity this whole incident brought to our lives. However, it also serves as a great reminder to look for humor in the midst of trials, as it can be found even in the darkest of times.

The rest of the afternoon was mostly quiet, but I remained uncomfortable. My breathing hadn't improved, and the hope of getting better soon was waning. Nevertheless, I was doing my best to fight off discouragement.

But then more disappointing news came. After further evaluation, the doctors determined the air in my chest wasn't lessening. The next step would be to insert a chest tube to allow the air to escape. Of course, I wanted to avoid this procedure if at all possible.

4:22 PM

Me: This chest tube insertion is supposedly painful.

John: Have they said if they were going to do the insertion?

Me: No, but it's not getting better. I'm guessing the doctor will determine if it's needed tomorrow.

John: Maybe it will get better by then. He hasn't called me yet today, but I will ask him about it when he does. That is if he calls me.

Me: He said he was going to.

John: Good. How are you feeling otherwise?

Me: Same. It seems like this is where I'm stuck for now.

John: My gut tells me that you will be turning the corner pretty soon.

John's gut feeling was indeed correct. I would turn the corner soon, but that corner was not at all what we were hoping for.

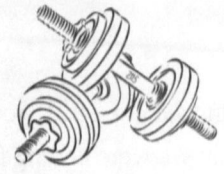

CHAPTER FOURTEEN

UNSTABLE O_2 SAT

Tuesday, April 28

Hours passed slowly.

Air still filled my chest, and my oxygen levels would drop every time I moved. Getting out of bed would cause the multitudes to come running, but I'm stubborn and honestly believed I could fight through this. Whatever "this" was. I wouldn't allow myself to give up. In my ignorance, I was making excuses for my symptoms and still downplaying the seriousness of my situation.

Unfortunately, throughout my extensive fitness education, none of the lessons addressed oxygen saturation. Therefore, I was unaware that levels under 88 percent are extremely dangerous.

When I stood to make my way to the bedside commode, my oxygen saturation plummeted to 64. The nurse ordered me back to bed and told me to stay put.

I said, "Oh, I'm going to move."

With a look of frustration, she replied, "I'm sure you will."

In my mind, moving would help me stay strong. The reality was my lungs couldn't handle the added stress, and I was most likely doing more harm than good.

After catching up on emails and browsing social media, I felt a conversation with the Tribe was in order. Since our workouts had been at 10:00 am since we'd been together, it was the perfect time to encourage them. I also wanted to break some tough news.

10:00 AM

Me: Time to work out!!! Let me see some pics!!!

Donna: Too late! Already done!!!!

Dawn: Go, Donna! So I have a call at 11, and then I'm picking up Joe from the airport! I hope to do some kind of workout later today. Don't want to disappoint my trainer.

Diana: I will try to take a pic when it happens. We did a 30-second push-up every hour, and my shoulders and pecs are a little mad at me today. I don't want to do the last set without doing it with my Tribe. Motivation is difficult when you're all alone!

Me: I need to break something to you. I've been holding on to it because it crushes my heart and makes me cry whenever I think about it. If my antibodies test comes back negative, I won't return to the gym for months. I will have to self-quarantine until there is a vaccine for COVID-19 or my immune system can rebuild. That will be as long as I'm on steroids, plus a month or two after. Steroids can last 3, 6, 9, or even 12 months for the type of pneumonia I have. It depends on my body's response. That means no family visits, no college graduation, possibly no family holiday celebrations, and definitely no gym. Of course, I'm shooting for three or fewer! But mostly, I'm praying for a positive antibodies test.

As I'm typing this with tears pouring down my cheeks, I beg you to pray for a positive test! I don't think I can live in isolation like that.

Rosy: Oh, Lana, I can't hold my tears reading your text. I can't imagine how hard it has been for you without knowing what's going on for sure with your body, but one thing for sure you can count on it's that God is with you, so please don't lose your faith and hope that everything it's going to be okay soon. We are with you all the way, and prayers have undeniable power. Keep on with your positive attitude. We love you so much!

Donna: Oh, dear God, Lana! I can't imagine what you're going through right now! This is so much for you to think about while you're trying to recover. I'm not sure I understand the medical reasons behind all of this, but I completely understand the feelings and the madness in all the possibilities. Like Rosy said, prayers are powerful, and we will band together to talk God's ears off. If there is ANYTHING you need, we are here for you. I love my Tribe!

Diana: My heart sank as I read all of that. I knew it was unpredictable, and they were still working on it, but I had no idea about the level of complication behind it. I don't know if I still fully understand, but I know what to cheer for. Let's pray that there are positive antibodies, and we will also pray that God will deliver a doctor who has the full answers and can heal you from all of this.

The part that hurts the most is that I know how physically and mentally strong you are; we have watched it for years now. But seeing you having a tough time like this hurts my heart. I know the Tribe will band together and celebrate the day we can all work out like us again. I truly miss every one of you, but we will wait for our little Miss Lana to come back stronger than ever. Your belief and devotion to God and trust that he is there to help you will see you through the darkest of times.

Dawn: It's just too much to take in, and I can't stand you've been holding it in, but I also wouldn't want it out to the universe initially. It does seem odd to pray for a test to be positive, doesn't it? We are all here for you and would never let you be totally isolated. Drive-bys have taken on a whole new positive meaning!!

Donna: When will the test be back, Lana?

Me: I love you ladies so much. I don't think you'll ever know what your friendship and support mean to me. Thank you for all your encouragement! The test results should be back hopefully tomorrow. They said 2-3 days, but the blood work didn't go to the lab until yesterday. I'll let you know as soon as I hear.

Donna: We can't pray hard enough! xoxoxo

It took a few minutes to gather my emotions after that conversation. But sometimes, a good cry helps to make things a little better.

Dr. Walls made his rounds, and we discussed what had happened earlier this morning with my oxygen saturation when I got out of bed. Based on our conversation and what he saw in my charts, he had the respiratory therapist increase the amount of oxygen I received.

John and I spoke for several minutes after Dr. Walls left. It was nice to hear John's voice, but we didn't have much to discuss. Other than what was happening with my health, there wasn't much happening in the world. Over the past week, John and two of our staff members did some deep cleaning at the gym. However, now that that was complete, the pandemic kept him home for the most part. Nevertheless, he was still making daily trips to the hospital to bring my lunch. He was glad to have something to do, and I was incredibly grateful that I could have a familiar, healthy meal every day.

Around 4:45 pm, I decided to attempt to stand to see how my body would react. Although my heart rate shot up to 121 beats per minute, my oxygen saturation remained at 95, and I was able to stand for almost a full minute. I was so excited that I took a selfie as I stood beside the bed and sent it to John. He and I had a video call to celebrate my accomplishment. However, my nurse wasn't as impressed with my efforts. As a matter of fact, I'm confident all the medical staff members wished I would listen to directives and stay in bed.

John sent the daily update to our family, along with the picture I shared with him.

6:51 PM - Family GroupMe

John: Today's update. Well, she made some improvement this afternoon. She stood for one minute, which is a minute longer than she could stand yesterday, and her oxygen recovery was pretty quick afterward, but it's still not where it should be. She took the deepest breaths she's taken in about two weeks. She still requires a high level of oxygen, and her heart rate is still substantially higher than normal. Her resting rate is usually in the 50s. Currently, it's staying in the 90s to the 110s. This morning, she had an issue where it jumped into the 140s for a few minutes, but that was before she started feeling stronger this afternoon.

She wanted me to send this picture so you guys could see that she is starting to feel a little better. I don't know that she feels quite as good as she would like you to think. But she certainly is feeling much better.

She's starting to set some really impressive goals now, so I know she's healing. By tomorrow her goal is to be able to walk all the way to the bathroom!

Kathy: That sounds wonderful. Things are going in the right direction! Pulling for her with all my heart.

Ali: Yay for improvement!!!!!!

Jessica: Yay!!!! Best news all day/week! So grateful for the progress. Continued prayers and happy thoughts coming your way!

Jeanne: Happy to see a smiling face! The steroids must be doing their job. Go big or go home!

John: Jeanne, it's funny you say that because we just had that same conversation today! She said that exact thing. There's still a long road ahead, but it's nice to feel like she's getting out of the ditch a little.

I can't thank everybody for the support you've provided during this time. It means an awful lot to both of us!

Julia: I heard that's what family is for.

I wrapped up the day with a final call to John and a quick journal entry.

My Journal

I had a very rough morning. My oxygen level dropped to the mid-60s, and my heart rate spiked to 142. My blood pressure jumped to 125/75 compared to my normal 90s/60s. No fever. I stayed very still. There's still air in my chest. Around 4 pm, I began to feel better. I stood up for one minute. I sat upright, pretzel style, in the bed for about an hour. I took several deep breaths without pain. Hopefully, I have turned the corner John mentioned yesterday.

I was encouraged by the day as I drifted to sleep. I felt my body was be-ginning to mend. But at this point, I wasn't sure what would happen next. I felt like a yo-yo. All I wanted was for the master of this never-ending game of ups and downs to grab hold of me and make it stop.

CHAPTER FIFTEEN

THE BATHROOM DOOR

Wednesday, April 29

The morning began on a brighter note than the day before. I felt I had made more steps toward recovery yesterday, which assured me today would be even better. And even though my oxygen saturation was still showing little improvement, I assumed it was just a matter of time before that changed, too.

John and I were on the phone when the nurse came for morning rounds. We ended our call sooner than I wanted to allow her to complete her duties. Shortly after, a physician assistant stopped by to share some news regarding my autoimmune disease tests. The bloodwork revealed no autoimmune issues. Considering what we knew so far, that was good news for the long term. There were still no results from the antibody test yet.

My appetite had grown a little, which led me to ask John to add another ounce of chicken to my lunch salad. Of course, he was glad to know I was a bit hungrier than I had been, and he assured me he would increase the salad's protein level.

It was only 9:30 am, but I was already bored. I was thrilled when Rosy initiated the morning's Tribe conversation.

Because the gym was closed, each of the Tribe ladies had been creating workout areas for themselves in their homes, but Donna completely renovated the space she had been using. Home gyms had become necessities during the pandemic if you desired to stay fit. Sure, outdoor activities were an option. But those aren't for everyone, especially if you enjoy lifting weights as much as we did.

Donna texted us pictures of her new space. I think it's fair to say I was a tad envious, but I was excited for her.

Our banter went on for quite a few minutes before Rosy wrapped up the conversation as easily as she started it.

> **Rosy**: See you tomorrow, girls, and Lana, hang in there. Everything it's going to be okay. You have a lot of people thinking and praying for you because we love you and need you.

I filled the rest of the day with as many distractions as possible. I sent business emails to our gym members and watched a few shows on Netflix. John brought my lunch to the hospital around 11:30 am. After lunch, the nurse changed my bedding while I sat in the chair and cleaned up as much as I could. Later in the afternoon, Mackenzie and I spoke on FaceTime.

The day was quieter than the previous days, which gave me time to reflect and pray. I continued praying for healing in my body so I could go home and return to my normal routine. I thanked God for my family and friends and their support and prayers.

Although my side of the conversations with God hadn't changed much, His took a turn, and I wasn't sure what He meant. The words He spoke penetrated my heart but also gave me pause.

"No matter what happens, We are with you."

I replied, "I know, Lord. You are always with me. Thank you."

"Yes, that's true. But remember, no matter what happens, We are with you."

I will never forget how loved I felt when He spoke those words to me. And yet, at the same time, how unnerving they were. What exactly was going to happen?

I pushed my thoughts aside and focused again on the task at hand–getting better. I was determined to walk farther than the two or three steps it took to get to my bedside chair. Since I was born, I've been determined, and almost nothing can stop me once I've made my mind up to do something.

I shifted in the bed until my feet were over the edge. Then I wiggled forward to place them on the floor. In one resolute motion, I pushed myself up and stood. After taking in as much oxygen as possible, I began my journey toward the bathroom.

I went as far as the bathroom door before my oxygen hose stopped me. Unfortunately, it wasn't long enough to completely cross the threshold! So, even though I never saw the inside of that bathroom, I was satisfied with my accomplishment and had to share it with the world.

I started with the Tribe. I knew they would celebrate my rear end crossing the bathroom threshold with me.

5:20 PM

Me: Victory! I walked to the bathroom. I couldn't go all the way in because my cables and hoses wouldn't let me. But my feet got past the doorway, and I turned around and stuck my butt in. I could've kept going had I not been tied to the wall.

Donna: OMGoodness!!!! That is great news! No oxygen crash? Celebration time!!

Me: Well, a minor crash, but I recovered quickly. The nurse was surprised by my ability to do it.

Donna: That's our strong girl! Take it slowly, and don't keep testing the limits. You're going to be fine.

Dawn: Oh, Lana, this is fantastic! Nothing weirder than a friend telling you that her cables keep her from going all the way to the bathroom. This is a crazy world we live in. Victories!!

Me: I'm trying to bust out of here. I've got things to do and people to ZOOM.

Diana: You made it all the way to the almost bathroom, but it wasn't your lungs holding you back! Thank the Lord that your prayers are slowly being answered! Did you get the test results back yet?

Me: No test results yet. Maybe tomorrow???

Diana: More prayers are a-coming!

Rosy: Wonderful news, Lana. That is amazing. We are so happy that you are getting better and better. I'm sure everybody there is very impressed with your progress.

I still couldn't contain my excitement, so I sent the same victory message to John, Mackenzie, Lauren, and Mom.

As I settled in to bask in my accomplishments, my food arrived. I had ordered the usual turkey sandwich with fruit and asked for mustard instead of mayonnaise. The sandwich and fruit were as expected, but once again, there was no sign of the mustard I had requested.

John's sister, Jeanne, sent a message in the family GroupMe to find out if there were any updates to report.

6:54 PM

John: Thanks for asking, Jeanne. Today has been another good day for Lana! She stood for three minutes and walked to the bathroom. The bathroom is only about twelve feet away, but she said she could've easily walked further. The steroids are clearly having a positive effect on her in the timeframe her pulmonologist suggested. When I spoke to the pulmonologist late this afternoon, he suggested that the middle of next week was not an unreasonable timeframe for her to be able to come home. She is shooting for Monday! (yes, Lana, I wanted to make sure I got that in there!) It's been really good to see her begin to recover and feel like there is an end in sight to how she has felt. We know there's still a long road ahead with therapy, but at least she won't be suffering from the symptoms. All of your thoughts, concerns, and prayers have been incredibly supportive. We both appreciate all of you and love all of you very much!

Ali: This is amazing to hear!

Julia: That's fantastic news.

Jeanne: That is wonderful! The prayers, thoughts, and medicines are doing their job!

Kathy: What a wonderful way to end the day.

John: She was definitely excited this afternoon with the progress she has made! One more thing. I know she's starting to feel a little better because she was pretty feisty today. In a good way!

Just before 8:00 pm, John texted to remind me that the popular show "The Masked Singer" was about to start. He and I always enjoyed watching it together while attempting to guess what celebrity was behind each mask. This evening, we shared our opinions over the phone while viewing it on our respective TVs.

Then, the final journal entry I would make for several months.

My Journal

I felt very good today. The therapist dropped my oxygen to 50 flow and 30/lpm. I would like it to drop every day. I still have a leak in my right lung. Time should heal that. I will try to find a way to be more mobile tomorrow. Keep pushing!

PART 2

THE FIGHT

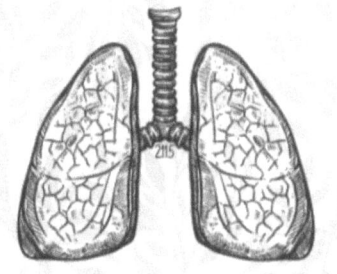

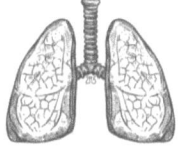

CHAPTER SIXTEEN

I NEVER USED THE MUSTARD

Thursday, April 30

Overnight, the amount of air in my chest cavity had increased, causing more discomfort and making it even harder to breathe. Wednesday had been uplifting, but all the talk of going home soon seemed like it might have just been talk. Now, all eyes were on me, and commotion from my medical team filled my room.

8:24 AM

Me: Don't wait for me to call—lots of activity.

John: I just spoke with your doctor, and they are going to send you down for a CT. I'm sure you're aware of that, but he brought me up to speed on everything. He will confer with a thoracic surgeon to see if they need to do a thin catheter to evacuate the air.

Me: I know.

John: I love you more than you can imagine. Contact me when you can.

Me: I love you. I wish you were here.

John: Me too.

I had wanted John with me the past week, but now it was becoming even harder to be away from him. Having surgery without him there seemed impossible. I wasn't sure if I could handle it.

A text message from Donna came within a minute of my text with John. Today was the day of our scheduled Zoom call to catch up. To my disliking, I doubted that I would be on the call. While fighting to breathe, I managed to respond in a few incomplete sentences.

8:25 AM

Donna: Update, please! And is everyone ready to Zoom at 2:00 today?

Me: Tough morning. More air outside the lung. May need a catheter to release it. Going for a CT scan. Emotions are flowing. I'm hoping to be able to join you this afternoon. Workout for me! Miss you all!!!!

Donna: Oh, gosh, Lana! I'm sorry for everything you're going through. Extra prayers, happy thoughts, good vibes, ALL THE THINGS! Maybe a catheter is best so you can get some relief. I hate that it hasn't resolved on its own. Still praying for a positive antibodies test.

Dawn: Sweet Lana, we wish we could hug you. You've been so strong. I would be crying every day, except that makes us even more exhausted, so don't listen to me. We all wish we could take this pain away. We will see you at 2 PM or any other time. You just say the word.

Diana: Lana, you WILL get through this. There is light at the end of the tunnel. It's so hard right now. We are hurting for you. Did they say if the air bubble will help aid the healing faster or just get you more comfortable? I hope you get some good news today. We are flexible to have the call anytime that you are ready.

Rosy: Lana, I know this is extremely hard for you, and I wish I could be there to give you a big hug. Please don't let this bump on the way to your recovery change your positive attitude. I'm sure you get this, and you are not alone. We have you in our thoughts and prayers every day, and very soon, we will be together again. We love you and miss you very much. I'm open for any time for our Zoom meeting.

I had told my friends from the beginning of my illness that I knew God was in control and would take care of me. I still didn't doubt that. But now, I was anxious about what was happening.

Through tears, my prayers reflected this fear, "God, I'm scared. Please heal my body. Give me strength to endure whatever lies ahead. Help me fight, Lord. I trust you to carry me through this trial."

The Lord's answer to my plea for healing was the same as yesterday, "No matter what happens, We are with you."

I remember thinking how vague those words were. They didn't explain anything, so all I heard was, "Hang on, there's more coming." That wasn't very reassuring.

As I processed my emotions of fear and discouragement, a text from my mother arrived.

8:56 AM

Mom: Heavenly Father, praises and thanks to you for the healing that's taking place in Lana's body. Thank you for a doctor that was willing to be open-minded. Thank you for nurses that care for her. Thank you for the one that came and prayed with her. Thank you for medicine. Thank you for her desire to be so healthy even before this. No matter how you choose to heal her, I am asking that it will be in such a way that you receive the glory. We will not say it was the medicine or her good health even though you may use those. It will only be that God healed her. We know you will be watching over her during all that may be ahead. May we honor you with our words and action. All glory is yours. Amen.

Me: A few setbacks this morning. More air around the lung. Going for a CT scan soon. May need the catheter to drain the air. Emotional!!!!!

Mom: Oh honey, I'm sorry. God has this. Hang onto that. If, and I say if, they have to use the catheter, it will make the healing go faster.

Holy Father, we know you are in control during this. Thank you that we can be sure of that. Lord, show yourself to everyone today. Please hear us as we ask for this to be gone and for her lungs to heal. You are the great physician. I ask that your peace wrap around Lana and cover her with calmness and assurance. Give her your word for her to stand on today, even for this minute. We still declare all glory is yours. Amen.

Jesus loves me; this I know, for the Bible tells me so. Little ones to him belong. They are weak, but He is strong. Yes, Jesus loves me. The Bible tells me so.

More tears rolled down my cheeks. That song, Jesus Loves Me, has been prominent in our family for years. My mom sings it to her grandbabies while she rocks them to sleep. It's like magic. No matter how much the kids fought sleep, the melody would lull them into a trance.

Sending me the words of this song was her way of reaching across the miles and holding me in her arms. I knew this, and I could feel her desire to be with me as much as I wanted to be with her.

I was too emotional to reply to her. I assumed we would talk later in the day. But unfortunately, I was wrong. That text was the last conversation I shared with my mom for over a month.

Mid-morning, John sent a vague request for prayers to our family. Based on their replies, I knew they were all on their knees once again. Every prayer helped ease my mind, and I was grateful to have so many who cared deeply for me. Yet nothing could remove my desire for all of this to be over.

John and I talked again around 10:30 am. Our conversations were becoming more clinical as my condition worsened. He shared what the doctor told him about the CT scan and procedure to release the trapped air. Finally, we determined that he would still deliver lunch as planned.

Shortly before lunch, Willis came in to check on me and make the necessary adjustments to my respiratory therapy. During his visit, I mentioned my mustard dilemma.

"I can't seem to get the cafeteria to send mustard with my meals, no matter how many times I ask. They keep sending mayonnaise, and I don't eat mayonnaise," I said with a grin.

"I'm a mustard guy, too. I think it's much better than mayonnaise. So don't you worry, Lana. I'll be sure to get you some mustard," he replied.

"Oh, you don't have to do that. I'm sure I can survive without it."

He smiled and said, "It's no problem at all, and it would be my pleasure to bring you some. No one wants to eat a dry sandwich. Or one with mayo."

"Well, thank you. My husband is bringing me lunch, so there's no rush. I won't need it until dinner."

While he checked my oxygen levels, he said, "You can count on having your mustard before dinner. I'll also let your nurse know your husband will be here soon so someone can be ready to meet him to get your lunch."

All of this was above and beyond his responsibilities. But, as I mentioned earlier, we bonded quickly. For some reason, he felt compassion for me, and I was grateful for his warm-heartedness.

John arrived with my salad right on schedule. He had become a personal DoorDash. My nurse, Teresa, met him at the entrance to the hospital, as usual, to pick it up.

12:03 PM

John: Teresa has your food, and I am back in the car. You should probably go ahead and eat instead of waiting for me. Just in case they come to take you to the CT.

I didn't want to eat alone. I enjoyed being on FaceTime with John while we had lunch. It was the closest thing to sitting at the table together. So I waited, and we ate lunch together when he returned home.

As we ate, I realized John had left off an essential element of the salad–the chicken. It didn't matter to me that he forgot, but it gave me something to mess with him about.

"How's your salad?" he asked.

"It would probably be better if it had chicken on it," I teased.

Surprised, he replied, "Are you sure there's no chicken on it? I could have sworn I put it on there."

"Oh, I'm sure. It's okay. I'm not very hungry anyway."

"I'm sorry." He felt terrible about his oversight, but we laughed about it in the end.

After we finished our meals, I decided I wanted to take a nap while I had a chance. So we said our goodbyes, and I adjusted to a position where I could breathe easier and relax.

Before I drifted off to sleep, I contacted the Tribe to let them know I would need to skip our scheduled 2:00 pm Zoom call because I hadn't had my procedure yet and wanted to sleep. They graciously accepted me bowing out and assured me they would be ready for a call whenever I was.

I slept for a little over an hour and felt re-energized. I reached back out to the Tribe, hoping they would be available for our Zoom call after all.

2:26 PM

Me: Nothing is happening yet, and I took a little power nap. Is anyone available?

Rosy: I'm here. Just came back to walk my dogs. Did they tell you how much longer to get the catheter in?

Me: They just said after 1 pm. Hurry up and wait. LOL. Do you still have the Zoom link? Would you like to jump on for a few minutes?

Rosy: I guess they are like the delivery people between 9:00 and 5:00 pm. *smiley face* Sure, let me try.

Donna: I'm here in the meeting!

Dawn: Just ending a call. I'll be right there.

Diana: I'm going to come to say hi!

The Tribe and I wrapped up our call a little after 3:00 pm. It was great spending time with them, and I'm glad we didn't wait any longer. Because, as with my mom, this would be our last conversation for quite a while.

At around 3:30 pm, it was finally time for my CT scan. There was a significant concern, though. The doctors were worried about whether my lungs could handle the procedure. My oxygen saturation was still very low, and a portable oxygen tank might not be strong enough to keep my oxygen levels up.

Willis arrived in my room with a handful of mustard packets and a load of gusto. "I brought you mustard. It will be here when you get back for dinner," he said with a wink.

He then turned his attention to the doctor, "If you get her down for the CT quickly, I'll put her on wall oxygen and get her through this procedure."

There was still hesitation, but after a brief discussion, it was a go!

"I'll take care of you," Willis assured me. "Are you ready?"

"Yep. Let's do it." I was definitely more confident in Willis' ability than mine, but I was willing to give it my all.

It took some effort to move me to the wheelchair, change my oxygen, set up the IVs, and maneuver all the cables for transport, but we managed. And then we were off.

When we arrived in the radiology department, the CT room wasn't ready. I sat in the wheelchair gasping for air and praying for that wall oxygen Willis had mentioned. The pounding of my heartbeat muffled the conversations around me. I closed my eyes, attempting to escape the suffocation I was experiencing. It was all I could do to remain calm.

Willis knelt beside me and touched my arm, "Are you okay, Lana?"

With my head in my hands and eyes closed, I gave him a slight nod.

"Hang in there. I'm going to get you through this." He stood and faced the doctor, "What's going on? We have to get her in there. Now."

"The room isn't quite ready. We know how critical the situation is. They're working as fast as possible," the doctor replied.

"They need to hurry." Even though his words seemed distant, I could hear his desperation.

Thankfully, soon after this conversation, Willis wheeled me into a cold room, where a kind, compassionate technician greeted me. The way she and Willis worked together was like a choreographed dance. Each of them moved and executed their parts as if they were one.

Moving from the wheelchair to the uncomfortable, hard exam bed took every ounce of effort I had left, even with assistance from the tech. By this time, I could no longer hold back my tears. Willis and the technician knew how difficult and emotional this procedure was for me, and they did all they could to encourage me to stay strong.

"We're almost there, Lana," Willis announced from the left side of my bed. "I promised I would get you through this, and I never go back on my promises. There, how's that?"

At last! That magical wall oxygen!

I gave him a weak thumbs up.

As Willis made the appropriate adjustments, he said, "You should start to feel a little better now. I'm not leaving this room. If you need anything, just let me know."

And he stepped aside as the technician took over. She gave me the rundown on how the scan worked, ensured I understood her instructions, and assured me she would do the scan as quickly as possible.

I entered the dark, loud tube and tried to be as still as possible. As tears continued to fall, I prayed.

"I'm scared, God. I want this to be over, and I want to go home. Please, God!"

"No matter what happens, We are with you."

It was then that those words completely penetrated my heart and soul. He wasn't promising me everything would be okay, only that He wouldn't leave me. I didn't know what would happen, but I was confident I would be okay even if my final breath were near.

For the remainder of the CT scan, I heard my mother's voice singing "Jesus Loves Me" and felt the Lord's presence by my side.

From home, John explained the situation to Mackenzie and Lauren and then updated the rest of the family again.

4:28 PM

John: I just wanted to let you guys know that they've taken Lana to do a CT scan and insert a catheter into her chest cavity. The air escaping her lung has increased, creating substantial pressure on her right lung. I think the lung has collapsed further than it was, and the doctors want to alleviate the pressure. We now have a thoracic surgeon involved. The catheter is supposedly pretty small and shouldn't cause too much discomfort.

As promised, Willis took great care of me during the procedure, but it was the last time I saw him. Despite his success, I was in acute respiratory distress. My lungs were failing faster than the medical team could understand or explain. Realizing that my condition could quickly worsen, the doctors decided that I needed to be closely monitored. So instead of returning to my room when the CT scan was complete, I was taken directly to ICU, where two lovely nurses waited to greet me. (And by the way, I never used the mustard.)

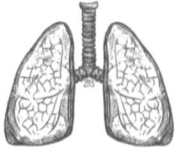

CHAPTER SEVENTEEN

THE WORLD WENT BLACK

Upon my arrival to the ICU, I made one final move from the wheelchair to the bed. The nurses maneuvered the cables and tubes, hooking them to the ICU monitors and machines. When that was complete, I was completely exhausted. Then came a directive I could have done without, "We need you to lay on your stomach. Your lungs will be able to function better that way."

I knew these lovely nurses were doing what was best for me, but the last place I wanted to be was on my stomach, face-down on a pillow. I have a slight case of claustrophobia, which certainly didn't help my situation.

I got as comfortable as I could despite my hatred for my position. Then, I closed my eyes and attempted to find a calm space in my mind.

Meanwhile, Donna updated the rest of The Tribe with the information she'd received from John.

7:30 PM - The Tribe (excluding me)

Donna: Hey, Tribe. John just called to give an update on Lana. She had the CAT scan this afternoon, and they found a secondary condition, Acute Respiratory Distress Syndrome (ARDS). Don't Google it! The catheter was put in, and her lung was re-inflated; however, they moved her to ICU because of the seriousness of her condition. She has been heavily sedated and is lying on her stomach to help her breathe. We can text her right now but know that she may not have the strength to text back. John went on to say that we are all very special to her and that she has never had a group of friends like this. Yada yada yada, sappy stuff that I can't handle right now. Keep praying. XOXO

Rosy: Love you, girl. She needs to get better. Thank you for keeping us updated.

Diana: Oh my word. I'm just seeing this, and I am so gutted.

Donna: It's so incredibly scary. I can't believe how quickly she's gone downhill.

Diana: I just Googled it!

Donna: That made things worse in my head.

Rosy: I'm thinking the same, Donna. I still can't believe how quickly everything changed.

Diana: I'm grateful they caught it, but tonight I will be praying for her that they can find the right medicine to heal her. This is too much.

Donna: I love you all and will be thinking of our little group through the night.

Rosy: Tribe united, praying together. Love you all.

Dawn: Oh, girls, I'm crying. This is just too much. This is all so surreal. Love you, ladies.

As Donna recommended, she and Rosy sent messages to me directly without expecting a response.

7:37 PM

Donna: Don't respond to me, okay? I know you may not have the strength. I just spoke to John. I love you, my friend. I will continue praying like a crazy lady. Keep the faith and know that God is definitely talking to you, so pay close attention. XOXOXOXOXOXOXO

7:49 PM

Rosy: Lana, I know you are having a hard time right now, but don't worry. You are in God's hands. There is a quote that always lift up my spirit, and I hope it will do the same to you. "God is never blind to your tears, never deaf to your prayers, and never silent to your pain. He sees, He hears, and He will deliver." Always in our prayers. Love you, girl.

As I settled in for a long night, a FaceTime call with John calmed my nerves, and I was finally able to find peace even as I lay on my stomach. Of course, our conversation was limited, but I was comforted by seeing his face. And his compassionate smile told me everything I needed to know—he loved me immensely and was utterly scared for me.

I was in no condition to relay information to John, so the doctor spoke to him directly and explained my situation. John then passed the information on to the family.

9:09 PM

John: Hello, everybody. Sorry for the late update, but it's been a hectic afternoon. Lana is in the intensive care unit and being monitored closely. She is struggling with a secondary issue called ARDS, which stands for acute respiratory distress syndrome. She's currently lying on her stomach because that seems to help with this particular condition. There is no treatment for ARDS other than making her comfortable and allowing her body to heal. They will continue treating her for organizing pneumonia in hopes that it responds better. They put a catheter into her chest cavity this afternoon and removed the air, which allowed her right lung to re-inflate. She is in good spirits despite being extremely sick. Thanks again for all of the prayers.

As usual, many replies with offered prayers came to him, for which he was very grateful. At this point, I had stopped monitoring messages.

The last visit from the doctor for the evening brought news I wasn't expecting to hear, "Mrs. Lamkin, your lungs are not improving, and you are in serious danger. The only option we have to help is to put you on a ventilator so your lungs can have a break and heal," he spoke with kindness laced with authority.

As much as I didn't want to admit it, I realized this was my only option. I replied, "I want to talk to my husband about this, please."

"Okay, but your call will have to be brief. Unfortunately, we don't have much time."

When John answered the phone, my true feelings came flooding out, "I'm terrified. They want to put me on a ventilator." My chin quivered as I whispered, "I don't want to do this."

He spoke in a tone I had become very familiar with over the years. One of strength and compassion, bold yet loving, "I know baby, but you have to. I love you so much."

I handed the phone to the doctor, and John began to ask questions about the procedure. The doctor stopped him and said, "We don't have time to discuss the details. This has to be done immediately. There's no time to wait."

That was the last I remember of that evening. I don't recall being prepped for the procedure or having any other conversations. The world just went black.

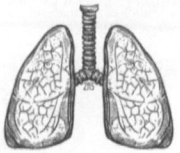

CHAPTER EIGHTEEN

GATHER THE FAMILY

The intubation that evening was a success, and the ventilator was doing its job. But my life still hung in the balance.

"Hello. This is John." It was 10:00 pm when the attending physician greeted him.

"Hi, Mr. Lamkin. This is Dr. Dartey-Hayford. I'm calling to let you know your wife's procedure is complete."

"Thank you. How is she?"

"She is stable for now but not out of the woods," he replied. "So, may I ask, do you have any children?"

John proudly answered, "Yes, we both have children from our first marriages. I have two daughters, and Lana has two daughters."

"Are they local?"

Concern began to fill John's thoughts, "My girls both live in the Concord area, Lana's older daughter is just down the road, and the youngest is at NC State in Raleigh." Then, with a furrowed brow, he asked, "Are you suggesting they need to be close?"

John heard the compassion in the doctor's voice as he answered, "Yes, I would suggest you have them near. We are doing all we can. However, we're concerned she may not make it through the night."

In shock, John hung up with the doctor and then made what he knew would be the first difficult call of the evening. He picked up his phone and dialed my mom's number.

"Lu, I just heard from the doctor. It's not good. They told me to get the family close. They aren't sure if she will make it through the night."

Nearly inconsolable, she fell to her knees beside her recliner and began to beg God to spare me. John empathized with her feelings because he was experiencing the same, but he couldn't find the right words to comfort her. He knew that nothing he could say would make it better. Struggling to stay composed, he remained silent as my mother sobbed uncontrollably.

When Mom was able to calm herself, they disconnected their call, and she was reminded of the vision God had given her merely a few days earlier. She had seen a majestic angel leaning over a hospital bed, his wings covering it from head to foot. Because of the angel's massive size, she couldn't see me but assumed I was there. The vision had been so vivid that she felt as if she could have touched his smooth feathers. Before the call from John, she had been confident that I would be okay. But after, she questioned the message she believed God clearly shared with her through this vision. She thought, "Maybe God wasn't telling me that Lana would be healed; perhaps this angel was present for a far different reason. Could he be there to take her to her eternal home?"

Taking a moment to gather her thoughts, she longed for my father's presence as she picked up the phone to call my sister. Though Cindy appeared to show little emotion, my mom could sense the pain she was hiding within. After their conversation, Mom reached out to her dear friend, Sharon.

"Hello?" Sharon answered.

Mom wanted to tell Sharon all that was happening but spoke the only words she could find, "She may not make it through the night."

"Oh, Lu. I'll make calls and get the prayer chain started." Sharon quickly called their friends before telling her husband she was leaving to be with my mom. She arrived at Mom's house within an hour.

Meanwhile, John made his second difficult call. After a brief pause, he contacted Mackenzie and Lauren. He told them what had happened as gently as possible and then directed Lauren to come home as soon as possible. Because Lauren was undoubtedly emotional, Mackenzie assured John she would talk to Lauren throughout her three-hour drive to Charlotte.

Although Covid was not the cause of my condition, it continued to affect our situation. Lauren would need to stay at Mackenzie's house while John remained isolated. The chance of him being allowed to be with me was slim, but he wanted to be ready if the hospital staff told him to come.

Plans were in place, but, as the older sister, Mackenzie felt the need to help Lauren think through what she should pack, "Do you have socks?" She had no idea why her first thought was about socks, but it did get her thoughts rolling.

Lauren replied, "Yes."

Considering the weather forecast, Mackenzie suggested, "Bring a jacket because it might get chilly. And throw in your rain jacket, too. Just in case."

"Okay. What else can you think of?" Lauren questioned.

Mackenzie scanned her closet to help her thoughts visually; her eyes stopped on her black dress. She approached her following sentence carefully, "I hate even to say this, but you may want to have a funeral outfit."

Hesitantly, Lauren replied, "Oh, you're right. I certainly don't want that to happen, but I should be prepared." She didn't have time for emotions, so she pushed them aside. She knew she had to get on the road.

Lauren's roommate, Mary, thoughtfully took Lauren's car to fill it with gas as Lauren wrapped up her call with Mackenzie. When Mary returned, she helped Lauren finish packing before she began her three-hour drive home. During her travels, a group of her close friends called and prayed for me and our family as she drove. As they prayed, she whispered her own prayer to God, thanking Him for the special gift of friends who know He is our hope when everything seems hopeless.

10:45 PM - Our Family GroupMe

John: Hello, everybody. I hesitated to send this out this evening, but I felt like the more prayers, the better. Lana is in extremely critical condition at this moment. She is sedated and on a full respirator with intubation. If you see this and pray for her, I ask that you pray she makes it through the night. Currently, that is the biggest concern.

John spent several hours praying and attempting to sleep before receiving the doctor's next call.

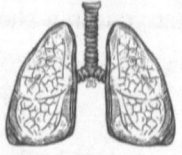

DON'T GIVE UP

Friday, May 1

John wasn't able to sleep. He wondered if he'd already seen me for the last time and contemplated what life would be like without me. He petitioned the Lord to let me live.

Finally, at 2:45 AM, John's phone buzzed. On the other end of the line was Dr. Theruvath. John anxiously answered, apprehensive of the news he was about to receive.

"Unfortunately, the ventilator isn't enough. Lana's lungs need more assistance. We want to put her on ECMO, extracorporeal membrane oxygenation. The ECMO machine will essentially become her lungs. It's our last line of defense. If we don't do this, she will not live."

John didn't hesitate to consent, "If that's our only choice, then do it."

Even with the doctor's explanation, John needed to understand more about Extracorporeal Membrane Oxygenation (ECMO). His internet search led to the following:

ECMO is a medical technique that uses a machine to pump and oxygenate blood outside the body, allowing the lungs and/or heart to rest or heal.

The machine acts as an artificial lung or heart, depending on the reason for its use.

ECMO is typically used in critically ill patients who are not responding to other treatments, such as mechanical ventilation. It is commonly used in cases of acute respiratory distress syndrome (ARDS), severe pneumonia, or heart failure.

The procedure involves inserting catheters into a large vein or artery, usually in the neck or groin, to access the blood vessels. The blood is then pumped through an oxygenator, which adds oxygen and removes carbon dioxide before returning the blood to the patient's body.

ECMO is a complex and invasive procedure that requires specialized training and equipment. It is typically only used as a last resort when other treatments have failed, and it carries significant risks and potential complications. However, it can be a life-saving intervention for patients with severe respiratory or cardiac failure.

After reading the text, John reflected on how accurately the passage described my situation. Then, he took a deep breath and sank deeper into the sofa, praying, "God, please don't take her."

A few hours earlier, Lauren arrived at Mackenzie's. Mackenzie helped her inside, and they embraced one another for several minutes. Eventually, realizing their exhaustion, they wiped away their tears and began settling in for the evening. They knew they had work and school responsibilities early the next morning, so they decided to go to bed.

As she began to drift to sleep, Mackenzie heard her phone buzz. She knew the moment it rang that it was John calling, so she grabbed her phone and answered. He told her he agreed to have me put on ECMO, and they discussed the details before ending their call.

"Thanks for letting me know. I'll tell Lauren. Good night, John."

"Good night, Mackenzie. I'll call you when I have more news."

"Thanks. I love you," she managed. Her tone reflected the confusion and fear within her. She knew she had to stay strong, but it seemed nearly impossible.

Understanding how she felt, John replied, "I love you, too."

After Mackenzie shared the news with Lauren, neither wanted to be alone. Lauren crawled into bed with her big sister, and they lay in silence next to one another, wide awake.

Mackenzie glanced at the clock and realized it was officially their dad's birthday. Her thoughts drifted, leading her to wonder how this day would look in the future. Would May 1st, a day that should be a happy occasion, turn into a reminder of the day her mom passed away?

As a tear rolled down her cheek, she whispered a one-word prayer to God, "Please."

John received the next update from the hospital at 4:45 AM.

"Mr. Lamkin, she made it through the night and is stable for now, but it's still touch-and-go."

Thankful to have cleared that hurdle. John reached out to my girls with the news. When they ended their call, Mackenzie and Lauren sat quietly together on the couch, taking in one breath at a time.

John's sister, Linda, who has a nursing background, sent an early morning message.

6:43 AM

Linda: Thoughts are for and with both of you this morning.

John: Thanks for the prayers. Overnight, Lana's condition worsened substantially. Even with the ventilator, her body could not maintain a reasonable oxygen saturation level. She is now hooked up to an ECMO (extracorporeal membrane oxygenator) as well as a ventilator. This device operates in place of her lungs. She has also been placed in an induced coma. Her oxygen levels with the machine are now at 98 to 100%, which is what she needs to have for her body to function efficiently. For her to survive, she will need to be in this state for approximately ten days. By the grace of God, she is alive, but she still has quite a fight on her hands. Her lungs are in complete failure at this time and have to heal for her to live without these machines' assistance.

Kathy: Needless to say, our prayers will continue throughout the fight. Let us know if you want or need anything. We love you both and are praying for both of you.

Jessica: I love you both very much and have been praying through the night - for Lana, you, strength for her fight, the girls, and so much more. My heart and continued prayers are with you.

Linda: Are the girls with you, John?

John: The girls are at Mackenzie's house. She only lives about 10 minutes away. We were on the phone most of the night, keeping in touch. They were trying to make sure and keep our house isolated just in case she could come home at some point. I'm not sure how much that will matter over the next couple of days because she will be in the hospital for quite some time.

Jeanne: Is there anything we can do for you?

Julia: How can we help?

John: I don't think there's much that anyone can do for me at this point. I will just be staying home and keeping up with her condition. I appreciate the offers, and I will certainly let you know if something comes up that I need help with.

Linda: Thanks, John. And as difficult as it may be, try to get some rest. My thoughts are with you, Lana, Mackenzie, and Lauren.

Kathy: Remember, you have us, and there is strength in numbers.

John: Linda, I will try to get some rest today. Kathy, I agree with you there is strength in numbers. All of the prayers are that strength.

Our family began contacting their friend groups and churches with John's permission, and prayers began to flood into heaven.

John received some encouraging news from the ICU nurse at 8:30 AM and immediately shared it with our family.

8:37 AM

John: I just spoke with Lana's nurse, and she told me that Lana is responding extremely well to the ECMO. It has allowed them to lower the oxygen rate on the ventilator, and she's doing well with that. She's awake enough at times to respond to the nurse and squeeze her hand when the nurse calls her name. I am going to the hospital this morning to pick up all of her stuff, and the nurse has said she would get me into the hallway outside of her room so that I can see her, but I will not be able to go in and touch her. She suggested I record something so Lana could hear it on her phone.

I also spoke with her doctor this morning, and he and the one who put her on the ECMO last night are both going to be in ICU around noon. He invited me to come and speak with them. Between the nurse and the two doctors, they are going to make sure I can see her.

There had been no time to contact anyone other than family, so text messages to my phone were still coming.

8:57 AM

Donna: Good morning, lovely ladies! Lana, I know you're probably tired of hearing the same questions, so give us an update when you can.

9:36 AM

Michelle: Good morning; checking in to see how you are doing.

Michelle and I have been friends since third grade. My second-grade year at Washington Elementary had been tough. I had made a few friends, but they weren't always kind to me. I didn't have what I would consider a best friend until Michelle moved to town. I remember seeing her and thinking, "I'm going to be her friend." So, I invited her to sit with me at lunch, and our friendship developed from there. We spent countless hours together; she was at my house almost as much as she was at hers. Through the years, we've never lost touch. Of course, life got in the way, and we didn't communicate as often as we should have, but she's always been in my heart and will forever be my friend.

Michelle's message would go unanswered until a later time. But John knew I would want the Tribe to have more details. This message was too heavy to text, so he picked up his phone and called Donna directly.

After Donna and John ended their call, Donna sent a message to the Tribe under a text conversation she named "Prayer Warriors."

11:31 AM - Donna to the Tribe (Prayer Warriors)

Donna: Sweet ladies, John just called. Miss Lana had a rough night and almost didn't make it. She is in critical condition, in an induced coma. She's on ECMO and has machines doing the breathing work for her. She is on massive blood thinners because of the ECMO, and the fear is a brain bleed, so they occasionally bring her out of the coma to check her neuro function. The nurse will be reading John's text messages to her when she is awake. We should not send any more texts because we don't want to muddy the waters. I have added John to this text chain so we can communicate with him and receive updates as a group. We need constant prayer for our warrior. I don't know what else to say.

John: Donna, thank you for sharing this update on my behalf. The only correction I will make is that I will actually be doing recordings of my voice that the nurse will play for her instead of reading them.

Diana: The first word out of my mouth was an expletive, and I think it would contradict the title of this group chat. I will add her to my extra prayers this afternoon. This feels unreal. I will be adding John to my prayers.

Dawn: John, it's Dawn. We are there with you in prayer and love and disbelief. It's wonderful that you are doing voice recording for Lana. I cannot imagine what you are going through, but she is such a fighter. I know we don't need to tell you that.

Rosy: John, this is Rosy. We are here for you, keeping you and your beautiful Lana in our prayers. Please remind her how much we love her and how much we need her. She is an incredible woman who has helped and inspired so many others. Thank you so much for keeping us updated.

It was time for John to head to the hospital. He gave himself plenty of time to drive uptown and navigate the additional Covid checkpoints within the hospital before meeting with the surgeons. Once he found his way to ICU, he was escorted to a conference room to discuss my condition.

The doctors explained to him that I was stable but still very ill. They were sympathetic to him and delivered the news as gently as possible.

"The ECMO is working for her, but we still do not know what is causing this crisis. Her condition will continue to be monitored very closely, and we will keep running tests to try to find the cause."

"Do you think she will live?" John matter-of-factly asked.

"We don't know. We'll do everything we can for her."

"May I see her?"

"Yes."

"Will I be allowed to come every day?"

"Because of Covid, that would not be allowed in most cases. However, she is extremely ill and is considered end-of-life. So I'm certain we can make that happen."

"What about her girls? Can they come to see her, too?"

"Of course."

Before walking John to my ICU room, the physicians explained to John what he would see when he entered my room so he wouldn't be surprised.

In the hallway outside of my room, he was directed to put on personal protective equipment (PPE) to prevent the chance of exposing me to any infection. Then, covered from head to toe, including a face mask, he passed through the sliding doors into my room. Although he thought he understood what the doctors had told him, he wasn't entirely prepared. He stopped and gazed at the numerous pieces of equipment keeping me alive. A heart rate and oxygen monitor sat near the head of my bed. Next to it, multiple bags supplying fluids, blood, and medications hung on an intravenous pole. Each line and tube attaching the equipment to me was bleeding slightly. Turning to his right, he examined the ECMO machine at the foot of the bed; his eyes followed the large tubes from the machine to the hem of my hospital gown, where a catheter tube ran alongside them. Before turning his gaze to my face, he looked at the ventilator sitting to his left, directly across the bed from where his examination of the room first began. He studied the ventilator tube entering my open mouth, the feeding tube in my nose, and the tape nearly covering my face holding it all in place.

Then his focus turned to me, the woman he knew so well buried beneath the medical equipment. Realizing I may never come home, he gently took my hand, kissed my forehead, and whispered, "I love you."

Because of the seriousness of my condition, he was only allowed a short visit. He didn't want to leave, but he knew he had to. On his way out, he confirmed with the nurses that he would be allowed to return tomorrow. He removed his PPE, stepped into the hall, and walked to the exit doors of the hospital. His thoughts were on the long road we faced ahead of us.

For the rest of the afternoon, John sat alone, processing. He received a few messages from his sisters but didn't have the energy to respond right away.

1:03 PM

Kathy: Hey, John. Just checking to see how you are doing. Love you.

Linda: Been thinking about Lana's mom and how she's doing. John, when you speak with her, please let her know that Meghan and I are thinking of her. Hope the doctors have some good reports.

Julia: Please let her and the girls know they're in all our prayers and thoughts.

The Tribe transferred all the love and support they shared with me to John and began covering him with it. And in a brief text to John, Donna expressed something I had been noticing for several weeks–aside from family, Donna, Rosy, Dawn, and Diana will always be the core, but my tribe had grown. God had been preparing an army for this battle while we were busy going about our lives. Isn't that just like Him?

4:11 PM

Donna: Hey, John! We have so many prayers working now. Lana's "Tribe" is much bigger than we thought, and every one of us is talking to God. Thank you for keeping us in the loop. It's never necessary to respond to our texts. We know you're concentrating on our little lady.

As the evening drew to a close, John managed to find the strength to call my mom once more to fill her in on what happened at the hospital. He also wanted to read the messages from his sisters to her. He then had conversations with Mackenzie and Lauren. And finally, he was able to reply to his messages.

8:31 PM

John: Nothing has really changed this afternoon. Her vitals are stable, and her oxygen levels are staying where they should. They are having a little trouble getting her blood to thin sufficiently, and they are working on that. I had a chance to speak with her doctors today, and they told me that other than her lungs, all of her organs are working well. I am going back to the hospital in the morning for a little while, and I may have more to report then. But for now, we just have to wait.

Jeanne: That all sounds positive. Have you gotten any rest?

John: I took a nap this afternoon, but to be honest with you, it was a bit restless.

Jessica: I can't imagine it was easy to see her like that, as good as I'm sure it was to be with her.

Jeanne: I'm sure resting is difficult. She is a fighter, and it's positive that her oxygen is maintained. Also, I'm glad they have her sedated so she can rest and heal. I will continue to ask for and send prayers. Love you guys!

Kathy: Several of my colleagues wanted you and all of her family to know that their prayers and thoughts were with the family. Several said that they would continue to pray for her, so there are a lot of prayers going up to God. And we all know what prayers can do. I'll pray for you to have a peaceful and restful night. Love you!

Julia: Still praying for everyone. Try to rest tonight. Love to all.

John: Thanks, everybody.

To finish his day, John sent one last message. This one was a recorded voice message that he sent for the ICU nurse to play for me. I'm confident his loving voice penetrated my heart and helped me fight even harder.

"Hey, sweetheart.

I just wanted to call and tell you goodnight. I love you. I hope you get a good night's rest and let your body heal. I so enjoyed spending time with you today, holding your hand and telling you how much I love you.

I also wanted to tell you how much people are thinking about you now and praying for you. It's crazy. You have many people saying just how much you've impacted their lives and how much you've meant to them. It's humbling to know that I'm blessed to be your husband.

I want you to remember that when you are in your mind tonight, remember what you told me about when you were in the CT machine and that you could hear God saying to you that He is with you and not to be afraid.

I want to tell you that you are immensely loved; you are a strong woman. Not just physically but mentally. You can fight. You're the best fighter, the most willful, the strongest person I know. That's what everybody else keeps saying, and it's true.

Don't give up. Keep fighting and healing.

I can't wait to see you again. I love you and hope you rest well tonight. I will talk to you tomorrow. They're going to let me come back tomorrow and spend more time with you.

Know that aside from God's hands, the human hands of the doctors and nurses there are taking care of you. They are very capable and very loving.

I love you, and I look forward to seeing you tomorrow. Sleep well, rest well, heal well."

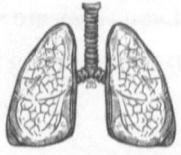

CHAPTER TWENTY

HOW'D WE GET HERE?

Saturday, May 2

When the sun began to rise, John decided there was no point in staying in bed. His mind was racing, and restlessness had taken control.

Being separated from a loved one when they are fighting for their life is one of the worst experiences a person can have, and John faced it alone because of the pandemic. Of course, he continued to communicate with our family by phone and text messages, but sometimes just having another person in the same room helps. All he could do was take one hour at a time.

Mid-morning, he went to the hospital and was allowed to spend 30 minutes with me. He held my hand and talked to me. Sitting next to my hospital bed and looking at my swollen, bleeding body was something he had never considered having to do. He couldn't wrap his mind around everything that was taking place. As he sat with me, he wondered how we got here. It had only been a few weeks since we were in the gym, excited about the future of our business and discussing when we might finally take that trip to Hawaii we were dreaming about. Boy, how quickly things change.

Our time together passed too quickly. Like yesterday, John didn't want to leave, but he wasn't allowed to stay any longer. He whispered goodbye and promised to return as soon as possible. And as he left the room, he prayed that that opportunity would come.

Before leaving the parking garage, he sent a text to the Tribe.

11:07 AM - The Tribe

John: Hello, ladies. I thought it would give you a bit of an update this morning. I'm just now leaving the hospital, and I had the opportunity to go in and hold her hand and speak to her for about a half hour. I know that she heard me because her eyes opened the first time I spoke. She recognized my voice. Throughout our conversation, I knew she could hear me because sometimes a tear would come to her eye. I told her how much people are praying for her, and I played a message that Lauren and Mackenzie had recorded for her. If you want to send her a voice message that I can play for her, just use your phone app and send it to me in a text. I will play it for her when I talk to her again. She loves each of you dearly, and I appreciate your support so much. She is stable and resting. Her vital signs are good, and she is doing exactly what she should be doing at this point.

Donna: This is uplifting news, John. I will get the teenager to show me how to send a voice message. I'm thrilled for the opportunity to tell her how much she means to me. I have to thank her for so much, but I'll keep my message short and save the huge list for when we can sit down for dinner as a group once again. Thanks for the update!

Diana: Her vitals are good! That is great news. It will be a journey to heal, but we will be patient for her to get better. I'm so happy to hear that you were able to go in and see her.

I will send her a voice text when I can find my words. Thank you for the update, John. We will continue to pray and ask for good energy to be sent her way.

Rosy: Thank you so much for the update. You can imagine how happy makes us to hear that she is doing better. We also understand how hard it is for you and for Lauren and Mackenzie at this time. So please don't forget we are here for anything that you guys need. Love you like family.

After sending the same message to our family, he put his phone down and headed home. To keep his inquisitive mind occupied, he spent the rest of the day researching ECMO and what might be causing my illness. And when he did take a break from studying, he used the time to pray.

Mackenzie and Lauren visited their dad. Of course, they wanted to celebrate his birthday, but it was impossible to be festive; their emotions were too strong to hold back. Although stoic, Eric's heart hurt as he watched his girls battle the thought of losing me. He did his best to encourage them as they wept.

Meanwhile, the medical team at the hospital continued their fight to keep me alive.

The day had been long, but it was finally coming to an end. John checked in with the ICU nurse before the evening ended and sent the update to our family.

11:02 PM

John: I spoke to the hospital a little while ago, and today has been a good day for Lana. They got her blood thinner dialed in today, and she responded well. The gases that they are removing from her blood with the ECMO improved. She is still critical, but at least she made a move in the right direction today. I will be going back to see her again tomorrow.

John climbed into bed that evening feeling like he was fighting for his next breath almost as much as I was fighting for mine.

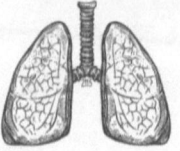

C H A P T E R   T W E N T Y - O N E

VISITORS

Sunday, May 3

Donna sent John the first message of the day. The love and concern of the Tribe for me and my family were evident.

8:09 AM

Donna: John, I pray that Miss Lana had a good night and that you got some sleep. We're here if you have updates you'd like to share or if you need anything. Please don't feel like you have to respond to every one of our texts (yes, we text a lot).

John: Good morning, Donna. I spoke with the hospital rather late last night to get an update on Lana. She had a good day yesterday and showed some improvement. They struggled to find the right amount of blood thinners, but they solved that problem yesterday. She responded well to that, and the numbers in the gases they are sweeping from her blood improved. Small steps, but at least positive steps. The love and prayers that are pouring in are amazing. God has her in His hands.

Donna: He certainly does, John! I know I speak for the group when I say that we are thinking of her constantly, praying for recovery, and thanking God for the gift of her life. Small, positive steps are a blessing!

Diana: I love hearing that our Little Miss Lana had a good day. Thank you for letting us know, John. God will hear all our prayers and is in control.

Dawn: Small but wonderful steps! So great to hear this. I'll pass this on to Shelley and Lynn, some of our Snap groupies.

Rosy: Thank you so much, John, for the update. Make me so happy that our beautiful Lana is improving. Little steps in the right direction. It's wonderful! I have all my friends and family in Mexico praying for her so God can hear our prayers from everywhere. Please take care of yourself, also. She is going to need you very much.

Word of my condition spread, and our friends began to reach out.

9:11 AM

Jeanne: John, I wanted to let you know that Walter Dixon, Fred Faris, and Dave Walton have reached out to me privately, wanting to know about Lana and you. Each of them said to send their regards to you and that they have the entire family covered in prayers. I've kept Dave informed of your updates because he and Lana had been texting last week.

Oh yes, I forgot I need to add Debbie Keller, Janine Crane, and Danny and Judy to that list, as well.

Most who contacted Jeanne were John's childhood friends, but Dave was a friend God placed in my life many years ago.

We met in Dallas, TX, in 1989. American Eagle had hired him in Myrtle Beach, SC, at the same time I was hired in Raleigh, NC, which put us both at the American Airlines training center at the same time. Our dorm rooms were in the same area, so we'd bump into one another often. Also, our graduating class was relatively small, so it didn't take long for us to get to know each other.

Once we completed our training and headed to our new jobs, we kept in touch. Then, after many years at the beach, Dave decided to move to Charlotte. That's when I introduced him to John and our family. That November, John and I invited him to Thanksgiving dinner, and in typical Lamkin family style, he soon became one of us.

Not long before my situation, Dave had faced a health crisis of his own. He understood what our family was dealing with and wanted to support all of us.

Friendships like ours with Dave are extra treasures from heaven.

As John read the text from Jeanne, he noted all the names she mentioned. However, he didn't reply because he needed to get to the hospital.

John spent an hour and fifteen minutes with me that morning. After seeing me, one of the doctors reviewed my X-rays with him. My lungs appeared to be improving. The differences in the images then compared to three days before were noticeable. And even though I remained in critical condition, the doctors planned to test my ability to function without ECMO the next day. They didn't expect that I would be able to come off of it entirely, but they wanted to find out how much I could tolerate. If it were possible for me to wean off of ECMO, they would then start to discuss removing the ventilator.

The hospital staff bent the visitor restrictions for us again, allowing my girls to come to see me. John made arrangements to bring them that afternoon.

Mackenzie had asked Lauren the night she arrived, "How will we process this if we aren't able to say goodbye?"

Being permitted to visit me gave her some relief from those fears. Because now, if the worst happened, at least she would have the chance to tell me she loved me one last time.

As they arrived at the hospital, Lauren didn't know what to expect within the walls of the medical facility. She first noticed how strangely quiet it was. All the chairs were vacant, the desks were unattended, and there were no nurses to be seen. Covid had left everything but patients' rooms empty. Being allowed into the silence where no one else was present emphasized the seriousness of my condition.

They made their way to the ICU. John went in to see me first. While Mackenzie and Lauren waited, they turned their attention to the soap opera playing on the TV in the waiting area to keep their minds occupied. Lauren gave a running commentary of what was happening on the screen above them, attempting to lighten the mood. She wondered if she was annoying her sister, but Mackenzie didn't say anything, so she continued to fill the silence with her words until John returned.

Mackenzie went next. She had hoped that she and Lauren would be allowed to go in together, but that wasn't an option. John did his best to explain to her what to expect. It helped ease the process, but nothing could have prepared her completely.

Fully covered in protective gear, she entered the room. She walked to the edge of my bed and stood. She looked around at all the machines and questioned how her healthy mom could be lying in front of her in a coma. Her eyes moved up and down my body, examining the multitude of tubes. She listened to the rhythmic hissing sound of the ventilator along with the beeping and low-humming noises from the other machines. Then she noticed the blood that came from my nose, mouth, ears, and around the tubes (caused by blood thinners). To her, I looked very small.

Trying to control her emotions, she began to talk to me. But she wasn't sure if I could hear her through the two required medical masks covering her face. She was told to try to remain positive. But standing there, seeing what she was seeing, she was lost.

"How am I supposed to stay positive when my mom is like this?" she wondered.

She touched my hand, but that didn't feel like enough. Then she remembered that when she was little, I would gently run my thumb over her eyebrow when she needed comforting. It always calmed her, so she placed her hand on my face and stroked my brow with her thumb.

When the ECMO nurse entered the room, Mackenzie tried to ask medical questions but soon gave up. The nurse couldn't hear her over the machines that filled the room with noise, and her words were muffled behind her masks.

She stayed with me for about 20 minutes and decided it was time to let Lauren come in.

"It's pretty much like John explained, but there are more tubes and blood than I anticipated," Mackenzie warned Lauren. Taking control of her emotions, she quietly said, "She looks so small."

Lauren took a deep breath, then inched her way to my bed. She felt like a toddler standing in a fine china shop. She was afraid to move, nervous she would break a Covid rule or accidentally mess up one of my tubes. She noticed the boots that looked similar to walking casts on my feet. John had told her about them; he had explained they were being used to help prevent what is called foot drop. It's when your ankles and feet become weak, and you can no longer lift the front part of your foot.

She looked closer at me. Mackenzie was right; I did look very small. But Lauren also noticed that I had never looked more like Grandpa, and as she fought back her tears, she thought, "This is my family."

There was no chair, which made it apparent this wasn't a place meant for visitors. Lauren began to cry. She didn't know what to say, so she apologized to me for crying.

I was covered with blankets, but a small part of my arm was peeking from beneath the bedding. Lauren placed her hand on my skin. She was overwhelmed by how cold I felt. The sounds filling the room confirmed that I was alive, but it didn't feel like it. She sensed I was in the "in-between," not present on this earth but not yet in heaven.

Before she said goodbye, Lauren examined how big the equipment was and again noticed how small I looked compared to the machines keeping me alive.

She left my room feeling content that she was able to spend time with me. Since she had been at school, she had felt far away, almost disconnected from the situation. Being here validated that she was very much part of everything.

The day was emotional for both Mackenzie and Lauren, but it was also good. They had had the opportunity to be with me, even if it would be the last, and as they left the hospital, they were both at peace.

Shortly after John returned home, the doorbell rang. He opened the door to a beautiful cake from our favorite bakery, Nothing Bundt Cakes, sent by the Tribe a day shy of his birthday.

7:00 PM - John to The Tribe

John: So, I guess since you know that Lana's not here, you would try to fatten me up a little bit? This cake is pretty awesome! You ladies are amazing, and I appreciate you very much!

Donna: Get a really big fork and enjoy every crumb, John! Lana is in full support of you eating sweets this weekend!

John: Well, you know, I might struggle to wait until tomorrow to eat any of this. I think I'll start celebrating my birthday tonight! The girls may be coming over to eat lunch on the patio tomorrow, and this will be an awesome cake to share.

Diana: We are so glad it arrived and the icing didn't melt! We know that tomorrow will not be the typical celebration for your birthday, but that just means you get two this year. I know Lana will want a second cake for you when she is able to return home. We miss seeing you both!

Dawn: I hope the girls are able to come over tomorrow. You know Lana would love hearing that. My daughter turns 25 tomorrow. Some good people were born on May 4th. You deserve every bite of that cake!

Rosy: Yes, John. Enjoy every crumble of the cake. Lana told us how much she wanted for you a happy birthday celebration. I'm sure she will be happy to celebrate your birthday again when she get back home.

John: Dawn, tell your daughter happy birthday. And when Lana gets home, I don't think I'm even going to worry about my birthday. I'm going to be all about celebrating her. I'm pretty sure we're going to do a virtual celebration when she gets home, and I'll be interested to see just how many people end up on it. You guys are awesome, and I love you for what you're doing for us.

Dawn: That would be so much fun! A virtual party to look forward to for sure!

He was right; he wasn't able to wait to have a piece of his cake. He sliced into it, but before indulging, he sent a picture of it to the Tribe.

7:36 PM

John: She must have told you what kind of cake I like! How can it be that she is fighting for her life and still finding a way to help me have a better one? That's my Lana.

Donna: She's that special. I think her exact words were, "He'll eat anything sweet." HAHAHAHA

John: True that.

After enjoying his slice of cake, he called my mom to tell her about the day. And then, once again, sent a daily update to the rest of the family.

8:36 PM

John: Let me start by saying I am using these daily updates somewhat like a journal. I want to keep you in the loop, but I also want to have a documented daily statement that I can aggregate. When Lana is able, I want her to be able to read what was going on while she was not aware.

So I took the girls to see their mom, and they had a chance to spend a few minutes with her. She was very heavily sedated and was non-responsive to them. She may have been able to hear them, but it was hard to tell. I had a conversation with the ECMO nurse and learned more about the process. She was scheduled for her first test tomorrow, which means they will turn the ECMO down ever so slightly and see how she responds to that.

Today she got restless, which led to a slight reduction of the flow in the ECMO. Her oxygen level dropped immediately, which leads the ECMO nurse to think she's not ready for a test yet. Tomorrow we will find out if they think she is ready or not. The nurse feels like she may be on ECMO for as long as two weeks. Her lungs have definitely healed some over the last couple of days, but she is still very critically ill.

The other thing I learned from the nurse this afternoon was that Lana currently has about 15L (33 pounds) of fluids in her body that have been induced for various reasons. In spite of that, she has virtually no swelling going on, which the ECMO nurse was very surprised about. The way she said it leads me to think that it was a positive thing.

Jeanne: We'll take any improvement we can get.

Kathy: Small signs of healing are major rewards in this situation so let us count small victories. Thanks to God for all improvements. Our prayers will continue, and be thankful for all God is doing. Love to all of you.

Julia: It's good to hear her lungs are healing. Still praying. Try to rest tonight. Love you.

Another day passed, and I was still alive. However, as Lauren sensed, I was in the in-between.

Our family: Justin, Jessica, Dillon, Inara, Ali, John, Lana, Mackenzie, Lauren
August 2015

Lauren, Lana, Mackenzie, Cindy, Lu
May 2018

Dale, Julia, Kathy, John, Jeanne
March 2015

The Tribe: Diane, Dawn, Donna, Lana, Rosy
May 2018

My daddy, John
June 2014

Vacation with John, Lauren, Mackenzie
June 2016

With my girls 1 month before Novant
March 20, 2020

Me and Donna at Snap Fitness Waxhaw
August 2015

Valentine's Date
February 2017

Warrior 3 yoga pose for balance
June 2015

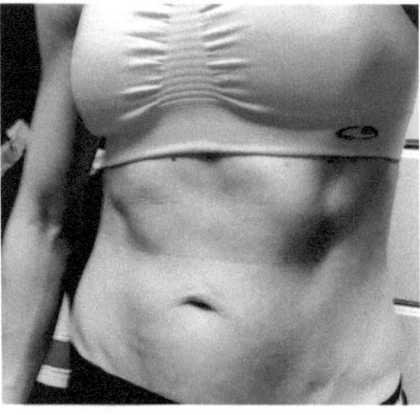

The abs I worked so hard for
June 2015

Showing the benefits of hard work
January 2016

Owners, Snap Fitness Waxhaw
June 2017

Easter brunch cut short because I wasn't feeling well
April 12, 2020

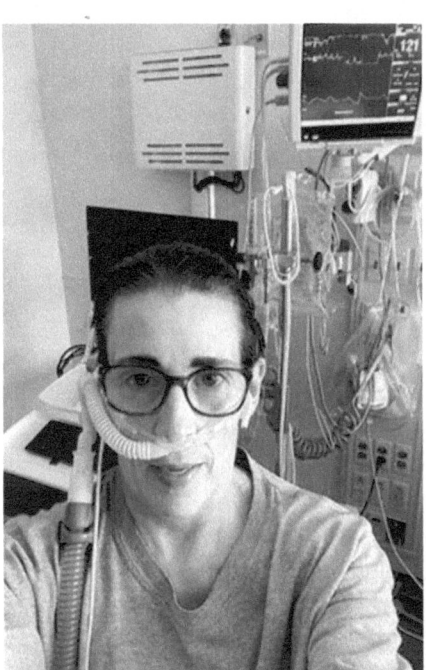

Still believing I would go home soon
April 28, 2020

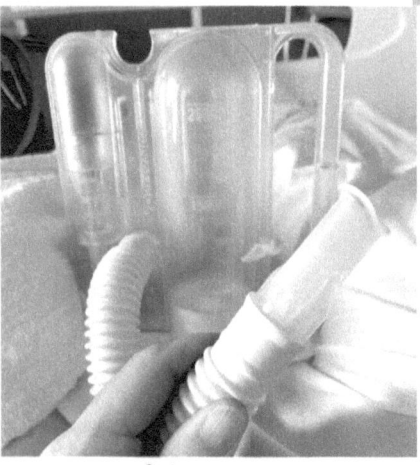

Spirometer
(aka carnival game)

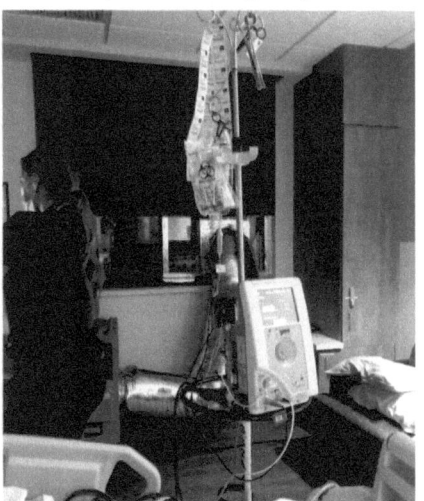

Novant ECMO machine
May 2020

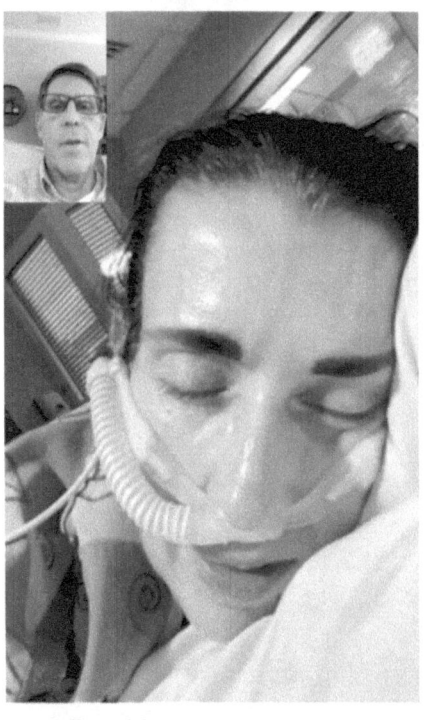

First Night in Novant ICU
April 30, 2020

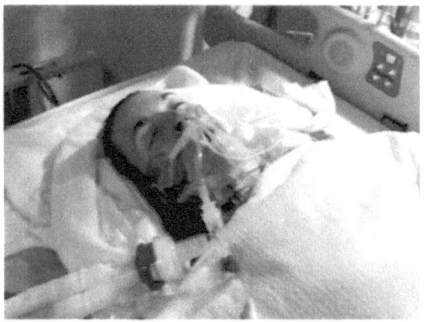

Considered end-of-life
May 4, 2020

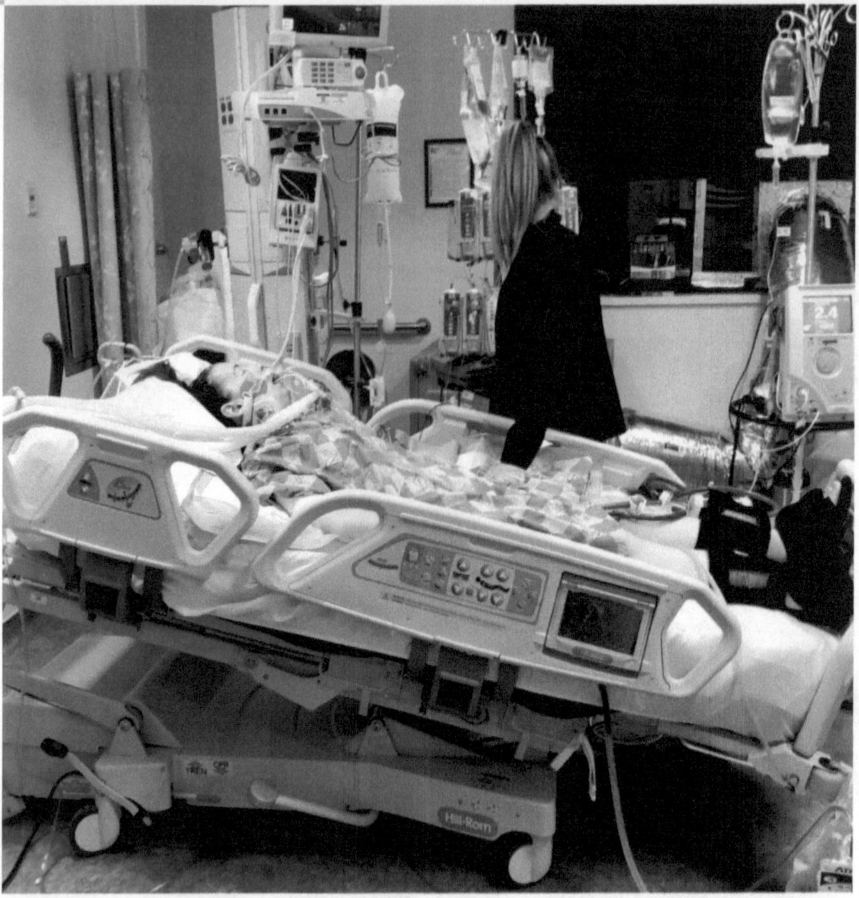

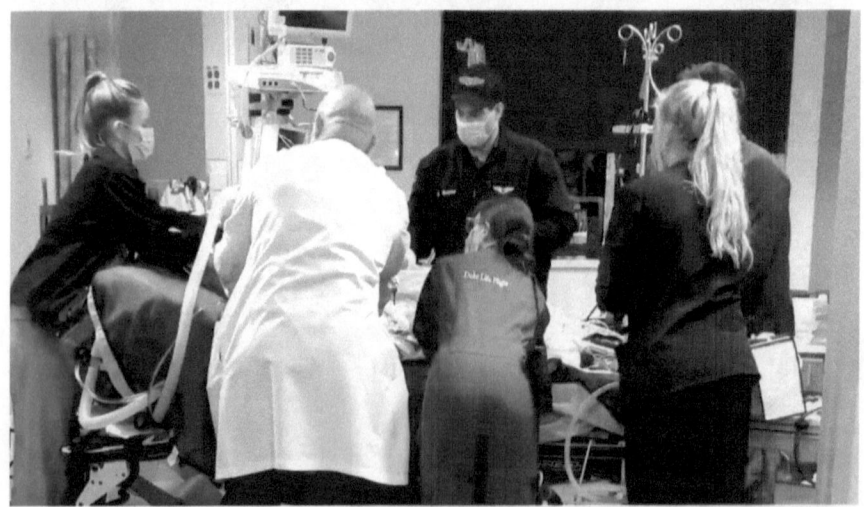

On life support at Novant Hospital
May 12, 2020

Duke and Novant teams transferring me to the gurney for Life Flight
May 12, 2020

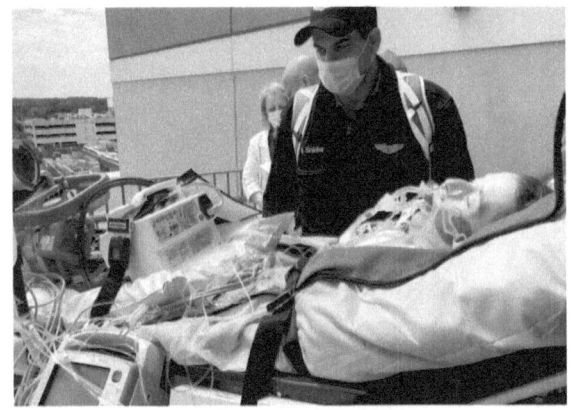

Moving to Duke Life Flight
May 12, 2020

Lift off to Duke
May 12, 2020

FaceTime with John, Mackenzie, and Mom
May 16, 2020

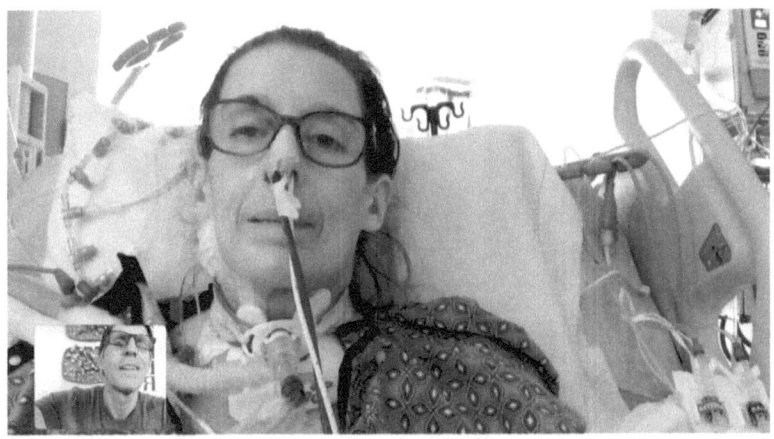

FaceTime with John,
May 22, 2020

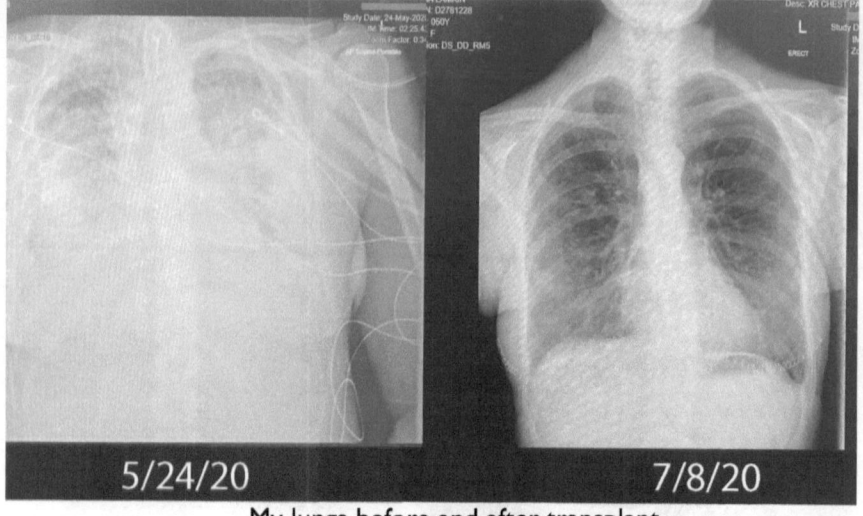

My lungs before and after transplant
(black indicates air)

5/24/20   7/8/20

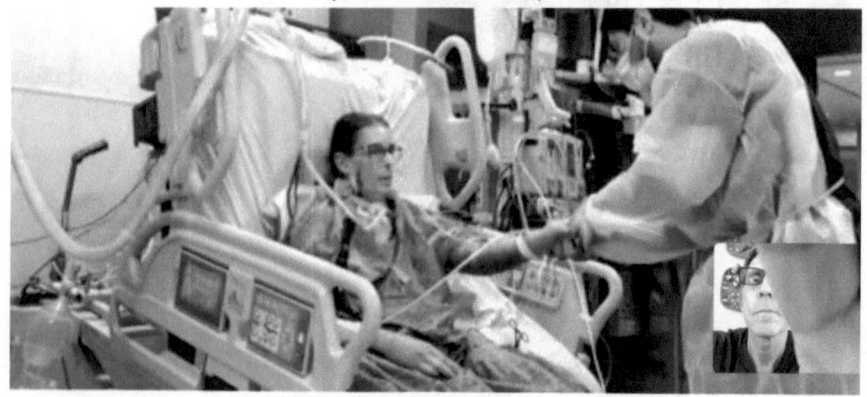

Physical therapy in Duke ICU
June 3, 2020

Machine used to help me walk
June 3, 2020

My view of photo wall
at Duke

14th wedding anniversary
First time together after 64 days apart
June 24, 2020

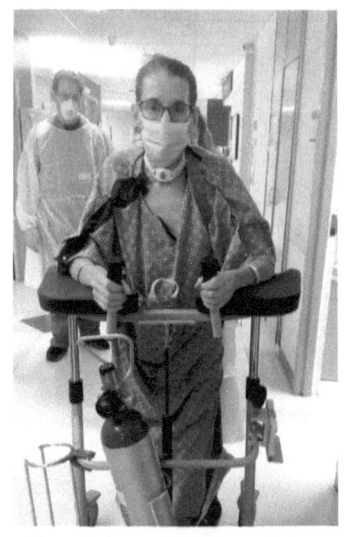

Regaining my strength by
walking at Duke
June 20, 2020

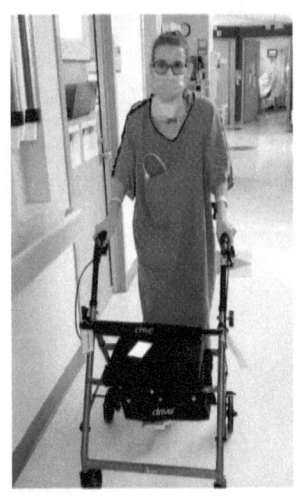

Upgraded my walking device
June 28, 2020

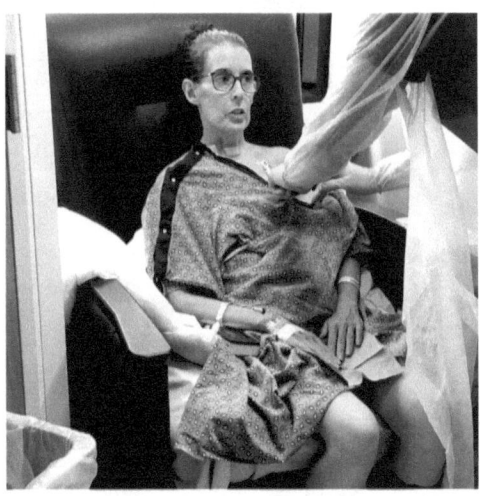

Port removal one day before to leaving Duke
July 2, 2020

Stairs leading into
rental house

Leaving Duke Hospital
July 3, 2020

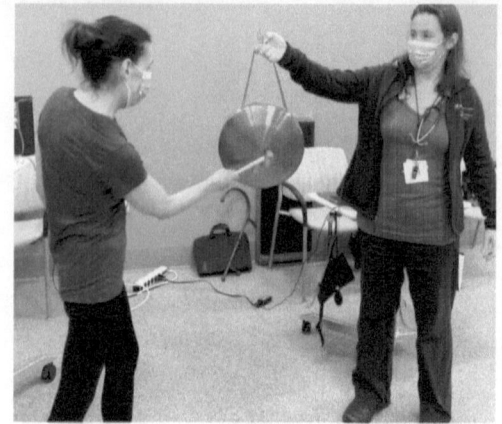

Graduating Duke pulmonary rehab
August 6, 2020

My cape from the Tribe

Signed poster created by Justin and Jessica

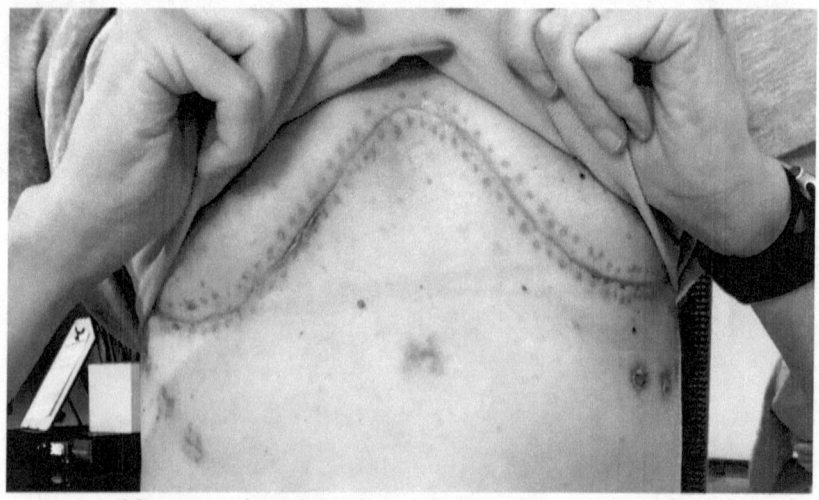

My scars after the surgical staples were removed
July 16, 2020

Reunited with the Tribe
Donna, Dawn, Rosy, Lana (Diana was at work)
August 24, 2020

First family gathering after
my transplant
August 2020

First time with my mom *(Lu)* and
sister *(Cindy)* after transplant
October 22, 2020

My mom and me
October 22, 2020

Birthday workout
December 14, 2020

Thanksgiving with family
2020

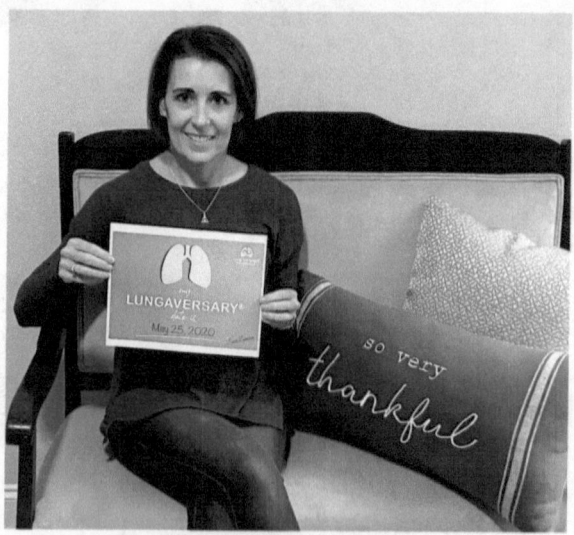

Lung Transplant Foundation
lungaversary acknowledgement

Mountains of NC
September 2021

Climbing mountains in
North Carolina
April 2021

Rosy, Bill, Donna, Steve, Lana, John
September 2021

Lana, John, Justin, Jessica, Ali, Dillon, Mackenzie, Lauren
Easter 2021

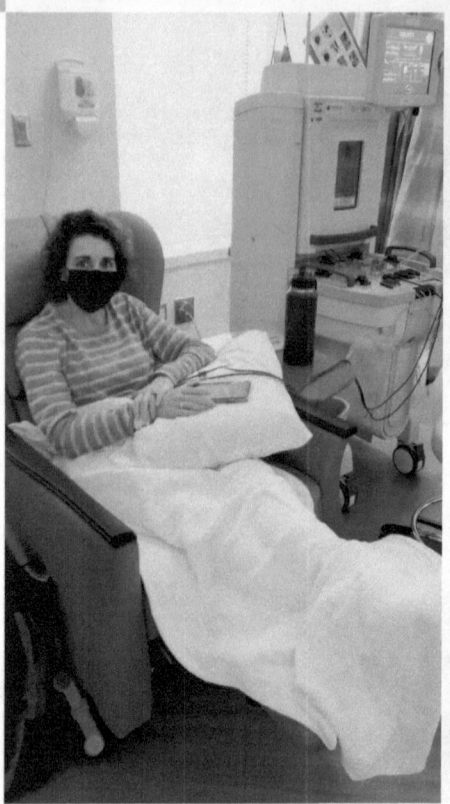

Six months post-transplant
November 2020

Monthly photopheresis treatment to
fight my chronic rejection
July 15, 2021

Speaking at First Baptist Church
Matthews, NC
November 2021

Speaking at Southbrook's women's event
October 2022

The Tribe:
Rosy, Diana, Dawn, Lana, Donna
March 18, 2023

John's birthday
May 4, 2023

Lana, Lauren, Jessica, Inara, Mackenzie,
Ali, Dillon, Justin, Matt, John
(candle math included - IYKYK)
July 10, 2023

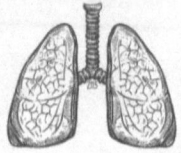

CHAPTER TWENTY-TWO

THE IN-BETWEEN

I'm sure you've heard stories of people experiencing a place somewhere between this life and the afterlife. I can confirm for you that stories like these are true. While doctors and nurses tended to my physical body, my soul was in the in-between.

It's taken me some time to piece together everything that happened while I was in the coma. My experiences felt like dreams at the time, but I now know they were real moments between heaven and earth. Most of them, anyway. Some parts developed from my humanness, but those parts, without a doubt, meshed together with what my spirit was encountering—my Savior. As I take you through this part of my story, I believe you will understand what I mean.

The first thing I remember in the in-between was being alone in a stark white hospital room. Above me hung a bright, ceiling-mounted light like those used during surgical procedures. It was large and round, with multiple LED bulbs shining down onto my bed. A large window at the foot of the bed allowed me to see into the hallway.

As I stared out the window, a man's shadow appeared on the opposing gray cinder block wall. (Imagine the shadow scene from Peter Pan when he snuck into Wendy's room, except this shadow was wearing a tunic instead of tights.) I knew immediately the shadow belonged to Jesus.

"Jesus, I want to see you," I begged.

With a hint of a chuckle, he replied, "You are seeing me."

"But Jesus, I can only see your shadow. I want to see YOU."

His words were gentle and understanding, "I know, but my shadow is all I can show you right now."

"Why?" This word came out as if I were a toddler wanting to have it my way.

"Because it's not time for you to see me. My shadow is enough."

And as quickly as He had appeared, He departed.

Now for the part where my human nature, and possibly heavy medication, interfered. It's almost too embarrassing to share, but I've never been one to shy away from a bit of humiliation and some comic relief.

Sometime after seeing Jesus' shadow, I was told I was going on a trip to Hawaii. John and I discussed going to Hawaii for several years before my medical issues. However, we hadn't made the trip because my focus was on the gym. So, as you can imagine, I was pretty excited about this opportunity.

When it came time to board our vacation airplane, I was wheeled on a gurney to a medical plane instead. The plane was full of medical equipment. Nurses to my right and left attended to all my needs, cleaned my wounds, and changed my bandages.

Another nurse boarded the plane, pulling an oxygen tank behind her. I was taken aback as she entered through the curtain separating the cockpit from the cabin. She looked just like my cousin's wife, Marci. Marci's not a nurse by trade, so I was utterly confused. I started to ask why she was there; then, I heard Dolly Parton's voice announcing our departure.

Yes, you read that right. I heard Dolly Parton. I warned you that heavy medication might have influenced some of these events.

Dolly had arranged a simulated trip to Hawaii so I could finally experience the vacation I'd always wanted. But unfortunately, as the simulation progressed, she realized I was too ill to continue.

Her efforts were exposed when she stopped production, "This isn't what we planned. She's much worse than we thought. We need to turn her over to a real medical team."

The set came down, and the walls of the studio airplane opened to reveal a team of cameramen and directors. Then the onboard nurses acknowledged their roles as actors, and a real medical team rushed in to take over.

Oh, and I can't forget to tell you that Kenny Rogers met Dolly plane-side as I was being swept away to the hospital.

I don't know for sure, but it would make sense that I had this "dream" while I was airlifted to Duke. But we're not to that part of my story yet. So I'll stop here for now and share more as we go.

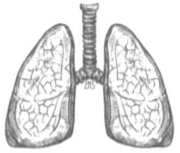

CHAPTER TWENTY-THREE

THE RAGING STORM

The life event we were facing had begun as a rain shower we believed would pass quickly. But now we were in the middle of a raging storm with no end in sight.

In the Bible, Matthew (8:23-27) shares about an evening when a furious storm came up on the lake. The disciples were terrified, but through the chaos, Jesus slept. When the men woke him, He rebuked them for having such little faith; then, He rebuked the winds and waves, and all became calm.

This Jesus, with the power to calm the seas, was on our side. Now my family had to have faith in Him to control this storm.

John continued to visit me daily. He sat by my bedside and talked to me as he held my hand. He encouraged me to stay strong and keep fighting. He prayed over me, asking God to change our circumstances. And each time he returned home, he prayed more.

As the storm raged on, it took a toll on John. He became tired, and his emotions began to stir. Sitting alone on the sofa, he began wondering what life would be like without me. It would be drastically different if he lost the love of his life, his best friend. He would miss our playful teasing and laughter; our home would be void of the joy that fills it daily. How could he stay in this house without me? Where would he go next? He wept as his mind flashed with images of what may become a reality.

On the morning of May 4, he wasn't sure how much time had passed since he sat down, but he knew allowing these thoughts to linger would only make the situation more challenging. And this was not how he expected or wanted to spend his birthday. So, he gathered his emotions and felt the time had come to reply to the unanswered text messages on my phone and the birthday wishes on his. He chose to begin with Michelle's text.

Monday, May 4, 9:56 AM

John (from my phone): Hi Michelle. This is Lana's husband, John. I don't know if you are aware, but Lana is in extremely critical condition and is on life support. I hear her speak fondly of you and will gladly bring you up to speed if you like.

Michelle: Thank you, John. I actually sent a message to Lu, and she told me what was going on, but thank you for getting back to me! Please know I am praying for you all, and I love Lana so very much!

After he had replied to the other lingering text messages, he waited for Ali and Jessica to arrive for a somber birthday celebration.

Our family birthday celebrations typically include all four girls, their significant others, and our granddaughter. We eat a lot, and we laugh a lot. But this one would be different. Covid restrictions were still in full swing, and because John didn't want to risk contracting any virus, he asked his girls to come alone.

Ali and Jessica arrived together early that afternoon. They knew their daddy was hurting, yet they could do nothing to make him feel better except offer hugs and heartfelt words. For that, John was grateful.

Jessica was confident John hadn't been eating as much as he should, so she did her best to convince him to eat more. But with stress comes a lack of appetite. Nevertheless, he promised her he was taking care of himself. Reluctantly, she accepted his reassurance and, together with Ali, tried to make his day as special as possible.

They spent a few hours with him, then said their goodbyes. He felt the weight of our home's emptiness again after they left. No matter what room he was in, heaviness lingered. In an attempt to lighten the burden, if only for a short time, John filled the rest of his day by playing guitar and reading while waiting for the doctor to call with another update.

Throughout my stay at Novant, the doctors were kind enough to call John daily to let him know how I was doing. After each conversation, he would then call my girls and my mom. And finally, he would message the rest of our family.

Monday, May 4, 6:25 PM - Family GroupMe

John: I just got off the phone with the hospital getting my afternoon update. Both early this morning and this afternoon, they wanted to move Lana around a little bit to clean her up, and each time she was a little feisty. It lets us know that she is aware of what is going on. I told the nurses that she typically doesn't like to be touched by strangers. As for her numbers, she is stable. She is oozing blood from all the incisions, her nose, and some from her mouth. As a result, they gave her three units of blood today.

Her oxygen levels have remained stable with the ECMO and are consistently 98 to 100%. One number that they are tracking is her tidal volume. As I understand it, that is the volume of air in her lungs. Before they will begin to take her off of ECMO, her number will have to reach 300. Yesterday that number was about 190, and today it is about 215 or 220. It did not come up this afternoon from this morning enough to make a difference.

While her lungs have shown some improvement over the last few days, the X-rays today were not substantially better than yesterday. That is to be expected based on the amount of damage in her lungs. Based on the bronchial wash and resulting lab work, they have concluded that she does not have COVID-19. They have done another antibody test. For some reason, they did not get results from the first one. They will follow up, but it was actually ordered before they did the antibody test.

I may have mentioned this, but I think it is worth noting that the doctors and nurses have been awesome. A new ECMO nurse and a new primary nurse were on duty today. They all enjoy learning about Lana and connecting with her as a patient. It's interesting to know that they find it enjoyable to treat them when they know more about them personally. As always, thanks for your thoughts and prayers! I love you all.

John's nephew and sisters replied with love, support, and offers of prayers. And within the stream of messages, Linda shared her medical knowledge to help everyone better understand tidal volume.

Linda: Sounds like she's got a really good team working with her! Please thank her caregivers from me, and I'm sure from all the others. I'm glad they want to know about her because that makes her a person, not a number. And to further explain tidal volume: it's how much you breathe in and breathe out in one respiration cycle. It can vary based on the size of the person. The fact that she's as petite as she is would make hers less than some big guy. The healing can take a while, but it's good that even though she didn't increase this afternoon, she didn't decrease either. Continued good thoughts to all of you.

As the number of text messages, social media messages, and emails from our friends and acquaintances increased, John realized he needed a better way to manage them. Since GroupMe was working so well to keep our family in the loop, he decided to set up an additional group for anyone outside the family who wanted to receive updates. He knew putting everything in place would take a day or so, so he got to work immediately.

While setting up the new group, John added my mom and sister to our family group. He was mindful of how much they needed encouragement from the rest of the family, too.

The following day John received news that was good on one hand because it would be a solution. But on the other hand, it was quite mind-blowing and frightening. The possibility of a lung transplant had now come into play.

Tuesday, May 5, 2:40 PM - Family GroupMe

John: I wanted to give an update for today. I appreciated the responses last night, and I'm sorry I didn't get a chance to respond to you guys. Linda, I appreciate you explaining tidal volume.

During my visit this morning, I spoke at length with the doctor and several of the nurses. Lana is stable, and her vitals continue to be strong. All of her numbers, with the exception of her lungs, are perfect. Her lungs are about the same as yesterday, which is better than they were three or four days ago, but it's still very slow going.

The request has already been made by the doctors at Novant to transfer her to Duke medical center. The ECMO unit at Duke is one of the best in the world, and she will have the top specialists available. Novant was doing a great job, but this is just another level of care that they can't provide. I am now awaiting confirmation that she has been accepted as a transfer.

The doctors are confident that she will be transferred. In fact, the medical flight team at Duke is on standby, waiting for the signal to go. At this point, I don't know if I will have access to her as I have here in Charlotte. If I do, they will work with me on housing. If not, I will have to determine how I speak to her daily so she can hear my voice. I'm confident that the team at Duke has already considered all the ways to do this.

Another reason to have her at Duke is if her lungs do not heal appropriately. Duke has a world-class lung transplant facility, and she would have to be in such a facility to be on the list for a transplant. We are several weeks from any decision like that, but we must plan for that contingency.

Lastly, you will see that I have added Lana's mom, Lu, and her sister, Cindy, to our group. I've been giving updates to them consistently, but we felt it might be easier to get it all into one place. As I find out details, I will let you know Lana's status as it relates to Duke.

Plans consistently changed, as had been the case since I arrived at the hospital. The physicians at Novant knew I needed more care than I could receive at their facility, but the ultimate decision belonged to the team at Duke. The decision came later that day.

Tuesday, May 5, 4:38 PM - Family GroupMe

John: I just got off the phone with the critical care pulmonologist, and they have been in constant contact with Duke today. Based on all the information they have shared, Duke is comfortable with her not needing to be transferred at this time. I definitely feel like Duke's response is reason to feel better about her current condition.

The care she is receiving through Novant is excellent, and the primary reason for sending her to Duke was to monitor her condition in case she needed to be put on a lung transplant list. But, again, the physicians at Duke do not think she is to that point. Duke is aware of Lana and will be in constant communication with the physicians at Novant.

Continued prayers and positive thoughts are greatly appreciated. Julia, I asked about blood donations; at this point, I don't think it serves much purpose. I really appreciate your offer and your thinking that way.

Mackenzie: So, she is staying here?

John: Yes, she will be staying in Charlotte at this point.

As much as John trusted the doctors and liked being able to visit with me every day, deep down, he felt that I needed to be at Duke, and he didn't understand why they chose not to have me transferred to their facility.

The ups and downs were almost too much to bear, yet he pressed on. He continued to set up the larger GroupMe page, and he thought of Mackenzie and Lauren's dad, Eric, and decided that he also belonged in the family group.

Tuesday, May 5, 4:43 PM - Family GroupMe

John: I just added Mackenzie's and Lauren's dad, Eric, to our family page. Quite frankly, I should have done this sooner.

Eric: Thanks

John: You bet

That evening, John had the day's final conversation with my nurse, Reagon. She was the nurse on staff the evening I was put on ventilation, which meant she was familiar with my case.

Reagon told John they had changed my sedative, and it was helping me to rest better. And as a result, the ECMO machine was not having to work as hard. She also shared that they had lowered the ventilation to the percentage of oxygen the average person typically breathes each day. She told him that my blood sugar had crept up to 180, and they would administer insulin to combat that change. Lastly, she explained that the combination of lower ventilator oxygen and the ECMO's lighter workload indicated some slight overall improvement. However, she cautioned him that my recovery would be slow.

Maybe we wouldn't need Duke after all.

After the call, John completed the final item on his to-do list for the day and sent the first message to the group he named "Lana's Update."

Tuesday, May 5, 7:00 PM

John: I have started this group to provide updates on Lana. So many people have asked about her and have been praying for her that it's hard for me to keep up with everybody. I thought I would start this group in an effort to communicate more efficiently. I am sure I have left a lot of people out of this, but I wanted to get it started. Please let me know if you know anyone who wants to be on here. Thanks again for all of the prayers and all the love! It has truly been humbling.

I have been speaking to her, playing recorded messages that have been sent to me, and playing music for her. I have prayed with her. I have prayed over her. I have read Bible verses to her. I have shared with her how much outpouring of love and support I have experienced for her and our family. I knew she could hear me a couple of times, but mostly she was non-responsive. I still believe she knows I'm there.

The group grew quickly, and notifications of new messages popped up faster than he could reply. Our friends, the pastors and staff members from our church, and patrons of our gym sent words of encouragement and thanked John for including them. Then, one by one, Novant nurses and friends of our friends joined.

The group grew to nearly 200 people. And many of those people shared our story with their families, friends, and churches. Of course, I didn't know it at the time, but tens of thousands of people from all around the world were praying on my behalf. Our pastor shared our need for prayer with the congregation, and churches I had never visited dedicated their services to me. A radio station in Ohio even told my story. To my knowledge, I don't know anyone who lives in Ohio. The love and support that poured out for us continues to overwhelm me. I can't begin to wrap my mind around why God chose to bring all these people together for me–a virtually unknown woman running a small gym in Waxhaw, NC. But that's His character. He often uses the broken, the meek, and the unknown (in this case, me) to show His love and mercy.

John read every message posted that day before turning in for another restless night. The difference with this evening was he knew the throne room of Heaven was being flooded with pleas for my healing.

Morning came quickly, and John felt an overwhelming urge to begin praying earlier than most days. He was uncertain why it felt more pressing than any other day, but he would learn later that God was orchestrating the timing of his prayers with my mom's prayers.

He waited for the sun to rise before he prepared to leave for the hospital, then navigated through what had become his daily routine.

Wednesday, May 6, 5:37 PM - Family GroupMe & Lana's Updates

John: I hoped to have my afternoon update with the doctors before posting, but I haven't heard from them yet. I just want to say that we serve a mighty God. Last night I struggled to sleep and was feeling restless and unsettled. This morning at

5:00, I found myself praying for some improvement and increased hope. Since I was up early, I decided to arrive at the hospital a little earlier than usual. I wanted to get there around 9:30 to 10 o'clock because that's when the doctors do rounds.

I saw the door to her ICU room open when I got there. I also saw her doctor and a nurse standing outside of her room. It seems that between early morning (maybe around five or 6 o'clock) and when I arrived at about 9:40, she experienced a substantial, almost dramatic improvement in her condition. Her doctor said he really couldn't explain it, but I could. We serve a mighty God!

Lana is still in critical condition and on ECMO and ventilator. But today was easily her best day in the last 3 1/2 weeks. I haven't spoken with them since noon, but they were talking about beginning the process of weaning her off of life support and getting her awake. This can take some time, but it's definitely a positive move.

The number that they watch so closely to determine when she will be able to breathe on her own is her tidal volume. The number they wanted to reach was 300. During the weekend, that number stayed in the upper one hundreds. On Sunday, it went to the low 200s and remained there until this morning. As of this morning, over a period of a few hours, it increased to the low to mid 300s. Again, the doctor couldn't explain what had changed or why she had improved so much. I can—answered prayers.

Make no mistake, she is still critical, and on life-support, but with her move today, she looked so much better. I have spoken to multiple doctors and nurses today, and they all agree that this morning was good.

Mom: I was awake from around 2:00, praying until a little after 4:00, and it was then that I felt enough peace to go back to sleep. It now occurs to me that is 5:00 your time. So I guess I was on prayer duty until you took over. All praise goes to our merciful and loving God.

Debra: Continuing heartfelt prayers.

Kevin K: Amen, John, and praise the Lord!! Continued prayers for a full recovery.

Janine W: She has a lot to fight for. Continued prayers.

Donna: It is right to give thanks and praise!

Christina J: Yes, thank you, Lord. We praise you for every bit of improvement!!

Judi A: Thank you, Lord! We serve a mighty God.

Kasey C: To Him who is able, we thank You!

Steve B: This is wonderful news! "If you remain in me and my words remain in you, ask whatever you wish, and it will be done for you." John 15:7

Shelley C: Praise God! John, was she alert and aware of you when you were with her today?

... followed by many other praises to our Lord.

John: Your prayers have been instrumental, and I can't begin to thank you enough. I will ask for your continued prayers for her healing and for her to come off of life support and to be taken out of her coma. I will also ask for your continued prayers for our family and me. This has been the hardest thing I've ever had to go through, and I can't imagine having done it so far without the support of so many people. We serve a mighty God!

Shelley, I always assume she can hear me even when she doesn't respond. I always let her know how many people are praying for her and how much love is being shown. I pray over her and with her every time. With all of that, she was still unresponsive to me today. They keep her pretty deeply sedated because she tends to get agitated when they lighten the sedation. For those of you who know her well, I'm sure that it comes as no surprise that she would get anxious and want to get something done!

The comments continued throughout the evening and into the following day, giving John the strength he needed to face another day.

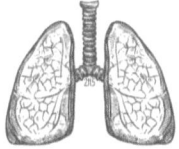

CHAPTER TWENTY-FOUR

THE STORM RAGES ON

On May 7, the doctors began to hone in on what might be causing my body's aggressive behavior. In their eyes, COVID-19 had officially been ruled out, and they turned their focus to my immune system. A diagnosis hadn't yet been determined, but an autoimmune disease called myositis was now being discussed, and there was hope they were headed in the right direction.

As always, John spent the morning with me at the hospital and reported the day's happenings to our family and friends through GroupMe.

Thursday, May 7, 7:01 PM

John: So today has been another day where Lana showed a little improvement. She is still incredibly sick, but every step, however small, gets us closer. They turned the ECMO down to basically its lowest settings to see how she would respond. She must meet three critical markers before they will remove her from ECMO. We've spoken about tidal volume and oxygen levels in her blood, but there is a third marker that measures how well her blood is removing the gases. The main gas is carbon dioxide.

Her tidal volume was slightly improved today, and her oxygen levels were holding steady even with less volume from the ECMO. Her ABG (arterial blood gases) was not quite high enough to remove her from the machine today. They will test her again in the morning, and if she holds up well throughout the day, they may take her off of ECMO tomorrow. It would be a major step forward if that could happen.

The other significant change today is the team brought in the nephrologist. I spoke to him at length, and he was amazed at how well her kidneys were functioning. He described her case as "bizarre." The doctors continue to be stumped by what has caused all of this. We have almost certainly eliminated COVID-19, as she has had four negative tests and one negative antibody test. I have had negative antibody testing, as well.

This evening, they will start the first of four days, where they will do a plasma replacement for her. A quick overview of plasma–it carries coagulants, antibodies, and various proteins. That is a very limited overview! As they replace her plasma each day, they will give her immunoglobulin shots to replace her antibodies and coagulants. The idea is to remove whatever part of her auto-immune system that has been attacking her.

I know God is with her through this journey. I don't know where it ends or what it looks like down the road, but I know it's in His plan. I continue to be grateful for the support and the prayers.

Donna: I think I'm going to order that cape for her. She is indeed WONDER WOMAN. Come on, Lana!

Linda: This all sounds very interesting and very encouraging! At this point, do they have any idea what is causing the autoimmune response and/or what caused the pneumonia?

John: As always, you ask such good questions, Linda. They no longer feel that organizing pneumonia was the culprit. They now feel like whatever is causing this autoimmune disease is something other than that. They are currently working on the thought that any organizing pneumonia that is part of this pathology results from the ARDS. Some speculation is that it could be some form of myositis, an autoimmune disease that attacks the muscles. It presents in many ways and doesn't always attack the muscles. Sometimes it attacks the lungs. The fact is they are all baffled by this case. If you want to talk more in-depth about the medical aspects, feel free to call me.

Linda: Thanks, and the same for you. I have a couple more questions, but I'm going to do a little research on my own and see what I come up with. (I always have more questions. The doctors I've worked with over the years always knew to expect them! Surprise! Surprise! LOL) Then, if I don't find the answer I'm looking for, I'll get in touch with you or text you and see what you know! Or, you can run it by the team. Also glad to hear that the antibody tests came back negative except for the measure of protection it might have given you both. The report from the nephrologist sounds excellent!

As a sidebar, Donna did indeed order the cape she mentioned. It is bright red with white satin piping along its edges. It has a glittery gold lightning bolt striking through a large white circle and the words "Super Lana" in black capital letters across the circle's width. It was an extraordinary gift and one that I will always cherish.

John was with me on the morning of May 8 when the second round of plasmapheresis was performed. He was still shocked by how broken my body had become in such a short period. He desperately wanted this treatment to work and for my lungs to heal so we could leave this nightmare behind us. And yet he knew as he looked at me that unless we were blessed by miracle, we had a very long road ahead.

While he was at the hospital, he was able to speak directly with the thoracic surgeon. The surgeon explained that there is a point when the side effects of ECMO begin to outweigh the benefits. Because it requires blood thinners, it leads to excessive bleeding. I had been receiving around three units of blood each day to replenish what I lost, so the doctor felt it would be best to remove the ECMO. They also wanted to determine if I could tolerate being on only the ventilator. However, if my body couldn't handle those circumstances, I would be put back on ECMO.

After speaking with a different doctor later that same afternoon, John sent out the following message.

Friday, May 8, 2:49 PM - Lana's Update

John: I just spoke to one of her doctors, and Lana is not strong enough or healed enough to come off of ECMO yet. She also has evidence of a slight infection that they will have to treat. The doctor said this particular infection is pretty common around the hospital and typically responds to treatment well. Still, she is in no condition to fight infection. He has also reached back out to Duke and is waiting to hear back from them. I will let you know what I find out. I have pleaded with God for over a week now to bring her through this and heal her. I remain anchored in the fact that it's His plan.

Shelley C: Holy Spirit, breathe your healing life into Lana's lungs and guard her from clots and internal bleeding. Thank you, Lord, that Lana has treated her body so well so that she can be strong to beat this enemy within. To You be the power and the glory!

Rosy: John, thank you so much for the update. We are always waiting impatiently for it. We will be praying for Lana, not stopping until her full recovery, and of course, we keep you and the girls in our prayers also. I'm sure your strong faith will take you through this hard time. God is on your side.

Kasey C: We acknowledge that You are able to do all that we are asking and more. We stand together, united in these requests, Father, and pray for Your will to be done.

Trish D: Come on, sweet Lana. Keep fighting! We love you!

Donna: I miss my friend, and I want her back.

Tammy M: Me too, Donna.

Shelley C: I agree. Missing Lana! One-of-a-kind woman. Inspiring and real. Encouraging and challenging. A rare human being loved by so many.

Kathy: I'm lifting all of you up to God and asking Him to provide whatever is needed to get Lana healed. Knowing He has the power to bring Lana out of this without any lasting effects. Love to all of you.

On May 9, significant changes began to take place.

Again, John was at the hospital as the plasmapheresis took place. My O_2 saturation level was good, but my compliance had decreased for some reason. Whereas my tidal volume was in the mid-300s over the past few days, it had dropped back to the low to mid-200s. There was no conclusion on what had caused the drop.

The evening before, a larger tube was placed in my chest to relieve the air escaping from the tear in my lung. During the procedure, the medical team removed approximately 700cc of blood that had pooled in my chest cavity. They took new X-rays after the procedure, and my lung appeared to show some relief.

John was hopeful that my compliance would improve after the blood and air were removed, but that was not the case.

However, Duke finally approved my transfer.

Saturday, May 9, 11:08 AM - Lana's Updates

John: Yesterday, the doctors here at Novant initiated the process of transferring Lana to Duke. The first time they started this process, Duke didn't feel like she was quite at a point yet where they needed to be involved. Multiple people have already reached out to me this time to get insurance information and offer housing suggestions. They've also given me literature to begin reading to prepare me for being her caregiver.

The reason for transferring her to Duke is so she can be in place for a lung transplant. She will enter the lung transplant protocol if they can't get her healed or are headed in the right direction to healing pretty quickly. To date this year, Duke has performed 61 lung transplants. The average wait time has been 17 days. The most recent transplant was only a 9-day wait after the patient was placed on the list. As critical as she is, the doctors here feel she will be placed very close to the top of the list. In speaking with one of her doctors last night, he said it is generally considered that Duke is the top hospital in the country for this situation. We are blessed by that.

Assuming everything goes through for the transfer and she goes to Duke, it will most likely happen Monday. I suppose there is some possibility it could happen this weekend, but I don't think the probability is very high. She will stay on ECMO when she first gets to Duke to see if there's any possibility of her lungs healing. Ideally, she would get to keep her own organs. I don't think they will wait long before they make a decision on whether or not she should have a transplant. It is still stunning how quickly this all occurred.

Lastly, I can't begin to thank everyone on here for the prayers. I know she is in God's hands at this point, and prayers are what we have. As I look back over time, I understand just how much He has been preparing us for this.

As they had been for days, messages of love and encouragement from a multitude of prayer warriors flooded John's phone.

Jenny S: John, my heart just breaks for you and your family. Lana is strong, and I'm praying continually for healing!!! Please know you are not alone on this journey. You and Lana have an army of prayer warriors petitioning our Heavenly Father on your behalf!!

Carol T: John, I'm praying when I have words and praying with no words of my own. I know Lana is hearing God's whispered words to her. She knows His voice. Be strong and courageous. You have an army lifting you up.

Donna: Yes, John. I truly believe God put everything in place for this moment. I saw Lana transform into a well-oiled machine, strong of mind, body, and faith. She is ready for whatever comes her way.

Rosy: John, we are here for you and your family. We know how amazing and strong is our friend Lana, so we are confident that with God on her side and this army of people who loves and prays for her and your family, she will get better soon. Love you very much.

Tammy M: My heart was troubled all through the night and into the morning for Lana and you, so I prayed. Now, I know why. We'll keep praying and holding onto our faith. The strength you both show on so many levels is inspiring to us all. Make sure to take care of yourself as best you can, John. Love to your family.

Shelley C: I pray that we all would rejoice in hope, be patient in tribulation and be constant in prayer. (Romans 12:12) Not in our own strength, for this is impossible. But ALL things are possible in Christ, so we will all lean into his mighty power and strength as we cover Lana and your family in prayer.

Lynn G: It is beautiful to see this large community of prayer warriors covering each of you, John. It reveals the goodness Lana has brought to her friends and community. We are all touched by her. Now it is my/our privilege to support Lana and your family in prayer. He is with you through all of this as He hears each of our prayers. Praying for strength, peace, and healing.

John was exhausted by the situation, but the support he received gave him the energy to study the information he'd received from Duke about the process. Plus, at some point in all the chaos, tests finally revealed the culprit causing my illness. I have a very rare autoimmune disease called dermatomyositis, accompanied by another rare condition called antisynthetase syndrome PL-7. So he had a lot to learn and more to do to prepare for my transfer to Duke, and he suspected it was just the beginning of what was to come in the weeks ahead.

When he had done all the research he could digest, he returned to the hospital to spend as much time with me as possible. He understood he would no longer be allowed to visit me once I was moved to Duke.

That evening, his mind wouldn't stop thinking about all that had happened throughout the day. Knowing he wouldn't be able to sleep right away, he took some time to send a final message for the day.

Saturday, May 9, 11:52 PM - Lana's Updates

John: I spent a couple of hours at the hospital this evening, and Lana seems to be doing pretty well, all things considered. She had a kind of tough afternoon today after they did the plasmapheresis. But her title volume had improved again and was comfortably over 300. Her gases and oxygen levels were good, and she seemed to be resting. She's still bleeding quite a bit, but they're managing that. Her hemoglobin had dropped some today, and that was most likely based on the bleeding. On the other hand, her heart and kidneys are really working well. It seems to me that it's especially important for her kidneys to continue functioning at a high level due to all the fluids they are pumping into her.

Throughout this journey, God has continued to put people in our lives at just the right times. Tonight, it was Hannah Flynn, Lana's ECMO nurse. I'm not even sure she knew how much she encouraged me. After speaking with Hannah tonight, I better understood the type of care she might get at Duke compared to Novant. The team at Novant has been great. Compassionate, attentive, kind... all the things you would want from a group that is taking care of someone you love so much. On top of that, they are very good at what they do.

Hannah shared with me this evening that the ECMO teams at Novant are designed to get patients from the most critical conditions into a position where they can be transferred to somewhere like Duke. At Duke, Lana will be dealing with doctors and nurses who do nothing else but ECMO. While I already knew that, it comforted me to hear it from her. I guess she made it more real or something.

When I was there this evening, I asked Lana to squeeze my hand if she could hear me. I wouldn't call it a squeeze, but she certainly moved her hand ever so slightly. I hope when I'm there tomorrow, she will be responsive enough for me to put my phone to her ear and have her hear Mackenzie and Lauren speak to her. It's Mother's Day tomorrow, and I know they will be missing their mom. My prayer requests for the evening are that you continue to pray for Lana's healing, especially her lungs and the bleeding. I would also ask that you give thanks for the doctors and nurses who have been taking care of her. Without them, I don't think Lana would be here with us today. Again, God has put so many of the right people in our lives during this journey.

One last thing. Don't forget to give thanks for all the moms tomorrow.

I'll be going back up tomorrow to wish Lana a happy Mother's Day.

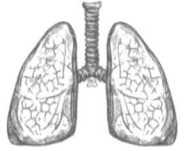

NOT A TYPICAL MOTHER'S DAY

Sunday, May 10

John wanted to be with me on Mother's Day, but before he prepared to go to the hospital, he wanted to check with the nurse about the timing of my day. There would be no reason to rush if there were procedures taking place that would keep him in the waiting area.

10:07 AM - Our Family

John: I spoke with Lana's nurse this morning to get an update and find out if they were doing the plasmapheresis this morning. In short, they are going to do the pheresis, so I will wait a little later today to go up there. As for Lana's condition, she had an uneventful night, and this morning all of her major measurements had improved. Her blood gases were much better, her compliance had improved, and her oxygen was at 100%. She was bleeding less, and her chest X-rays showed improvement. This has been quite the roller coaster, and I'm not getting ahead of myself, but it's always good to know that she has made some forward progress.

Happy Mother's Day, moms. This Mother's Day is far from ordinary for anyone.

Usually, Mackenzie and Lauren spent Mother's Day with me. It's one of my favorite days of the year. But, most likely, they don't realize how much I look forward to it and probably won't understand until they are mothers themselves.

Life changes when you have children. Suddenly, you have a tiny human to care for, and it's no longer all about you–your focus shifts to this precious little life God placed in your care. Sometimes you wonder if you have what it takes to raise them, and it's all you can do to keep your head above water. But there are so many moments that make all the struggles worth it–their first words, their first steps, their first day of school, their first dance, their first car, and all the other firsts along the way. Mother's Day isn't about receiving accolades for being a mom. Instead, it's about basking in your children and reflecting on all the blessings their lives bring to yours.

I remained in a coma, completely unaware it was Mother's Day.

Mackenzie had planned to make an in-person visit, but she had been sneezing some that morning and decided it would be best to stay home. She thought she was suffering from allergies but didn't want to take a chance. So instead, when she knew John was at the hospital, she called him, and he held the phone to my ear so she could wish me a happy Mother's Day. When she was finished talking to me, John played a voice message from Lauren for me.

Even though I don't recall them talking to me, my girls did their best to let me know they were with me. And knowing the efforts they made makes Mother's Day 2020 one I'll never forget.

After John played Lauren's message, he spoke with my doctor and shared the uncertain update with our family.

Sunday, May 10, 2:14 PM - Our Family

John: I just spoke with Lana's doctor a few minutes ago to get an update from his viewpoint. Her compliance has been good today compared to what it was yesterday. But, in his opinion, her lungs really haven't shown much improvement day over day. She's clearly doing better than she was a week ago, but she's nowhere near coming off of ECMO. Novant will not be doing any more plasmapheresis. I have no idea what they will do at Duke. Assuming nothing goes sideways, and she does indeed go to Duke tomorrow, they will begin making their own assessment of her and determine what techniques they will employ. I should know more within the next couple of days about how they feel regarding her lungs getting an opportunity to heal versus having a lung transplant. I continue to pray for the healing of her lungs.

Mother's Day greetings and well wishes poured in through GroupMe. My mom made her first entry into this group's stream.

Sunday, May 10 - Lana's Update

Mom: This is Lana's mom. I want everyone to know how encouraging it is to know all of you are lifting her up to the Father and asking for her healing. I believe God is letting her feel all the love everyone has for her. Someday soon, we pray she will be able to see and read all the prayers said on her behalf. Only God knows the reason for this journey she is having to travel, but He is blessing her during it. Thank you for loving my daughter. All glory is His.

It had been a positive, uplifting day for John and our family. But once again, things changed quickly.

Sunday, May 10, 5:24 PM

John: Lana needs our prayers right now! They're concerned that she has gotten an infection because she has a fever and her heart rate is very high. They put her on an extremely strong antibiotic but right now, she is struggling.

Linda: Didn't they start antibiotics the other day or something because they thought she had an infection? And if so, is this an exacerbation of that or something different?

John: Linda, we're not sure what caused this. She has so many tubes in her that the infection could be coming from virtually anywhere. She was managing this through antibiotics already. They have added vancomycin in the last hour because she started running a fever. A couple of minutes ago, her heart rate was in the 140s, and her systolic blood pressure was approaching 200. Her oxygen levels have dropped pretty quickly. And her fever is holding firm.

In the last 2 to 3 minutes, her heart rate has come back down into the 80s, and her blood pressure has dropped back down. The nurses were scrambling for a while, and I'm not sure they're finished. They are watching her very closely now.

After sending this message to our family, John reached out through the Lana's Update GroupMe again, and prayers flooded Heaven's gates.

Sunday, May 10, 5:42 PM - Lana's Update

John: I just spoke with the nurse, and they have given her more sedation. She had become very agitated and was trying to move. She has not started the vancomycin yet, so that didn't cause a reaction. She has calmed down some, but her heart rate and blood pressure are still higher than they should be. Three nurses are working with her consistently right now, and it is taking all three. Thank you for your quick response with prayers. I know God heard.

Knowing the dangers of what was taking place, John pleaded with the Lord to heal me and then sent out another update.

6:51 PM - Lana's Update

John: Lana has had a pretty rough afternoon, but they have her heavily sedated now, and she seems calmer. Her heart rate is still a little high, but her blood pressure seems to be a bit closer to normal. They have iced her down some, and her fever has come down. They have given her some additional products to help her oxygen levels. I can't tell you how much I appreciate the response from everyone who was praying for Lana this afternoon. All of you who know her well know just what a fighter she is. Tomorrow, God willing, we will get her to Duke and pray they can turn her around. I don't know how God intends to use her through this experience, but based on what she is going through, I can only imagine it will be powerful.

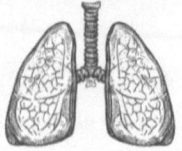

CHAPTER TWENTY-SIX

FIELD SURGERY

Monday, May 11

My numbers had improved enough throughout the night for the medical team to try to wean me off ECMO. Unfortunately, my body still couldn't handle it. On the brighter side, because I was now receiving vancomycin (the most powerful of all known antibiotics), my white count had dropped from 20k to 12k (the high end of normal is 11k), and my fever was gone. The nurses navigated the delicate balance of heparin to lower my blood pressure and norepinephrine to keep it from dropping too low.

It had become clear that I would not be transferred to Duke yet. Insurance approval was still pending; until that came, all plans remained at a standstill. The Novant team expected to receive the final documentation later in the day and would present it to the team at Duke the next morning in hopes of receiving approval for transport.

As the day progressed, my heart rate and blood pressure became unstable, the bleeding increased, and more air filled my chest. Something had to be done, and that something was emergency surgery.

Monday, May 11, 4:35 PM - Our Family & Lana's Update

John: I know I continue asking for a lot of different prayers from everyone on here, but I know how good you are at it. The thoracic surgeon who has been on her case is going into her chest, where they have inserted a tube. She has a lot of bleeding and air escaping into her body. They are going to try to determine where all of this blood is coming from and try to stop some of the bleeding. Because she's on a blood thinner, bleeding is to be expected. Over the last few days, she has experienced increasing bleeding from that chest tube, and they would really like to control that. Again, prayers are greatly appreciated.

I was too fragile to move to a surgical room; the risk was too high. So the team set up a mobile operating unit in my room. As John stood outside my door, he watched numerous surgeons and support personnel enter. Through a small window, he could see nothing but the monitors announcing what was happening in my body. He watched as my blood pressure shot up to 190/120; he heard the alarms ring out. Then, as quickly as my blood pressure rose, it plummeted to nearly 50/30. More alarms proclaimed the dangers. My heart rate increased to nearly 200, then suddenly dropped into the 20s. He felt like he was watching from worlds away, yet he was only feet from me. His body felt numb, yet his heart ached. All he could do was pray that God would guide the surgeons' hands and allow me to survive.

He guarded his words when he shared the situation with our family and friends. He wanted to protect them from the fear they would experience if they knew my condition was dire, nearly as bad as the evening I was placed on ECMO. What good would it do for them to experience that pain again?

May 11, 5:00 PM - Our Family

John: I can see Lana's blood pressure and heart rate from where I sit but nothing else. They have several people in her room, the doors closed, and they are working with some urgency at this moment.

Mom: We're there with you in our hearts, John. God is holding her and you.

5:38 PM - *Our Family*

John: They are still at it doing the surgery on Lana. I think they have located the source of all the bleeding and are working to rectify that. It seems that the tube that had been in her chest had created some scarring, and the scarring was bleeding. They removed almost 2L of blood from her chest cavity. A lot of the blood was old blood. Her vitals have remained stable during this time, and it seems the doctors have also done a good job of keeping her oxygen saturation levels high. I'm pretty sure they have re-inserted a new tube and, hopefully, will have much less blood flow with this one.

5:45 PM - *Our Family*

John: I just spoke with one of her doctors who came by just to check on her and give me an update. He said she's doing really well, and he is hopeful that this will potentially help her ability to get off of ECMO. There is absolutely no way to know that or any guarantees of any kind, but we know that 2 L of blood will inhibit her ability to expand her lung fully. I'm pretty sure they will do X-rays as soon as they are finished so they can see how it worked out.

Linda: 2 liters is a lot of anything extra to have in your chest; blood or any other fluid. It sounds quite hopeful that they have that corrected now, and I agree the ECMO and the ventilator should work much better. I'm thankful that she was in such good shape going into this, and her heart is strong.

Finally, Dr. Theruvath came out of my room. He and the rest of the team were drenched with sweat, evidence of how frantically they had been working. The surgeons cauterized several places in my chest that were bleeding, but there was so much blood they couldn't be sure where it was all coming from. They also added dressing to help restrict the bleeding. As a result of removing the blood and re-inserting a new tube, ECMO performed better. It was turned down to its lowest setting and working well. All-in-all the emergency bedside surgery was a success.

6:26 PM - Our Family

John: I've had an opportunity to get some additional information. Her X-rays were substantially better than before the surgery. She's also doing extremely well at this moment, with the ECMO turned down to its minimum. I think there's actually some optimism around here that she may be able to come off of ECMO tomorrow. She still has a tremendous battle in front of her, but coming off ECMO would certainly be a big victory.

At the end of what could have been a sorrowful day, an online celebration of thanksgiving took place instead.

6:37 PM - Lana's Update

John: It seems that Lana's case is pretty well known around the hospital. One of the people from another department who had been working with her before she got critical came by to visit me and said there are people all over the hospital praying for her. Regardless of the outcome, I know God has a plan for her. I still have no idea what it is, but I know it will be great!

Diana: Thank you for sharing the good news, John. It looks like Lana is working hard to figure this out. I will continue to ask God for her to stay on the path to recovery. Thinking of the whole family tonight and asking added prayers.

Kevin C: He hears, He knows, He loves, He cares! God is for her, and God is with her! Thank you, God! We trust You!

Tammy M: John, thank you so much for these detailed updates. Thank God for all the progress of the day! Can you imagine the symphony of prayer landing on our Father's ear for Lana and all involved in her care? It is incredible to be a part of this, and we give Him praise and glory in all things!

Donna: I haven't gone this long without talking to her since we met. I hear her voice in my head constantly (especially when I slack off), and I look forward to hearing her in real life again soon. She is a strong, faithful woman, and I bet she has found a way to pray under this heavy sedation.

Randy W: Thanks for the updates, John. I can't imagine what you're going thru, but rest assured, you're not alone. There are many beside you praying for positive results. You and the girls "hang in there."

Betty K: Thank you for the updates. As you said, God has a plan. In times of trials, it is hard to understand why? But we know God has it under his control, and we have to believe in his love and keep our faith. In good times, we thank Him for His goodness and love, and we should do the same in times of trials. He is the same God and is always with us. John, I am so very touched by your faith and love in God. You are lifting us all up by your words of Lana's progress and your faith. Lana is so very precious to each of us, and thank you for sharing with us. Try to get some rest.

Shelley C: Thank God that He never sleeps and is always working His will with power and authority for the good of His people. Rest well, Lana. Your God has you firmly in His grip!

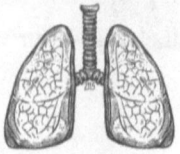

CHAPTER TWENTY-SEVEN
MORE IN-BETWEEN

As Shelley pointed out, I was undoubtedly in His grip, but it seems as if this was a moment of my "in-between" when I was also fully in His presence.

The room was dark as I lay quietly in my hospital bed. My mind told me I should be looking for the Light. Just then, the room was illuminated by a bright white glow coming from above to my left. I immediately turned toward it; I was drawn to it. As I gazed upon its beauty, I knew without a doubt the light was my Savior, Jesus. Beside Him stood an unrecognizable figure. I sensed it was a man. The light overwhelmed his features, yet he felt familiar to me.

Dad?

My dad passed away on February 20, 2015, due to complications brought on by carcinoid cancer.

On the Sunday before he died, my sister sent me a text that said, "I think you should come home. Dad is getting worse."

I immediately dialed my dad's cell, "Hey, Daddy. I want to come to see you soon. I know there's a winter storm coming in a few days. Would you like me to wait until it passes, or would you rather I come today?"

"I think you should come today."

That sentence said everything I needed to know. Dad would've told me to wait if he didn't believe his health was deteriorating quickly. Two hours later, I was on a flight to St. Louis, Missouri. Unfortunately, the storm arrived about the same time I did, and driving to my hometown was treacherous. I gripped the steering wheel tighter than ever as I navigated I-70 in whiteout conditions.

Finally! I pulled into the driveway, jumped out of the car, and made my way into my parents' house.

"Holy snow!" I exclaimed as I entered through the front door.

Typically, this would have gotten a giggle from Dad. But this time, he just looked at me, lost in pain.

I sat on the couch near him, longing to take his hurt away, "Can I get you anything, Daddy?"

"I'm fine."

Those words again! The older I get, the more they infuriate me, especially when I know they aren't true.

Mom woke me around 5:30 the following morning, "I think we need to take your dad to the emergency room."

I jumped out of bed and helped Mom gather what she thought we would need to take. She then assisted Dad as I bundled up in my minimal North Carolina girl winter gear. Finally, I made my way through the shin-deep snow covering the driveway to their detached garage. Pulling the car to the front door, I prayed the roads were clear enough to get to the hospital.

Shortly after our arrival, the medical team discovered a hole in Dad's intestine. Surgery was the only option to keep him alive, but it couldn't be done in our small-town hospital. Due to the blizzard, Life Flight was grounded, so Dad was taken by ambulance to a hospital in St. Louis, and my family followed in multiple cars. Once we arrived and were all in his room, we discussed the options and risks. Although there was a likelihood he might not survive the surgery, Dad decided to proceed.

Small tumors caked together in his abdomen prevented the surgeons from repairing the tear. After a few days in the hospital, Dad returned home by ambulance Wednesday afternoon for hospice care. On Friday around 10:00 PM, as my mom held his hand while she slept in the chair beside him, he took his final breath on earth and his first breath in heaven.

I've always been told there are no tears in Heaven, no sadness. So why would God allow Dad to visit me now, in my time of distress? Wouldn't it break his heart?

As my mind raced with questions, I felt the loving hand of Jesus touch my left cheek. Then, he gently turned my head away from Him toward another light down and to the right.

Over the years, I've become familiar with the funny side of Jesus. This time was no different. I knew He was pointing me back to this world, and the vision He used to show me His intentions made me laugh. It was an illuminated Snap Fitness sign, of all things.

But I was still drawn to His light. Each time I looked back toward Him, He gently turned my head in the other direction.

And then it was over. It ended the way most dreams do. They just stop, and you continue to sleep.

Many months later, while praying, I asked God why Dad was there to witness my suffering.

He answered, "Oh, sweet girl. Your dad knew you'd be happy whether you stayed there or if you came home to Me. Neither outcome could upset him because he's experienced both and knows both are very good."

As I've explained to John, my "in-between" was a peaceful place. I felt no urgency to come back or to move on. I believe what I experienced helps me to be more at ease about death, what it may feel like when it happens, and how easily it will be to transition from my human body. Of course, I'm still not ready to die. But there is comfort in knowing what lies ahead.

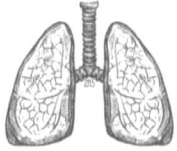

C H A P T E R   T W E N T Y - E I G H T

LIFE FLIGHT

Tuesday, May 12

John planned to arrive at the hospital at the same time he had the previous days, but he received a call mid-morning from a Novant nurse that changed that.

"Hi, John. This is Cassie. I'm unsure if you're aware, but Duke's life-flight team is coming to transport your wife this morning."

Surprised by the RN's news, he replied, "No, I had no idea."

"They're en route as we speak. It will take them a while to prep her once they arrive, so you have plenty of time to get here," she shared. "I'm off duty today, but I'm going in because I want to be there when she leaves."

"Thank you so much for letting me know. I'll be there as quickly as I can. See you there." He was already headed toward the shower as he spoke.

When John arrived in my room, Duke's team had already begun working with me.

The process of transporting a critical patient is tedious and time-consuming. The current machinery must be changed to the transporting hospital's machinery. For me, that included many monitors, a ventilator, and ECMO. In theory, it seems like it should be simple—unplug everything and replug everything. But when you consider precisely what all this machinery was responsible for, it's easy to understand how complex this task was. These machines were keeping me alive. Moving someone on ECMO is extremely risky; one mistake could have dire consequences.

As he waited for the work to be completed, he sent a message explaining what was happening.

> *10:32 AM - Our Family & Lana's Update*
>
> **John**: I'm at the hospital this morning, and the transfer team from Duke is here. They are currently disconnecting her from Novant machinery and connecting everything to their equipment. They will be putting her on a life flight. It will take approximately 55 minutes to get from here to Duke. I would ask that you thank God for the blessing of the people here at Novant, the flight team for Duke, and the doctors and nurses who will take care of her there. I will also ask that you pray for her continued healing, as well as peace and comfort for our family. When she leaves here, I'm not sure when I will be allowed to see her again. I continue to rest in the fact that God is in control and has a plan.

He then spent time soaking in the comforting words of the numerous prayers being lifted to our Father.

> **Kathy**: Father, hold Lana and her medical angels in your hands as they make the flight to Duke. Bless the medical team at Novant for the wonderful care they have taken of Lana. Please provide strength to Lana to make the trip. Be with our family and give us endurance and peace for the next part of this journey. Thank you for the blessings you have given and for the healing that will come. In all things, we know you have a plan. In Jesus' name, amen.

Lori M: Lord, we may not understand the reasons for what is happening, but we trust You. We know You make no mistakes, and You will be glorified in what Lana, John, and their families are going through. Hear our prayers and envelope this precious family and all who love them tightly in your arms. Protect them. Bring them a peace that has no explanation but You as the answer. We ask you for complete healing for Lana. Thank you, Lord, for the hands that can heal her. I also ask that Lana can feel John's presence when he is unable to be with her. In Jesus' precious name I pray.

Dave: Prayers for you, John, for strength and continued faith. Remember to take care of yourself. Lana is as tough as they come and will fight with every inch of her being. She will need you healthy and strong when she comes home. Prayers of thanks for the incredible medical team at Novant that God continues to keep them safe. For the transfer team and pilot for the amazing work they do. And now for the Duke staff that God uses them in healing Lana.

It was around noon when I was moved to Duke's gurney and wheeled out to the medical helicopter.

John knew I would want to see the process if given the opportunity. So he shot a video and took a few pictures. I'm thankful that he knows me so well. I've revisited that footage many times, carefully observing the medical team as they methodically disconnect and reconnect my lifelines to Duke's equipment. It's like watching a scene straight out of a medical show, except it's me on that gurney, being wheeled out to the helicopter. My heart aches when I think about how John must have felt as the chopper lifted off, disappearing from sight. Even though it brings tears to my eyes each time I watch it, I'm truly thankful that we have that video.

Another thirty minutes passed as the equipment and passengers were secured, and the aircraft was cleared for takeoff.

Once the helicopter was out of sight, John left Novant Hospital for the last time, hoping he'd have the opportunity to see me again.

Upon arriving at Duke, I was taken directly into surgery. The purpose was to revise the ECMO cannulation, moving it from my groin to my chest. The surgeon also performed a tracheostomy and addressed the excessive bleeding in my chest. These procedures would allow me to begin weaning off sedation, enabling me to move my body.

The medical team at Duke was kind enough to speak to John often, which helped to lessen his worry a little.

2:20 PM - Our Family & Lana's Update

John: I have spoken to multiple people from Duke in the last bit, and they are preparing Lana for surgery.

This morning I would estimate her body weight to be about 85 pounds. That does not count all of the fluids that are induced. Because she had such low body fat, her loss is predominantly muscle.

As I started speaking with the team of medical personnel at Duke, I found them to be extremely caring about me. It certainly helps to create a more peaceful feeling for me. It goes without saying that they are doing everything they can for Lana. I continue to feel blessed that we are so close to Duke, as they are arguably the best in the world at what we are dealing with. As always, the incredible support and prayers we have received cannot be overstated.

Before this journey goes any further, I want to say thank you to the team at Novant for taking phenomenal care of her and me. I cannot imagine a more caring or loving group of people. I don't think they understand how much they have blessed me during this time. No matter how much I could ever try, I can never repay them. As you send up your prayers, be sure to give special thanks to God for this group.

Mom: As her mother and on behalf of her sister, I want to also thank them for caring so much for Lana and John. Being hundreds of miles away, it blessed us to know she was in such capable hands. Thank all of you from the bottom of our hearts.

Shortly after acknowledging the Novant staff, more evidence of God's hand in our journey came from our friends, Tripp and Elyse. Elyse's sister is a clinical pharmacist at Duke and would eventually be my pharmacist. Until then, Dr. Hinkel, their good friend, would be the pharmacist handling my medications. Not that either would give me special treatment over other patients, it was just comforting to know God had prepared these special people for us to encounter along this long road. And we would soon discover multitudes more.

Though their calls were helpful to John during my transition, it was all he could do to keep up with all the details from the staff at Duke, which included the news that a lung transplant would indeed be necessary for me to live. He systematically contacted our girls, my mom, and then Eric. Assuming how distraught John must be, Mackenzie, Jessica, and Justin decided to visit and have dinner with him. He was comforted by their presence and thankful not to spend the evening alone.

After they left, he sent a final update before he settled in for the night.

11:30 PM - Our Family & Lana's Update

John: It's been a long day, but I wanted to provide a brief update on Lana for our Prayer Warriors. Her surgeries today went pretty well. But unfortunately, it's been determined that she has very little chance of surviving without a lung transplant. I spoke with the doctor who will be doing the transplant, and he informed me that she would be one of the highest-rated candidates in the entire country. A tentative timeline is to have her listed on the national registry by the end of this week, and with the level of her illness, it's entirely possible there could be a transplant done next week.

I will provide additional detail tomorrow when I have had a chance to rest and clear my thoughts. Thank you for your kindness and support through this trial. Make no mistake, I still believe that God has a plan for Lana and for me.

Goodnight everyone.

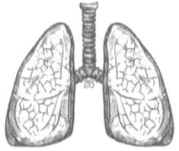

CHAPTER TWENTY-NINE

SHE'S AWAKE

Wednesday, May 13

Along with calls to Mom and the girls, numerous conversations with an array of people from Duke and our insurance company filled John's day. He spoke with a psychologist at Duke to share all he could about my personality and positive outlook on life, so they would be prepared to work with me, and he talked to the director of the transplant unit. He also had a call from one of my former Novant doctors asking how I was doing. The doctor didn't say exactly, but John believes his call was to check on him, too.

The preparation process for a double-lung transplant is complex. There were many moving parts, and it was John's responsibility to ensure they aligned. Unfortunately, the task only added to his exhaustion.

Ali had some time available and decided to try to ease John's overwhelm by bringing him lunch, which became an early dinner instead. Unfortunately, because of the chaos, they couldn't make time to eat until around 3:30 pm. But then he was able to relax and enjoy Ali's company.

They spent a few hours together. The weather was beautiful. The skies were clear, and it was 80 degrees, so they decided to take a drive in my convertible, which hadn't been started since my last day at the gym in March.

They drove around on country roads, breathing in the fresh air and talking about everything and nothing.

John cherished his time with Ali. It had been a while since they had had alone together, and it was a much-needed escape from the medical world he had been dropped into.

When the day was finally winding down, John was able to send out an update.

9:14 PM

John: I spoke to Lana's nurse a couple of hours ago, and Lana is about the same. They did a CT scan today for the purpose of taking body dimensions. I think the nurse expects that Lana will pretty well stay in the same condition until it's time for the transplant. She did tell me that they had taken an additional step to try to remove some of the subcutaneous air from her body. It's been a very busy day speaking with different people from Duke.

Ali came over today and brought me some lunch, breakfast, or dinner, depending on how you look at it. Between her, Jessica, and Mackenzie, it's been really good to have them over. I miss having Lauren here. Just so you know, I am lying in bed dictating these comments. Hopefully, I will get a better night's sleep.

God continues to put loving, caring people in my life right now. It's incredible to know just how he is taking care of me at this time. He is my strength.

My request for prayers is that you continue to give thanks for the teams at Duke and Novant. I would also ask that you give thanks for all of the people who are on this text stream praying for us relentlessly.

Finally, I would ask that you pray for all of those at Duke who are going through the same type of trauma as we are. Knowing that some of them do not have faith in God is truly sad. I'm not sure how they could do it without Him.

John didn't realize it, but his daily messages gave others hope. He was encouraging them by sharing our darkest moments. As a result, they saw God move in ways they never had before, miraculous ways. They saw that our faith came from nowhere other than the Lord.

> **Trish D**: John, I don't know if you are meaning to, but reading your words gives me strength, hope, and clarity. I can only hope that if I were ever in your shoes, I'd handle it with as much faith as you have. Thank you for walking the walk. Rest easy *allowing us to witness* you walking the walk.

As Mackenzie read the messages, she remembered her discussions with John that day about the doctors wanting to bring me out of sedation to explain where I was and what I was about to undergo. She wondered if that was still the plan and turned to John for clarity.

> **Mackenzie**: Are they still going to try to take Mom out of sedation to talk to her first?

> **John**: Mackenzie, they've been trying a little bit since after the surgery yesterday, but she hasn't responded very well. She begins coughing, probably due to the tube that was down her throat for two weeks. They are going to continue to lighten her sedation and see if they can get her awake. It will probably take a few days to do that. Even if they do, she most likely won't be in any mental state for several days to

make any decisions or give any clear thoughts. She's been sedated for a long time now.

Mackenzie is a caregiver by nature. From when she was little, I witnessed her "mothering" those around her. One particular incident stands out in my mind. She was probably four years old, maybe 5, and I had dropped her off in her Sunday School room. While chatting with one of the other moms, I noticed the arrival of a new couple with their reluctant daughter. The little girl was hesitant to enter the room filled with kids she didn't know, so she clung to her mother's leg. Mackenzie also noticed the new family and took it upon herself to welcome her soon-to-be friend.

She approached the girl she had never met and said, "I'm Mackenzie. Would you like to play with me?"

The little girl slowly nodded her head. Then Mackenzie put her hand on her new friend's back and led her to the area where she had been playing. It was a precious moment that not only put the child at ease but also added a smile to her parents' faces. And it made this mama very proud.

Now, over 20 years later, Mackenzie wanted to take care of me. John's answer made sense to her, but she remained hopeful that I would wake up soon. Her concern came from wondering if I would have the chance to decide my own fate, to choose to have a lung transplant or not. She was reasonably sure I would give the go-ahead, but she felt it should be my choice. She also didn't want John to carry the burden of the decision alone.

Only time would tell, and she wouldn't have to wait long for her answer.

As John was ending his day and getting ready for a solid night's sleep, his phone buzzed. It was the hospital. He hesitated to answer because it was late, and it concerned him that something may be wrong.

"Hello," he said.

"Mr. Lamkin?"

"Yes." His reply was guarded.

The nurse shared her name and then said, "Your wife is awake and would like to talk to you."

The next twenty minutes were the best we'd shared in two weeks.

11:47 PM - Family & Lana's Update

John: I know I said I would be crashing early tonight, but that is not the case. The hospital called me, and I had an opportunity to speak with Lana this evening. She is awake. She couldn't talk to me because of the tracheostomy, but I had a chance to speak into her ear and pray with her for about 20 minutes. The nurse then put it on speaker for me to tell Lana good night and that I love her. The nurse said that Lana nodded her head and mouthed the words I love you too. When I told her we have a FaceTime date tomorrow at 11:00, she nodded again. Kind of hard to go to sleep after that!

When I spoke to the nurse for a few minutes to get an update on Lana, I asked her how she was handling being awake and what her understanding was of the situation. She said the first two questions Lana asked were where am I and where is my husband. I had already told the doctors and the psychologist that those would be the first two questions she asked. I'm glad to know that the Lana I know and love is in there. We serve a mighty God!

I ended up spending the next hour and 20 minutes talking to Lana's mom and our girls. It's the best conversation we've had in a couple of weeks. So many prayers answered and so much to be thankful for.

Excitement is the best way to describe the messages he received in return.

Kathy: I think I would be up dancing! If you're going to lose sleep, that's a pretty good reason. Sounds wonderful. Prayers and love to you and the family, which includes everyone fighting for her. Good night, little brother.

Barb S: Oh wow! How exciting! Such joy in knowing your sweetie is awake and understood you. Continuing to pray! Praying for you as I know it's hard to be so far away and still many unknowns. But praise God for this beautiful gift.

Raina N: That is incredible! Praise Jesus for this news! Such a great way to end the evening.

Kasey C: John, what a gift... for both of you... I'm without words... so thankful for God's grace, presence, and provision!!

Mia C: That is amazing, wonderful news! What an answer to prayer! I'm still praying for a miraculous intervention!

Adrienne B: Wow... just WOW!!!

And the messages kept coming the next morning.

Thursday, May 14, 7:13 AM

Julia: That's the best early morning message we've gotten in a bit. I stood in the kitchen and read it out loud. AND Kathy, I did a little dance. It was ugly, but I didn't care. I had cause for celebration.

Jeanne: Oh, this is indeed happy news! I know you're looking forward to 11 o'clock and your FaceTime visit!

Lauren B: That is such awesome news! I am so happy you were able to talk and pray with her! She is such a fighter! All of us at Novant continue to pray for you both!

Shelley C: Your love, Lord, reaches to the heavens, your faithfulness to the skies. Your righteousness is like the highest mountains, your justice like the great deep. You, Lord, preserve both people and animals. How priceless is your unfailing love, O God! People take refuge in the shadow of your wings. They feast on the abundance of your house; you give them drink from your river of delights. For with you is the fountain of life; in your light, we see light. Ps 36:5-10

Praising the Lord this morning for Lana's awakening, I will keep praying for His Hope to be securely planted in your hearts that He is faithful and will supply our every need every time. Thanks for this good bit of news, John! Love to Lana.

Donna: I've said from the beginning that this woman is doing burpees in her head! She is fierce and has prepared herself for this moment with her physical, mental, and spiritual strength. I thank God she was able to communicate with you, John! Today, this is everything!

Sherry T: Tears streaming down my face as I read your miraculous news this morning, John. All I could think about is how happy I am for you, and to God be the glory! It's still a long journey, I know, but your Lana is on her way back.

Dave: John, this news brings tears to my eyes. Hearing your voice is the best medicine Lana can get right now. And I know it helped your heart and spirit. Lana has thousands of people praying for her. My sister called me last night and told me she asked for prayers for a friend in need at church. They said no and said they were dedicating the whole service to Lana's health, your well-being, and strength and clear minds and steady hands of the surgeons.

Please tell Lana, like everyone else, I am thinking about her nonstop and sending all my prayers and support for added strength to fight through to a full recovery. Big Hug.

These are only a few of the replies. I'd love to share them all with you, but there's much more story to tell.

At 2:20 AM, John's phone buzzed, alerting him to another call from the hospital. With each call from them, his heart skipped a beat. Would it be good news or bad news this time?

"Hi, Mr. Lamkin. Lana's awake and would like to hear your voice again. Are you able to talk to her?"

John replied without hesitation, "Absolutely."

The nurse placed the phone to my ear, and I listened to John speak. Because it was the middle of the night and it was quiet (for the most part), he would occasionally drift off to sleep. Then an alarm would sound from one of the machines I was hooked to. The sound would wake him, and he would talk to me again. To my pleasure, this went on for two and a half hours.

There's something about his voice. From the day I met him, I could spend hours listening to him talk. When we were dating, he would call me the moment he got in the car to come to pick me up, and we'd talk until he'd arrive. The same would happen when he headed home at the end of our date. He would call me on his lunch break, on his way to a meeting, and when he drove to an appointment. If he was in his car, we were on the phone together. Hours upon hours, we spent time talking. We still do. His voice is like music to my ears.

There's something about his voice that relaxes me and makes me feel safe. That evening was no different.

When we finally ended our call, John snuck in a few hours of sleep before facing another day of navigating through all the information needed by our insurance company and Duke, followed by attending virtual classes, along with Mackenzie, to learn how to be my caregiver after my transplant.

Then, as scheduled, our 11:00 am FaceTime call began. I hadn't seen his face since the evening of April 30. You can only imagine how happy I was– heavily medicated but extremely happy. It was another event worthy of sharing on GroupMe.

Thursday, May 14, 2:50 PM - Our Family GroupMe

John: So I really thought I was going to get sleep last night, but it didn't work out quite as I thought it might. I got a call from the hospital at 2:20 AM with the nurse telling me Lana wanted to hear my voice. No problem. That lasted until 4:50 AM. In my world, that was better than sleeping. Today, Mackenzie, Lauren, and I had an opportunity to Face-Time with her. I think she was pretty lucid in the moment, but I'm not sure if she will remember it later. After we spoke with her, we spoke with one of the doctors and then both of them together.

He explained to her where she was, what was going on with her, and that she was in the hospital to have a double lung transplant. He would ask her if she understood, and she would nod her head yes. I'm pretty sure she was aware of what he was saying.

I spoke with her and told her that I had researched, asked countless questions, and had come to a very clear understanding that it was the absolute best thing for her. She had been a bit teary this morning, but I would guess, knowing her, that it was her lack of clarity regarding her situation. I think now that she understands what is in front of her, she will have a chance to accept it, set her goals, and pursue them with the single-mindedness she possesses in abundance.

Mackenzie and I started classes today because we will be primary and secondary caregivers.

I've always told people that our family is extremely tight. The word I use is clannish. Even when we're apart for a while, we rally around each other when the time comes. You guys have been incredibly supportive through this entire journey, and I can't say thanks enough. I love you all.

He then sent the same message in the Lana's Update GroupMe with a slightly different ending.

Lana's Update GroupMe

John: A couple of thoughts for today. We had a sermon recently that Shane (our pastor) gave that talked about debunking myths regarding the Bible. One of those myths was, 'God will not give us more than we can handle.'

We know that's not true. We know that He will not give us more than He can handle. Throughout this season, people have commented to me how strong I seem. I will tell you that I am about two words from crying most of the time. My strength through this time has come from knowing that God loves me, He loves Lana, and He has a plan for us. My prayer today is that you know He loves you.

John was right; I had a lot to process. It was overwhelming enough to wake up in a different hospital, but the added news of having to have my lungs replaced was heavy. Breathing in the unexpected, I had to take some time to try to clear my head (despite all the medication) and come to terms with all that had happened while I was out.

I needed a double-lung transplant. Me! One of the "fittest people I know." I didn't have the strength to walk this path; it would all come from God.

"No matter what happens, We are with you." Those words resonated more deeply now. I was in the throes of the most challenging battle of my life to date, but I knew Jesus was carrying me. As the Bible promises in Deuteronomy 31:6, He will never leave or forsake me. I didn't question this promise for one second.

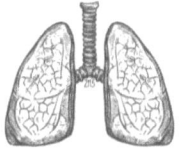

CHAPTER THIRTY

TIME OUT

Friday, May 15

Typically, transplant patients begin the process months before receiving their gifted organs. A long-term illness and drawn-out wait certainly aren't what anyone would want, but in our case, the problem was quite the opposite, and time was running out quickly. The team at Duke was trying to get everything done within a few days. It had been a mad scramble for Duke and John. Most days, John was inundated with the large volume of phone calls, gathering necessary information, and responding as quickly as possible. But he also felt blessed that we lived close to one of America's best lung transplant centers. It was another example of God's plan for us.

John had spoken with our transplant coordinator, and Duke hoped to get me listed for a transplant today. The only hurdle left was getting the final approval from insurance. So, Duke sent a medical package to our insurance company for their review and approval. According to our coordinator, Sandra, they were one of the insurance companies with a designated transplant department, which would make the process move swiftly. And if all went according to plan, we would have approval quickly.

He told our family where we were in the process and added a special prayer request.

May 15, 7:41 AM - Our Family GroupMe

John: My prayer requests this morning are that you would give thanks for all the people at Duke who are working so hard to get Lana a new set of lungs. I would also ask that we give thanks to God for placing us so close to the resources for that to happen. Please also pray that the insurance approval gets through the system as quickly as possible and that Lana gets the best set of lungs for her in the quickest period of time. As always, I am humbled by your support and your prayers.

I also want to thank all of you for taking care of me during this time. I know I have been physically isolated for the vast majority of the past several weeks, but I haven't felt isolated emotionally or spiritually.

My sister then shared a little of her guarded heart with us (you can bet I will tell you about it every time she gives us a peek in).

Cindy: This makes a big sister's heart sing with so much joy and peace at the same time. Coming from someone that holds all my emotions in, this has made me face this day with happiness! John, you are such a rock in this situation, and I can't thank you enough for taking such good care of my sister. Being so far away makes me feel helpless and so out of touch with everything. Taking such good care of my nieces in this time of need. It is so hard to watch a family member go through such difficulty. Lana has always been

my ROCK, and she makes me smile and laugh. Thank you
with all my heart and love!!!

That post melts my heart every time I read it. We may not be as close as
some sisters, but we don't love each other any less than those who are. I know
she's always one phone call away and will be by my side anytime I need her.

As the day progressed, things didn't go as anyone expected or planned. I
realize this put my family and medical team under undue stress, but I decided
I needed a break while everyone was scrambling to put the pieces of my transplant puzzle together. I couldn't communicate this with anyone and wasn't
fully aware of what I was doing. I must have needed a few minutes (or a little
longer) to gather myself.

I recall thinking, "I want to be left alone. No more poking and prodding.
No more X-rays. No more anything. Just leave me alone!"

So, I stopped.

My actions didn't stop any of those things; they only increased the activity around me. But I had checked out and was no longer aware of what was
happening in my room.

12:32 PM

John: We need prayers. I just got a call from Duke, and as
of this morning, Lana has not been able to move her extremities. She can still mouth words and nod her head in response. They have run numerous tests today to check for issues like stroke, spinal pressure, additional syndromes, etc.
So far, they have found nothing in all their tests indicating
damage that could be treated. They will also consult a
rheumatologist to determine if her Dermatomyositis could
be causing this level of weakness. If it is determined that she
has neurological damage, it could preclude her from getting
a lung transplant.

As the day went on, nothing changed. I was moving nothing from the neck down. I honestly can't be sure that my desire to be left alone was causing my inability to move or if something more serious was happening in my body, but it caused an absolute uproar. I was tested for stroke; they tested my spine to see if there was pressure on it and looked for potential drug reactions. There was a possibility that all of the steroids I was on in such a short period could have been causing steroid-induced myopathy (weak muscles). They ran tests to see if additional autoimmune issues were causing it. Continuous and ongoing consultations were happening between my attending physician, neurologist, and rheumatologist.

Every test they could think of was being done, yet there were no conclusive answers. The decision was made to postpone putting me on the transplant list. John shared the disappointing news with our family.

6:14 PM - Our Family GroupMe

John: The plan is to continue trying to solve the problem of what is causing her weakness while giving her an opportunity to get stronger. The attending physician, Dr. Reynolds, who manages the transplant department and is a teaching doctor, said this might turn out to be a blessing. They have done multiple scans today, including scans of her lungs. He said the top of her lungs look good, but the bottoms are struggling. He also told me that even though it is somewhat of a long shot, there could actually be potential for her lungs to heal enough not to need a transplant. He was very careful to make sure to let me know that it was a long shot but still possible.

When boiled down to its essence, there currently seem to be three potential outcomes. One, she stays on ECMO for a while and gets strong enough to have a lung transplant. Two, she stays on ECMO for a while, and her lungs heal enough to not need a lung transplant. Three, she doesn't recover. I ask that you pray that she gets strong and her lungs recover. Maybe God put a stop to her being listed today because she doesn't need a lung transplant, and he is going to heal her.

While he waited for another update from the hospital, he remembered the suggestion to gather cards and photos to put on the wall of my hospital room. He, Mackenzie, and Jessica devised a bigger plan: create a poster with pictures of our family and me and have everyone sign it. This effort would take time, which John didn't have. Jessica would take the lead.

8:09 PM

Jessica: Please upload family photos. We'll pull them together into some sort of collage format with an agreed-upon phrase.Dad, we'll run the final version by you for approval and probably go with something in a standard size, like 24"x 36".

As family photos began arriving through GroupMe, John received a call from my nurse. Much to his relief, I had started pushing back against pressure and was moving my arms.

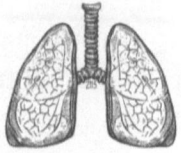

CHAPTER THIRTY-ONE

GRID VIEW

Saturday, May 16

Dr. Reynolds called John as soon as he left my room after his morning visit with me. "We ran every test we could think of. I have no medical explanation for why Lana couldn't move her body yesterday. Or why she is better today."

He told John that I was doing very well moving all my extremities, but because I was alert and stronger, he wanted to postpone listing me for a transplant. The reasoning behind waiting was to see if I would get even stronger still. I had been under sedation for so long that there was no way of knowing how much of my weakness was caused by the medication or how capable I was on my own. So they planned to bring in a physical therapist to work with me and try again to remove the ECMO. In addition, if I did have to undergo a transplant, I needed to be as strong as possible to survive it. If I were any weaker, I wouldn't be able to withstand such a major surgery.

John was convinced that God used my lack of movement to slow the process. He shared his convictions about God's healing power with Dr. Reynolds and the medical staff at Duke.

We all know that many who study science don't always agree with our spiritual beliefs. But in this case, God had put us with one of the best transplant pulmonologists in the world, who also happens to be a believer. It was comforting to know. We not only could rely on Dr. Reynolds for excellent medical care, but we also knew He understood our hearts and welcomed conversations that included our Christian beliefs.

As I've grown to know Dr. Reynolds, I trust him completely. And as he has gotten to know me, he trusts my opinions and allows me to take the lead (for the most part) with my care. He's learned I will do whatever it takes to keep my body as healthy as possible. But at this point, he still had no idea what a fighter I was. He would, however, learn quickly that I mean business.

No one knew how I would respond to rest and physical therapy. My lungs were severely damaged and potentially would never recover enough to avoid a transplant. But everyone agreed that the decision would be God's and that giving me a little extra time was the best approach.

My family and I met via Zoom at 11:00 AM as planned. My mom joined us for the call this time. I became more lucid as the sedatives cleared my body, and I was grateful to see and communicate with the people I loved most. John was amazed by the improvement from 24 hours ago.

Later in the day, my ECMO settings were reduced to test my tolerance. It didn't go well. I became agitated (I was told), which made my blood pressure and heart rate unstable. I was moving around enough that there was a concern I would decannulate the ECMO. Since it was the only thing keeping me alive, I was lightly sedated again to keep my anxiety at bay and ECMO in place.

Mom was happy she could talk to me on our call but was also aware of how critically ill I remained. She held tight to her faith, continued to pray, and shared some encouragement with the others.

9:15 PM

Mom: "The wonderful thing about praying is that you leave a world of not being able to do something and enter God's realm where everything is possible." ~ Corrie Ten Boom

BREATHING IN THE UNEXPECTED

Her message touched the hearts of many, leading them to bow their heads and enter God's realm on my behalf once again.

John called the hospital around 10:00 PM to check on how I was doing. Although I was tired and didn't have much to say, the nurse brought the phone to me and allowed John to say good night.

Sunday, May 17

We had another Zoom call scheduled for 11:00 AM, and John got an idea right before our call began.

10:48 AM - Lana's Update

John: Lana's love language is words of affirmation. I'll share a link where you can send Lana an email, and they will read it to her and put it on her wall. It's easy, and it's free. She is alone there and needs to be encouraged. She needs to know how important she is. If you have a few minutes, please consider sending her a message.

Also, I know this is short notice, but we have a call with Lana in 15 minutes. I would love to be able to read messages to her describing how she has impacted people. If you have a short message you can share where she inspired or served you, I would love to read it to her. Thank you!

Over the next several hours, stories from friends, clients, and acquaintances flowed in. Even a few of the nurses from Novant shared their thoughts. John wasn't surprised by what he read. He already knew my heart was to encourage and guide others, but the messages reinforced that. I felt the warmth of friendships as he read each to me. He had given me the unique gift of words of affirmation that filled my love tank.

When we ended our call, he immediately sent an update.

11:28 AM

John: Thanks to everyone for the messages. She absolutely loved being read to and having people encourage her.

She was very alert today. It is amazing to see how much stronger she becomes each day. Unfortunately, while her body is growing stronger, her lungs continue to struggle.

During our call today, she stopped everything to get a message to us. She wrote the word "grid" to let us know she wanted a grid view on the computer so she could see each of us on the screen at the same time. When I spoke to the nurse this morning, he didn't think she would be strong enough or have enough motor skills to convey by the written word. But, again, she defies normal through her incredible willpower.

John only touched on our "grid view" exchange. He didn't share that it took several minutes and everyone's efforts to figure out what I was saying. And then to decipher what I meant.

On my device, the Zoom call was set to show only the person speaking, and their face filled the screen. I didn't like that at all. I wanted our call to feel as close to being in the same room as possible. I wanted to see everyone's expressions as we chatted. I knew there was a setting to have all the call attendees on the screen. It's called gallery view, but the only word I could conjure up was "grid." I was so determined for my screen to be set the way I wanted it that I could focus on nothing else.

While John, Mom, and Lauren were trying to interpret what I was mouthing, I noticed Mackenzie looking at me intently. I realized she was my only hope. I focused my eyes on her and prayed she could feel my inner cries for help.

I pointed to the letters on the alphabet board the nurse was holding and she relayed what she saw, "G?" I nodded.

Back to my board. "R?" I nodded again.

My confidence grew, "I." Yes!

"D."

I looked back to Mackenzie. Come on, kiddo.

"Grid?" I smiled and waited. "I don't know what you mean, Mom."

AUGH!!! This would be my last attempt. I pointed to the screen and back to the scribbles on my board. Again, I stared directly at Mackenzie.

Her eyes lit up, indicating she had solved the riddle, "She wants it in gallery view so she can see all of us."

I let out a sigh of relief and gave them a thumbs-up. That's my girl. I knew you could do it!

From that point on, when we got on a call with a new nurse navigating the setup, Mackenzie would start by saying, "Be sure it's set to gallery view so she can see everyone."

As the day went on and I became more alert, I began thinking of things I wanted to have with me as I healed; whenever that may be. Some of my requests were reasonable, and others, not so much. Honestly, who needs a makeup bag in ICU? But John wasn't about to tell me that I was being ridiculous. Instead, he packed everything I requested and drove the two hours and 20 minutes to Durham to deliver them. God love him.

Besides asking him to go out of his way to deliver the unnecessary items, I also requested that he sing to me.

10:34 PM

John: I spoke with Lana through a nurse for about 15 minutes this evening. We had a good conversation. Tomorrow on our 11 o'clock Zoom call, I have committed to singing for her. I asked her if she would like me to sing, and the nurse said she nodded enthusiastically. Because I walk around the house singing all the time, I'm guessing it will remind her of home. I also asked her if she would like me to bring her phone, iPad, and get-well cards to the hospital. Again, the nurse said she gave an enthusiastic nod. We have no idea if she is strong enough yet to pick up her phone or iPad for any period of time, but they will be there for her when she is.

She did request an additional item. She wants me to bring her makeup bag. Her nurse said that there are plenty of nurses who would love to help her by doing her makeup.

Her lungs are still not working well enough to be off of ECMO, but she is clearly regaining the spark that makes her Lana. How I love that woman. I have no way of knowing if God will ever heal her lungs, but I sure am thankful for the work He is doing for her spirit.

I would ask that you continue to give thanks for her improvement. People heal at Duke beyond what the physicians can understand. Her doctor told me it had happened before, and it will most certainly happen again at some point. Let's pray that Lana is one of those people. Ours is a God of healing and miracles.

Something I haven't mentioned about John is that he was a professional musician in his life before me. He traveled the country singing with bands and even did some studio work in Nashville. He put his vocal career aside shortly before we met. But He tells me there's always a song playing on his inner jukebox. And, as he mentioned in his message, he often sings it aloud. I hadn't heard him sing in weeks and welcomed hearing his beautiful vocals.

The evening ended with a message from my dear friend, Tammy.

10:37 PM

Tammy: What a way to bring this night to a close. Thank you for allowing us to be witnesses to your love story in this time of crisis. We know you love each other tremendously, even before this. This experience grows a love much deeper than words will allow. It warms my heart, and I can't wait to hear about your day tomorrow! We give praise to our God and continue to pray for Lana's recovery and a restful night for you.

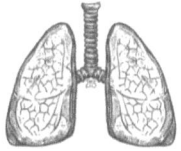

CHAPTER THIRTY-TWO

DO IT

Monday, May 18

It's easy to begin to doubt God's plan in situations like ours. Despite our prayers for a miracle, my body continued to struggle, with ups and downs that left us uncertain about the future. Doubt crept in, even as we tried to trust in God's plan. God had shown us numerous times that He was working, yet my mother's faith in receiving a miracle wavered as she watched me suffer day after day. But then, something happened that gave her hope.

As she slept, my mom dreamed that God showed her clear, healthy lungs. She had been at the feet of Jesus, praying that He would heal my lungs. This dream seemed to be evidence that my lungs would indeed be well again. She woke up filled with excitement and confidence, convinced that I would soon be able to breathe deeply once again. It felt like a message from God, a sign that our prayers were being answered. But as time passed and my condition remained unchanged, that hope gave way to disappointment and confusion.

We knew God was working, but it was hard to keep doubt at bay. Every day, it gnawed at our faith. We had asked for a miracle, yet it seemed my lungs would never recover. We had to decide whether we would continue to trust God's plan or allow ourselves to lose faith altogether.

Ultimately, we chose to keep the faith, although it was a daily exercise.

John had received a "so-so" medical report from the hospital. He shared the technical details on GroupMe for the nurses who were following. His message included terminology most of us would struggle to decipher, but a reply from one of the nurses who cared for me at Novant confirmed the news was encouraging. Even with a report that received a thumbs-up from medical personnel, the fact remained that I still needed a transplant to survive.

The criteria to become a lung-transplant recipient given by the *International Society of Heart and Lung Transplantation* are as follows:

> Being a lung transplant candidate includes having end-stage lung disease AND the following:
> - Physical ability to survive for 90 days following transplant
> - Medical likelihood that you will survive five years after transplant
> - High risk of death if a lung transplant is not performed within two years

It was obvious that I met those qualifications. The final determining factor was my lung allocation score (LAS). The lung allocation score is used to estimate a lung candidate's medical urgency and expected post-transplant survival rate relative to other patients on the waiting list for a lung transplant. It's the number that determines your place in line on the list. The higher the score, the closer to the top of the list you are.

Because of my situation, I was not able to undergo all of the tests that determine the LAS. For those tests, I was given the average score. When all was said and done, my LAS was 92 out of 100, which is very high. My doctor believes that would have been higher if they could have completed all the tests. But a higher score wouldn't have mattered much. With a 92, I was considered a high priority and was placed at the top of the list. I would receive lungs quickly.

Later in the afternoon, Dr. Reynolds contacted John to tell him that he had a conversation about the transplant with me. John wanted to have one more opportunity to speak with me before a final decision was made. If my family was satisfied that I understood and agreed, we would move forward.

After John shared this update on GroupMe, a special message of encouragement came from our new friend Nicole.

4:27 PM

Nicole: Transplants are miracles, too!!

John: Nicole, you are right. Lung transplants are miracles. For those who don't know, Nicole is a double-lung transplant recipient and has been an incredible blessing to me. She has been in pretty much exactly the same position that Lana is in and is living a healthy lifestyle today.

Nicole's words were a lifeline for my family. As we waited for a miracle, she reminded us that God's plan often unfolds in unexpected ways. We might not receive the outcome we hoped for, but that didn't mean we wouldn't receive a miracle. Perhaps the miracle we were waiting for was already happening, but we were too blinded by our expectations to see it. As we grappled with the uncertainty of my condition, Nicole's words gave us hope and strengthened our faith that no matter what happens, God was with us.

Nicole divinely came into our lives. Nicole lives a few houses down the street from John's sister, Jeanne. Jeanne and Nicole knew each other from neighborhood events but not well. Amid a random conversation, Jeanne mentioned my situation. Nicole shared with her that she had gone through a very similar situation a few years earlier. Recognizing the value of her insight, Jeanne asked for Nicole's contact information, and she generously agreed to connect with us. We felt like we had been given a gift from above in the form of Nicole's wisdom and experience.

John reached out to Nicole shortly after Jeanne met her; she has been a wonderful friend to us ever since. Having her in our lives was more evidence of God's plan being orchestrated far before the events that were now taking place. And she was among the first people I visited when I returned home.

A Zoom call with my family took place at 6:30 PM. The conversation remains foggy in my head, but I remember wondering what a double-lung transplant would be like and questioning if it was something I wanted to do. John asked me if I needed time to process my thoughts before making a final decision.

I've always been someone who follows the rules, and for a long time, I thought I had the rules of a long and healthy life all figured out: work out hard and eat healthily. But it became clear those rules no longer existed; working out and eating right hadn't worked. And now, it was as though new rules had been put in place without my knowledge or consent, and the stakes were now much higher. The new rule was simple: get new lungs or die. It was a harsh reality to face. So yes, I needed a minute to process my thoughts.

I don't know exactly how long it took for me to make my decision. I do know the decision didn't come without first praying for the courage to boldly trust God. During my prayer time, He spoke the words that He had weaved many times throughout my hospital stay, "No matter what happens, We are with you."

"I trust you, Lord," I whispered back. Then I asked the nurse to send a text to John.

10:07 PM - Text to John

Me: Do it.

As soon as John read my text, he shared the news.

10:38 PM - Family and Lana's Update

John: I just got home a few minutes ago and called the nurse to check on Lana. She was resting after what I would assume was an exhausting day for her. My conversation with Lana this evening was difficult. Having to see her come to grips with her situation made it tough. She didn't know exactly what had happened to her, the disease that she is suffering from, how long she has been sick, or the amount of time that she has missed. Asking her questions to see what she knew and explaining all of these things to her was heartbreaking. And we had about 20 minutes to do the whole thing. Then let's pile on to the situation by making her be alone other than limited video time. I can't imagine what she's dealing with.

I was driving home and got a text message that popped up on my phone. When I looked at it, it was from her. I had taken her phone to her today, and she had asked the nurse to text me with it. It simply said, "Do it."

She is an absolute warrior. The plan is to list her tomorrow, and she knows that. She also knows that this surgery will probably happen in the next few days. I would ask that you pray for her strength, both physically and emotionally.

We have another video call with her tomorrow at 11 o'clock. If any of you would like to write some words of encouragement directly to her, we are going to read them to her on that call. I also took her a big stack of cards today that we have received from so many of you. The support and kindness that have been shown to our family has been overwhelming. God has provided an incredible group to pray for us and lift us up during this time. We will be forever grateful and humbled.

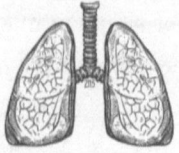

CHAPTER THIRTY-THREE

LISTED

Tuesday, May 19

This is the day I would be placed on the transplant list. If you expect the listing process to come with a big bang, I should warn you, you may be somewhat disappointed.

It began as every other day had. Nurses and doctors came in and out of my room. Vitals. X-rays. Medications. The machines beside me made the same noises they had been making day in and day out. And John made his morning call to the nurse like he did each day. The storyline remained the same–ups and downs, in need of new lungs.

9:41 AM - GroupMe

John: I spoke with the nurse a few minutes ago, and she said Lana seemed to get a little more rest last night than she has the last few. She's still not resting particularly well; I'm sure she is anxious. They continue to chase her heart rate. Her kidneys are very efficient, and she processes fluids very quickly and at a high volume. As a result, she tends to get dry, which requires them to give more fluid than is typical. This could be causing her increased heart rate.

The nurse today was the one who was with us on our call last night. She asked Lana about her "Do it" text, and Lana confirmed it this morning. She also agreed that Lana seemed to be hearing and/or processing, for the first time, what she is facing. I know how strong she is, but I also know she's by herself there, and that's not how she functions best.

We have a Zoom call with her at 11:00. I should get a better idea of her frame of mind then. I continue to pray for her to be brave and know that God has a plan for her and He is with her.

During our 11 o'clock Zoom, John noticed that I wasn't as cheerful as I had been the previous few days. He recognized a look in my eyes that he's seen many times before. I had my target acquired–get new lungs and go home. I was in fight mode. He knew I was tired and likely angry, but he also knew those two things would make me fight even harder.

Sometime that afternoon, Dr. Reynolds called to tell John I was officially on the transplant list. BANG! I thought I would throw that in to spice it up for you because that's all there was to it. There was no pomp and circumstance, just a quick call to give the formal announcement. "She's been listed."

John sent out the news via GroupMe, as he had so many times before.

5:16 PM

John: As of this afternoon, Lana is officially on the list to receive her lung transplant. Because her score is so high, the surgery will happen pretty quickly, probably within a few days. Once they get a call that there's a set of lungs, I will have just a few hours to get to Durham to be in the area when she has her surgery. I would ask for prayer that she can rest and be still while she waits. I will also ask for prayer for the family who has to endure a tragedy for her to receive those lungs. As you pray, please give thanks for the fact that this is even possible. God could have placed us anywhere in the world, and yet here we are.

Since I can't be with her because of COVID-19 restrictions, I will stay in a hotel room while she's having surgery. Once the situation changes and I go up there to be her caregiver, I will find a short-term month-to-month situation. No idea when they will lift the restrictions.

I have texted with Nicole as recently as today. I've also spoken with the hospital, and they've given me a suggestion for where to stay if I have to come up quickly for her surgery.

John and I spoke on FaceTime around 6:15 PM. It wasn't a normally scheduled Zoom call, so I assume one of my kind nurses made it happen because I still wasn't strong enough to hold my own phone. Most likely, the nurse had placed my iPad on the tray table in front of me and dialed John's number. ICU Nurses are indeed amazing human beings! They go beyond their call of duty to ensure their patients feel cared for. Or at least, that's been my experience.

Our unplanned FaceTime was worthy of one final message for the day.

6:59 PM - GroupMe

John: I just had a really good FaceTime with Lana. We spoke for about 30 minutes, actually. And when I say we had a conversation, I mean just that. She has excellent control of her facial muscles, and it's really pretty easy to read her lips. I've been told that is not always the case. She also had physical therapy today and managed to support her weight with her legs for a few seconds. Her nurse and physical therapist were blown away, considering where she has been for the last month. Knowing Lana, it doesn't surprise me. I am so proud of her!

Mom: That's my girl!!!!

Michelle H: Thank you so much for these updates. I am very proud of her as well, but like you, not surprised. She is one of the strongest people I know!! I will be praying for Lana and you, the girls, Duke Medical team, and the poor family that must lose someone!!

John: Michelle, the part about the family having to lose someone is really tough. I just pray that they know Christ and will rely on Him to get them through the hard times as well.

Tammy: I also pray the donor and their family know Christ. Such an emotional roller coaster, and so many things to pray over.

Throughout the day, amidst what had become normal activity, my thoughts were consumed with my donor and their family. It weighed heavy on me that in order for me to continue living, someone else's life had to end. The gratitude a recipient feels towards their donor is difficult to express. At some point, a stranger made the decision to donate their organs and save lives, and their family must carry out their wishes moments after their passing without much time to say their goodbyes while numerous people anxiously await. It is a strange feeling, waiting for someone else's passing so that you can receive a part of them. My emotions were all over the place, ranging from anticipation to guilt to sorrow.

Along with my emotions, my intellect searched for reasoning to explain why God orchestrates our lives in such a manner. These thoughts didn't shake my faith or lead to uncertainty. Instead, they left me reflecting on how our human minds will never have the capacity to comprehend His divine omniscience.

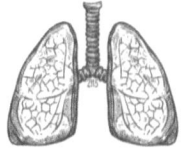

CHAPTER THIRTY-FOUR

ANXIETY AND A BIRTHDAY STICKER

The days leading up to my surgery after being listed for transplant were pretty much what you'd expect. My friends and family kept earnestly praying for a perfect match and for John to stay strong. They also prayed for the person who'd become my donor and their family. As soon as John spread the word about my listing, messages of support started flooding in. Seeing the love and encouragement pouring in from all directions was incredible.

Wednesday, May 20

8:26 AM - GroupMe

Sherry T: I pray for Lana to be strong and at peace with her decision and to allow God to bring the perfect lungs into her body. I pray that God will wrap his loving arms around Lana, and she will feel his strength, and at this very moment, she will know she's not alone. I pray for the family that will grieve their loved one to give Lana the opportunity to continue her ministry and know their loved one's gift will go on giving in God's glory. God, please give John, Mackenzie, Lauren, and Lana's mom peace beyond our understanding. And in the hours ahead, as they wait anxiously for that call, there will be many signs given to them to comfort them that God is in control. He has a master plan that only He knows and can understand. I pray for the medical team; God bless their minds, hands, and hearts and remove any distractions. I pray that in the hours before Lana's miracle happens, if anyone on her medical team does not know Christ, they will come to know Him before her surgery.

Donna: When I am lost for words, I steal the lovely prayers that are shared in this group. Thank you, all, for sharing your faith and spreading the Word. I know that Lana appreciates our focus on God's plan in this chain of beautiful messages to her and her family.

As much as I disliked the war I was in, I was thrilled that it brought my family and friends to the feet of Jesus. I knew that among the countless people standing on the battlefield with me, several who hadn't been in a prayer posture for some time (if ever) were on their knees. Isn't it interesting that when we are forced to face the reality that our time on earth isn't permanent, we run to the One who longs to give us an eternal future? So even as the battle raged on, my soul was content as the battle raged on because I was confident God was using it to change hearts and give everlasting life.

Prayers meant more to me than anything, but I was also delighted to receive daily cards and letters. John sent many of them to the hospital, and I would spend time reading them when I had the energy. He also opened several and read them to me on our FaceTime calls.

The Tribe took the time to get together (outside and socially distanced, of course) to capture a few group photos for me. Rosy then designed a couple of small posters and delivered them to John. I cried when he showed them to me. I loved the sentiment behind them and the women in them! And as soon as the posters arrived at the hospital, I asked a nurse to hang them on the wall at the foot of my bed. They were hung among photos of my family and artwork from our granddaughter. What a gift that was. Every time I opened my eyes, I was able to look at the faces of my loved ones.

I continued working with a physical therapist and was finally successful in sitting up for several minutes. I'm sure it was difficult for most to understand the magnitude of this accomplishment. Even knowing I had been in a coma and hearing that I was incredibly weak, my physical condition was impossible to picture unless you witnessed it firsthand. I remember feeling as if my body would fold in half and I would fall flat on my face. I had indeed gone from "the healthiest person I know" to one of the sickest people you could meet, someone who couldn't sit up or breathe on her own.

Even though I was still struggling physically, I kept pushing myself. My mind was becoming more alert as I continued to get past the fog of the sedation. John realized how much clearer I was thinking when I asked him how payroll at the gym was being managed. He chuckled and thought, "That would be just like you, worrying about making sure people get paid." Then he assured me our accountant had it under control.

I told him I was scared while we spoke on FaceTime later in the afternoon. However, the type of fear I was experiencing was different than you might think. I wanted to explain it to him but couldn't quite wrap my mind around it. Plus, I didn't have the stamina to have such a deep conversation. Fortunately, our friend Nicole, who had been through a lung transplant with very similar circumstances, helped to paint a clearer picture.

10:16 PM - GroupMe

John: I had a good FaceTime conversation with Lana this evening. She's getting stronger, and that will serve her well for her surgery. Tonight she told me dealing with the idea of all that has happened and what she's facing is scary. As strong and brave as she is, she is scared, and I feel for her. I will ask you to lift her in prayer tonight, asking God to ease her mind and give her peaceful sleep.

Interestingly, I find this time scary, but I'm not scared. And while Lana said it was scary, maybe she's not scared. Maybe I just assumed that. Both of us have strong faith, and we spoke at length about that tonight. She told me that God has spoken to her and told her not to be afraid. She said there were times when she could clearly hear His voice telling her that He was with her.

Nicole: I can tell you from experience that the anxiousness is very different from fear. It is more of a physiological as opposed to a psychological anxiousness because of the distress her body is under and her inability to breathe. The day before my transplant, I scribbled on a piece of paper, "New lungs? I don't think I can do this anymore." I showed it to my doc when he was rounding. He said, "Yes, you can." From that point forward, they more or less knocked me out. Her body is getting tired; it has been fighting. New lungs are coming!!!!!!

Nicole was spot on.

Thursday, May 21

Mackenzie's birthday. Since she moved out of our home, we haven't spent every one of her birthdays together. But there has never been a year that I was prevented from being with her because of illness or a worldwide pandemic; until now.

I've always tried to make my girls' birthdays special by telling them "Happy Birthday" numerous times throughout the day. I'd shout it from the kitchen while they were hanging out in their bedrooms, send texts randomly during the day (even if they were home), and, of course, say it every time we came face-to-face with one another. They thought it was fun when they were little girls; then they became teenagers, which made it annoying. They're young adults now, so they embrace it again. I'll even go so far as to say they actually like it again.

I wanted to let Mackenzie know I was thinking about her. Even though I couldn't bombard her day with birthday wishes, I was determined to send her a message. I was still very weak and didn't have much dexterity. I maneuvered my phone to my left hand, hoping I could steady it, and placed my right index finger at the bottom of the screen. With all my might, I flung my hand upward, hoping my phone would recognize the motion as a swipe that would unlock the screen. I'm in! Thank goodness for face recognition. I then began poking at the screen, praying my finger would land on the icon I was aiming for. Success; the messaging app is now open. It was time to search for Mackenzie. Why in the world did I think it was a good idea to give this child such a long name? Next, I needed a cute sticker to send; search b-i-r-t-h. Okay, great. It knows what I'm looking for.

After nearly an hour of wrestling with my phone and hands, I finally managed to paste a Bitmoji sticker into the text message and hit send. Shwooooo, off it went. The previous text I'd sent her was on April 30 from ICU; a simple heart followed by four kiss emojis. This birthday message was simple, but to Mackenzie, it was the best gift she'd receive all day. Through tears, she typed her reply, "Thanks, Mom! I love you so, so much!"

That evening, like so many times over the past few weeks, The Tribe stepped in to care for my loved ones in my absence. They sent Mackenzie flowers and cake to help her celebrate. She enjoyed their gift, but I probably enjoyed it more. Their actions were evidence of genuine, God-appointed friendship.

John sent a brief summary out at the end of the day.

10:27 PM

John: I just had my final call of the day with Lana. I can tell she's really tired. She told me tonight her legs are getting stronger faster than her arms. I don't want you to think she is in any way, shape, or form strong. Her arms aren't strong enough to pick up the phone by herself, and her hands aren't strong enough to do more than send the one text today. She told me tonight that God had made it clear to her that her lungs would come when her body was ready, but she doesn't know when that will be. She has always had an incredible ability to hear God's voice. Tonight, I am giving thanks for God holding her close and for the fact that He chose me to walk this journey with her.

I realize not everyone believes in direct messages from God, but I do, and I was confident that my new lungs would be available in the Lord's perfect timing. I just needed to keep fighting to be strong enough to receive them.

Friday, May 22

I was feeling trapped. Trapped in a body that I didn't recognize, one that no longer functioned the way I had become accustomed to, trapped by all the tubes and machines keeping me confined to one space, unable to move without assistance from a team of nurses. The stress of physical therapy was exhausting. Even though I knew His plans were perfect, waiting for God's timing was getting more difficult by the hour, and my anxiety was getting the best of me.

While I am eternally grateful for the love and care I received over the past several weeks, I was overwhelmed by the enormous amount of attention I was getting, or better yet, required. I wanted it all to stop–the frequent visits from medical staff, the tracheotomy care, the beeping and buzzing from the machines, and the questions–How are you today? Do you know where you are? Are you feeling anxious? Do you want to talk to your family? Do you remember you have a Zoom call today? Do you think you can squeeze my hand harder? AUGH, all of the questions! They were overwhelming. But not wanting to disappoint anyone, I answered each one to the best of my ability.

ECMO was doing its job, but the more stressed I became, the less effective the machines became. So when I began experiencing low blood flow with ECMO, which can lead to inadequate oxygenation, the medical team jumped into action to lower my stress and improve the ECMO flow.

The light sedation I was given provided me with a sense of peace. And each time I had a moment to myself, I would go to the quiet place in my mind where I could talk to God. That place is where I found peace, where God reassured me that He was with me no matter what happened. In that space, I was given the desire to continue fighting.

Despite the turmoil that was taking place inside my mind and body, my doctor was satisfied with my progress.

5:13 PM

John: As a family, we had a Zoom call with Lana just a while ago. She's had a pretty tough day today, and you could tell she's pretty sedated. I asked her earlier today if she wants to get moving with her surgery. Her answer was a definite yes. For those of you who know her well, you know when she acquires her target, she is about as determined as any human alive. I also spoke with her doctor this afternoon, and he was extremely impressed with how she has progressed physically over the last week, even though she considers herself to be profoundly weak. A week ago today, she couldn't even wiggle her fingers or toes, and today she managed to lift her entire leg. I continue to give thanks for all of you and all of your prayers. I continue to pray for the people who are going through this, aside from us. We've both wondered why God chose her but, as always, Lana and I continue to rest in the fact that God has a plan for us.

Even though we'd received a good report, I felt like a rag doll by the end of the day. What little energy I had earlier had been depleted, so when John and I spoke later that evening, I asked him to read the cards that he'd received. No questions would be involved, just words of affirmation that I desperately longed to hear.

11:31 PM

John: I had my final conversation of the day with Lana a little while ago. She is so tired and so weak tonight. They had moved her around to change her sheets and clean her, etc. It clearly exhausted her. In spite of that, she wanted me to read her the cards that came in the mail today, as well as comments from this page. She loves hearing them. I know you have written encouraging words to her, and I have read them to her every time. If you're so inclined, I would love to have some really inspiring things to say to her tomorrow from these comments. I would ask that you pray for her that she might get some rest tonight and have more strength tomorrow.

Following John's request, messages of encouragement flowed in. I hadn't truly realized how God had been using my story for His purpose until I received these messages. Some said they had prayed more since my illness started than they had in years, drawing them closer to the Lord. Others shared scriptures, while another used words I'd often said to my gym workout groups to encourage me.

Lynn G: I always loved when working out with you that you would see us/me flail, and you would say, "It's okay, rest, then join back in when you are ready." So I repeat those words to you, Lana. "Rest. Join back in when you are ready."

And finally, a few of my dearest friends drew beautiful word pictures.

Judi A: God has you in his hands and will cradle you as you have held and cradled others.

Nancy J: Lana, you can, with complete faith, say, 'God knew I had this lung issue, and He knew when it was going to become evident to me. He's in control, and I trust that!' God is walking right beside you through this journey.

Jan G: Friends of friends who do not know you directly are thinking about you and praying for your well-being every day–multiple times a day and even in the wee hours of the night. Those prayers are exponential. I know that I'm waking between 2:30 and 3:30 am most nights. I have no words, so I prayerfully sit with you - like a night watchman would. I'm not unique; I'm sure others do the same, too. Your lives and connection to us are so precious.

I've always been strong-willed, but as the days went on, I drew my determination from the deep well of love and support surrounding me. Sure, God was using me in the lives of others, but boy, was He ever using others to help me fight for my own.

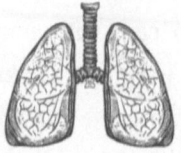

MY LUNGS ARE COMING

Saturday, May 23

While my body was getting physically stronger, my lungs continued to weaken. Breathing was getting more difficult, even on the ventilator and ECMO. On our FaceTime calls, John read cards and messages to me as I struggled to keep my eyes open. Fighting for life was taking its toll, and as much as I wanted to survive, I was exhausted.

I think it's funny (in a profound way) how God prepares us for specific moments in our lives—for example, pregnancy. Most women enjoy the experience of their child growing in their womb (once they get past the morning sickness). Then they begin to think about the birthing process and wonder if they're capable of doing it, and the thought of being pregnant forever doesn't sound like such a bad idea anymore. But I'd say it's around the 37th week when thoughts shift again, and because the entire pregnancy process is becoming miserable, their fear begins to subside. They don't care how the baby comes out. It would be okay if it were extracted through their nose. They just want it out.

God brings us to places once He has prepared us to face obstacles we never before imagined we could withstand. And that's where I was. I had concluded that cutting me in half and putting someone else's lungs in my chest sounded like a pretty good option. I never once in my life thought I would pray to have a double lung transplant, but now I was ready for it and wanted to get it over with.

John's conversation that afternoon with Dr. Reynolds gave him more hope that my lung transplant would be successful and we could return to a somewhat normal life after my surgery.

5:57 PM

John: I spoke with Lana's doctor today. When she first arrived at Duke last week, they were scrambling because they were concerned about her condition. Because she has gotten so much stronger in the last week, he feels confident, along with the surgeon, that they can be much pickier about her transplant lungs. He said because she was so fit before and he knows she will want to be that fit again, they want to be very particular and make sure she has really strong, healthy lungs. He indicated they want to use her as an example of what can be accomplished. It seems that her temporary lack of ability to move last Friday was a definite blessing. God continues to let us know he is still in control and hasn't left our sides.

As I've mentioned a few times, I worked very hard on my health and fitness before my illness. Along with God's grace, I know being fit saved my life. That's why I haven't stopped imploring others to become their healthiest version possible. Not only do we feel our best when treating our bodies well, but our lives may someday depend on it.

Sunday, May 24

John wanted the process to move along, as I did. Finding rest was difficult for both of us; the difference was I had the benefit of sedation. When he called the nurse around 9:00 am, she told him I hadn't slept well but was now resting.

While I was at Novant in Charlotte, I was prescribed blood thinners to ensure the ECMO machine functioned with ease. The downside was that these blood thinners caused quite a bit of bleeding. I received countless blood infusions to replenish the blood that was lost. At Duke, they would have given me more infusions to keep my hemoglobin levels in check because my oxygen saturation was dropping. But since I was already on the active transplant list, that wasn't an option anymore. Another infusion would have changed my blood panel, and we needed all my levels to stay the same to make a good match in order to go into surgery as soon as donor lungs were available. We were all hoping that the wait wouldn't be too long.

9:04 AM

John: I pray that today is the day God provides her with the perfect set of lungs.

Dr. Reynolds assured John that new strategies were being employed to keep me as strong as possible without compromising the transplant pool. Knowing Dr. Reynolds was a man of faith and was praying for me, along with everyone else, also encouraged John. Faith and prayer were the only things holding us together.

I don't recall the exact time, but as God had done so many times before, He spoke directly to my heart, and I had to share the message with John. "My lungs will be here soon."

In a supportive tone laced with a hint of reservation, John replied, "I sure hope so, sweetie."

"No, God told me. My lungs are coming."

John had witnessed my confidence in the Lord's messages many times since he's known me. As a result, he has come to understand that when I say

God told me something, we need to prepare because it will happen. And this time was no different.

After receiving a call from the hospital later that evening, John immediately contacted our family with the news he had received. Then he shared it in GroupMe with everyone who was following our journey.

10:50 PM

John: I just had a call from the hospital. They are going to look at a set of lungs for Lana. I don't know where they are, but the coordinator said she would call me at about 6:00 or 7:00 in the morning and let me know if it is a dry run or if it is a go. She said the lungs look really good on paper, but the doctor will make the final determination when he harvests them and inspects them. Pray for the best!

Because Lana is so sick, her risks during surgery are a bit higher than someone who is not as sick. I would ask that you pray for the surgery to go well when it happens. I would also ask that you pray for the family who has suffered the loss that will provide Lana's lungs.

It's very common to have a dry run, which is when the patient is called to the hospital for the transplant procedure, but ultimately it's determined the lungs will not be a good fit for the recipient, so they return home and wait for their next possible opportunity. The higher the lung assessment score, the higher the chances of dry runs occurring. If you remember, my score was very high. The lungs are different than any other organ—they are exposed to the environment. The donor's lungs must be evaluated for function, quality, and size, and they can have no sign of pneumonia or blood supply loss. Therefore, although lungs were available, there was still a chance that they might not be suitable for me.

Even with the chance for a dry run, John and Mackenzie prepared to travel to Lauren's apartment in Raleigh, about forty minutes from Duke. Although they weren't allowed to be in the hospital (thanks again, Covid), they both wanted to be close. So they planned to leave Charlotte as soon as they received word surgery would take place.

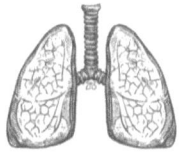

CHAPTER THIRTY-SIX

IT'S A GO

Monday, May 25 - Memorial Day 2020

It's a go!

John and I prayed together over FaceTime and ended our call moments before Dr. Reynolds entered my room around 8:30 am. He greeted me and immediately pulled his phone from the pocket of his medical coat, dialing John's number without delay. He wanted to give us the news together that the donor's lungs were good and already on the way to Duke. Once the call ended, John and Mackenzie wasted no time getting on the road to Raleigh, eager for this critical step in our journey to take place.

I wish I could recount every detail of that day from my perspective, but I don't remember anything about the day, other than our quick meeting with Dr. Reynolds. I don't even recall being wheeled to the operating room. My surgeon, Dr. Haney, had already informed John that my memory of the day and the preceding weeks would be hazy at best. In retrospect, it's probably a blessing in disguise. I can't imagine the fear and anxiety I would have experienced without the calming effects of heavy sedation.

During pre-transplant caregiver classes, John and Mackenzie learned that lung transplant surgeries typically take eight to twelve hours. However,

Dr. Haney felt my procedure would take closer to six hours. Even with the shorter surgery time, he cautioned John that the procedure was still incredibly risky. Others would not have survived all of the intense medical experiences that I was going through, much less an additional surgery as invasive as a transplant. He, like so many of the people on my medical care team, believed that my fitness level had played a major role in helping my body push through. So he maintained a positive outlook that it would also serve me well during the transplant.

While the lungs were en route, I was taken to the OR, and the surgical team began prepping to remove my ailing lungs. Since my donor's lungs had quite a journey ahead, starting the procedure before they even arrived made sense. After all, the less time those lungs spent outside a cozy chest cavity, the better.

Throughout the day, friends and complete strangers prayed for me while my family anxiously awaited updates regarding my condition. In an effort to keep herself occupied, Lauren had been working on a jigsaw puzzle, and when Mackenzie and John arrived at her apartment, they joined her in the puzzle-solving distraction. Meanwhile, my mom spent the day alone praying, ready to answer every call from John.

Surgery began around noon, and John's phone buzzed around 2:30 PM with the first update.

2:41 PM

John: They just called with an update. They are sewing in the first lung, and everything is going according to plan. She said Lana is doing well. Let's continue to pray that it continues to go well!

At 4:30 PM, the coordinator called with the next update. She shared the reassuring news that both lungs had been successfully transplanted, and the surgery had gone smoothly. John couldn't help but be amazed, thinking, "Wow, that was fast! It only took four and a half hours."

After speaking with my mom and ensuring she was informed, John promptly reached out to the rest of our family and friends, sharing the encouraging update with them.

5:40 PM

John: I just got the latest update. Both lungs are in, and everything has gone according to plan so far. We were told that Lana is doing fine at this point, but they will be watching her very closely for the next couple of hours.

Mackenzie and I will head by the hospital on our way home (since we're not allowed to see her) to drop off cards and some pictures that Inara (our granddaughter) drew. That will probably be around 6:30 or 7 o'clock.

The final call came from my surgeon, Dr. Haney, just before 6:00 PM.

6:11 PM

John: Mackenzie, Lauren, and I just got off the phone with the surgeon, Jack Haney. He was upbeat about the outcome. He told us that Lana was stable the entire time and, overall, things went well. They are looking to start weaning her from ECMO as early as this evening. Once she is off of ECMO, which could take a day or two, they will begin to wean her off the ventilator. That could take a week or so.

According to Dr. Haney, the lungs she received were younger than her and appeared to be in very good condition. They were also a good size, and they did not have to prune them to make them fit. There was some concern that they would have to leave her chest open for suctioning, but that didn't turn out to be the case. They closed her, allowing them to take her off sedation. They may have to go back into her chest in a few days to clean out the bleeding, but that's not certain.

All in all, it seemed to go about as well as could be expected. He was optimistic about her rehabilitation. He has spoken to the physical therapist who has been working with Lana, and he's basing his optimism on the reports, in part, from the PT.

I can't thank you enough for all of the prayers and support today and before now. This page has been a blessing to our family and Lana as I continue to read your comments to her every day. We know that God is in control of this, and His plan will be the one that we follow.

A collective sigh of relief was nearly palpable. I had received a miracle, the breath of life. While I was patient number 2115 in Duke's lung transplant program, the praises lifted to Heaven, along with prayers asking for peace and comfort to flood over my donor's family, were countless.

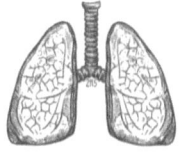

CHAPTER THIRTY-SEVEN

BACK TO THE OPERATING ROOM

Tuesday, May 26

Although my transplant was successful, there were a few bumps to follow. John stayed in touch with the nurses at the hospital throughout the evening and into the following morning. I was still bleeding quite a bit and had received several units of blood, platelets, and coagulant. To find what was causing the bleeding, I would be taken back to surgery, where the surgeons would partially reopened my chest to have a look. This surgery wasn't nearly as risky as my transplant, but it wasn't something anyone wanted me to go through.

Other than the bleeding, I was doing well. My heart was strong and steady, my kidneys were working efficiently, my oxygen saturation and my blood gas levels were excellent, and my blood pressure was doing very well without any medication. However, I was still sedated and given an IV for insulin due to elevated blood sugar.

As John anxiously awaited information about my surgery, he shared his reflections with our group, which stirred some uplifting conversation.

9:01 AM

John: At this point, all I have is my faith and the faith of those who are praying for us. Any pretense of anything else has long since been stripped away. Truthfully, I don't understand how anyone could go through this without the knowledge that God is sovereign and that He loves us. I pray every day that my updates will have an impact on someone to come to that understanding.

Vera L: Listening to "Alive and Breathing" by Matt Maher and thinking of you, Lana. You must be anxious to be so done with surgeries, machines, and all of the other things that have become part of daily life. You're almost there, sweet one. God always finishes what He starts. He loves you with tender compassion. He turns sorrow into joy. He knits together the tissues that have been stitched into place. He brings healing and renews strength. He will carry you through and give you a deeper joy than ever before. You are deeply loved.

Donna: John, you are certainly helping me understand what faith is…

John: Donna, know that Lana's faith is just as strong as mine could ever be. Every time we speak, we pray. Throughout this journey, she has told me that she has heard God's voice consistently.

Betty: John, your faith and Lana's, has had a great impact on so many who know Christ but are now learning how to trust and believe. My prayers are for strength and peace and rest for you and Lana. God is working miracles through this journey you and Lana, and her family are on.

John received word from the hospital around 3:00 PM that I was being prepped for surgery.

3:13 PM

John: The surgery will take about two hours. Hopefully, they will be able to get the bleeding stopped so they can begin weaning her from ECMO. Other than the bleeding, she seems to be doing as well as could be expected for someone who was basically cut in half yesterday. Those were the surgeon's words, not mine! If this surgery goes well, the anesthesiologist said they would take her out from under sedation this evening.

I was out of surgery by 6:00 PM. Dr. Haney was pleased to note there was minimal new bleeding, although he did need to remove a significant amount of blood that had accumulated from the previous night and earlier in the day. He was optimistic that he would not have to go back in for another wash. A chest tube was inserted on the right side to aid in drainage. The next step was to gradually reduce my reliance on ECMO later that evening, as long as there were no indications of drainage from the tube.

All-in-all, the report regarding my lungs was very good!

The latest update brought good news. I was still in critical condition, but my overall progress was positive. Although it was a bit challenging for me to expand my chest due to the size of the incision, the bleeding had significantly subsided. Plus, my oxygen saturation level and blood gasses remained consistently excellent, suggesting strong lung function. As a result, the ECMO support was reduced to its minimum level, and the favorable blood indicators supported the possibility of being taken off ECMO by tomorrow. But before that could happen, an epidural would be administered while I remained under sedation.

This was the first time in several weeks I wasn't fighting for my life.

PART 3

THE FINALE

CHAPTER THIRTY-EIGHT

PAPIER MACHE

Wednesday, May 27-Saturday, May 30

The following day, I was finally taken off of ECMO, and the cannulas were removed. My newly transplanted lungs were performing flawlessly, a testament to the incredible gift I had received. I remained under sedation, allowing my body to rest. Though the battle had been won, the war was far from over. The path to recovery stretched out before me, demanding patience and perseverance.

Weeks of being bedridden had taken a toll on my muscles, leaving them weakened and atrophied. Even my diaphragm struggled to regain its strength, unable to fully support breathing without the ventilator. But progress was underway, and the weaning process began. The ventilator was put into pressure support mode, providing only minimal assistance as I started breathing on my own. For more than a month, I had depended on machines to support my breathing, so the idea of letting go of that aid was downright scary. While I had faith in the medical team and their expertise, I still doubted my body's capabilities. But the initial trial run went remarkably well, lasting nine hours without the ventilator. Of course, there was still a lot of work to be done, and completing the transition from ventilation to independent breathing would take a few days. But the nurse described my accomplishment to John as very, very impressive.

Within three days of my transplant, I started physical therapy, ready to tackle the hurdles that lay in front of me. In addition to muscle atrophy, I also had to contend with some gastrointestinal issues caused by medication and tube feeding, which disrupted therapy on more than one occasion. While I was assured that many fellow patients faced similar issues, it was a humiliating reminder that dignity often takes a backseat when you're reliant on others for your care. But amidst it all, I found strength and resilience, knowing this was just a temporary phase in my journey.

On Thursday, May 28, John and I had our first FaceTime conversation since the day of my transplant. It was a moment of pure relief, and it was hard to tell who felt more overjoyed that I had finally crossed over to the other side of this nightmare. Both of us were beaming with excitement, eagerly anticipating the day I would finally be discharged from the hospital.

The rush of emotions that flooded over me after receiving this second chance at life was overwhelming, to say the least. Gratitude filled my heart as I marveled at the miraculous gift I had been given. But amidst the gratefulness, an unexpected visitor arrived: anger. It took hold of me, momentarily overshadowing my gratitude. My thoughts spiraled, and the weight of my emotions left me drained and lethargic, dampening my motivation for physical therapy and my interest in engaging with others. I became lethargic, didn't want to do physical therapy, and wasn't interested in speaking to anyone. I kept my emotional turmoil to myself, which naturally led to growing concern from the doctors and nurses witnessing the sudden change in my temperament.

John, always perceptive and understanding, quickly identified the issue. He recognized that when anger took hold of me, I needed a moment of solitude to work through it. And that's precisely what was happening. I gazed upon a body that felt foreign, unrecognizable, devoid of any evidence of the hard work I had put into being fit; all those years of pouring my energy into maintaining a healthy physique seemed to vanish into thin air. I was now adorned with scars, sure that more lay ahead. My new reality revolved around a daily regimen of medications with side effects that matched their potency.

So yes, I was angry and needed time to process it all. But it was a necessary step in coming to terms with the new chapter of my life, a chapter that held its own set of challenges and adjustments. And with the unwavering support of John and the understanding medical professionals by my side, I knew I would find my way through these emotions.

Then came delirium. Hallucinations were not uncommon after such a major trauma and the medical staff was accustomed to dealing with and treating them. But it wasn't easy on my family, especially the hallucination I experienced, which is now rather amusing to talk about but likely left John and Mackenzie scarred for life. To be fair, they never expected to receive a call from me, insisting that the past several weeks had never happened.

Imagine the scene: I found myself standing at the entrance of Jesus' tomb. The stone that had once sealed the tomb had been rolled away. Something odd caught my attention. The stone was made of papier mache! In that moment, a peculiar belief took hold of me—I became convinced that if the stone was fake, everything around me must also be an illusion. None of the recent weeks had truly occurred. The illness and transplant were nothing more than an elaborate theatrical production. With this newfound conviction, I decided that I had endured enough and it was time to go home.

I called John and insisted he come to pick me up and take me home immediately. My call caught him off guard, which led him to do what came naturally to him. He tried to reason with me to no avail. He explained that I couldn't leave the hospital because I had just undergone major surgery and I needed to stay there to heal. I didn't want anything to do with reason; I wanted to go home. So I hung up on him and called Mackenzie, pressing her with the same outlandish demand. She, however, wisely played along. She told me she would come as quickly as she could. A sense of relief washed over me, and I was convinced that Mackenzie believed my delusion. It seemed that my escape from this dreadful place was finally within reach.

With a newfound sense of hope, I nestled into my pillow and anxiously awaited her arrival.

Following my conversation with Mackenzie, a doctor arrived to handle the situation. Unfortunately, the details of their intervention remain a foggy haze in my memory, and once again, I cannot remember any specifics. Given my slightly disoriented state, it's safe to assume that some form of sedation may have been administered. Yet, I can only speculate, as my recollection remains hazy at best.

After my frantic calls, John insisted I speak to a psychologist or counselor to help me navigate the mental toll of everything I had experienced. It was undoubtedly a wise suggestion, considering the magnitude of the trauma I had endured.

It took a few days before counseling began, but when it did, it became evident that I needed to receive information typically provided prior to a transplant. Usually, individuals preparing for a lung transplant are required to attend pre-transplant classes, where they gain insights into the intricacies of the transplantation process. They learn what to anticipate before, during, and after the procedures. In my case, however, I had had none of that; I was flying blind and learning as I went along.

It was nice to finally have some idea of what we could expect to happen next. However, the information wasn't all sunshine and rainbows. It brought up new concerns, particularly the looming possibility of rejection. Perhaps this wasn't the ideal news to be confronted with at this point of my journey, but as they say, you take what life throws at you, right?

After taking in the worldly insights on how to deal with my circumstances provided by the psychologist, I felt there would be a better way for me to handle it. I went to the Lord for some good old-fashioned quality time. I took my anger, fear, and grief to the foot of the cross. After the Lord and I reflected on my emotions together, I was able to stir up some fierce determination to carry on with recovery. From that moment on, there was no looking back. Despite knowing that there would still be ups and downs along the way, nothing was going to stand in my way. I was ready to face whatever challenges came my way.

CHAPTER THIRTY-NINE

A LIFT TO THE CHAIR

Sunday, May 31-Monday, June 1

While my mood had improved physically, I was far from feeling well. Fluid had accumulated in my lungs, causing frequent coughing. To add to the discomfort, I was adorned with many medical apparatuses. Seventy-two staples held together the "W" shaped incision positioned directly beneath my breasts, spanning from below one armpit to the other. Nine chest tubes protruded from my body, a trach occupied my neck, an IV resided in my arm, and a feeding tube snaked its way up my nose. Needless to say, my overall state of being was nothing short of uncomfortable.

On a positive note, a speech therapist visited and provided me with a speaking valve, offering a means to communicate verbally once again. Of course, I needed to learn how to use it effectively, but having the opportunity to speak, even in a limited capacity, brought me a sense of relief.

Recalling the time spent in prayer when dealing with my anger after my hallucination, I drummed up the desire to do some exercises in my bed without my physical therapist being there. And later that day, I managed to remain off the ventilator for a solid twelve hours. John interpreted this as a sign that I was working through my grief.

I was making some progress, although I had a long road ahead of me. Still confined to the ICU, the key to my release was regaining the ability to walk (with assistance) down the corridor and back to my room. In my mind, it felt like a monumental task, comparable to conquering Mount Everest. But before I could even dream of scaling mountains, I needed to focus on the fundamental task of sitting up on my own. During my initial attempt, my physical therapist helped me move to the end of the bed to sit. I felt as if I were going to topple over and faceplant. So, add that to the list: no core strength.

June 1 was the first time I had a FaceTime conversation with John while sitting in a chair. He was stunned to see that I wasn't confined to my bed.

Now, getting into the chair was nothing short of an adventure. It required the coordinated efforts of three nurses and a lifting device that practically filled the entire room. First, the nurses would wrangle me into a lift sling that resembled a chair hammock. Once securely positioned, the sling would be attached to the lift arm. Then, using controls, the machine would hoist me from the bed. Next, one of the nurses would roll the lift across the room until I was dangling over the waiting chair, after which a controlled descent commenced.

Honestly, it all felt like a bit of an overkill. I wondered why they couldn't just pick me up and carry me to the chair. I only weighed around 75 pounds, for goodness' sake. But in fairness, I did have a multitude of unhealed wounds, so I suppose the extra caution was justified.

John and I talked until my body signaled the need to lie down again. The amount of time I could withstand being upright was limited to fifteen or twenty minutes, so the sling was left under me while I sat in my chair. We ended our call, and the moving process was repeated to transfer me back into bed. Naturally, with each repetition, the procedure became somewhat more familiar, but it was yet another aspect of my recovery that I couldn't wait to leave behind.

Later in the afternoon, I returned to the operating room for a procedure to remove blood from my chest, a step that required attention in spite of Dr. Haney's previous optimism. Additionally, the surgeons performed a bronchoscopy to extract a piece of tissue no larger than a breadcrumb from my lung for evaluation, ensuring the absence of any infection. They also used suction to remove as much secretion from my lungs as possible during the procedure.

After the procedure, John sent an update to our family, keeping them informed of the latest developments.

Monday, June 1, 6:52 PM

John: I spoke with the surgeon, and Lana's surgery went fine. He said her lungs look awesome!

I also had conversations with multiple people today about helping her understand what she has missed regarding pre-transplant training. I'm very optimistic that they will take great care of her.

Finally, I was told today that Duke is reviewing its visitation policy and may be relaxing it soon. Either way, I think I will have an opportunity to go see her once she is out of the ICU.

The possibility of the Covid restrictions being relaxed filled us with excitement. We knew how much my recovery would improve when we could be together again.

CHAPTER FORTY

CLEARING HURDLES

Tuesday, June 2-Saturday, June 6

As I healed, my feistiness, determination, and personality started to return. It was becoming evident to everyone that I was ready to fight my way back and make the most of it.

I've never been a morning person, and that includes mornings in the hospital. But I suppose when you're battling to get your life back, you don't have the luxury of being too particular about the schedule. Physical therapy began each morning between 8:00 and 9:00, a little too early for my liking. My ideal time for a good workout is 10:00 AM. However, I had to accommodate the therapist's schedule, and I felt grateful not to be one of his patients scheduled for 6:00 AM.

Fortunately, John was able to join me via FaceTime for the majority of my sessions. His encouragement motivated me to fight harder...most of the time. There were moments when I longed to move independently or not move at all, and having a cheerleading section reminding me of my weaknesses was the last thing I desired. However, without fail, once therapy concluded, I was grateful he had been there.

Once I successfully regained the ability to sit up, the next milestone was standing, which proved to be immensely challenging. My leg muscles had significantly weakened, making it difficult to support my body. Consequently, we began the process with a stand-up lift. The lift featured handles for me to grip and pads to support my forearms. The therapist and an assistant would help me transition from the bed to the lift. A strap was then placed around my hips and attached to the lift for security. While the machine did most of the work, it still required all the effort I could muster to stand. On my inaugural attempt on June 3, I was instructed to aim for a five-second stance. Remarkably, I managed eight seconds and felt like an absolute superstar.

The amount of time I could comfortably remain seated in a chair was increasing noticeably fast. In addition, I gradually prolonged my usage of the speaking valve, allowing me to communicate for longer periods. The healthcare team also provided me with a device called a spirometer, emphasizing the importance of consciously inhaling air to blow into it in order to enhance the strength of my lungs and ward off any potential bouts of pneumonia. Overall, my recovery was progressing well, albeit not as quickly as I would have liked.

During FaceTime calls with my family, my sense of humor began to resurface. We shared many laughter-filled moments, often revolving around my valiant attempts to speak while everyone else seemed to be participating in a hilariously surreal lip-reading experience.

One family conversation will forever be etched in our collective memory. For some inexplicable reason, as we chatted, my thoughts meandered to the difficulties of attaining truly restful sleep in the hospital. This unexpected mental detour triggered a delightful trip down memory lane, escorting me back to my childhood days. I found myself transported back to those years when I would exhaust all my energy in spirited play and then, when sheer exhaustion inevitably set in, seek refuge in the warm embrace of my mother's lap. Resting my head against her chest, I would effortlessly drift into a peaceful nap. To fully grasp the profound comfort of that cherished space, it is important to mention that my mother possesses an ample bosom (a trait that was not bestowed upon me). Nestling in her lap was akin to sinking into a deluxe, heavenly pillow of softness and plushness.

As these thoughts passed through my mind, I mouthed, "I'd like to have Mom's boobs."

Everyone appeared perplexed for a moment, and then Mackenzie asked, "Did you say you wanted Grandma's boobs?"

I nodded.

"Like, instead of your own?" she questioned.

"No! To take a nap on," I clarified, gesturing to demonstrate a sleeping position with my head and hands.

Naturally, that sparked a wave of laughter and playful banter about breasts before we smoothly transitioned to another topic. However, it gifted us with a remarkable anecdote and marked our first collective moment of pure joy as a group in quite some time.

On June 4, I managed to stand for a total of eight minutes, predominantly without relying on any support. I was able to make tiny movements from side to side, which may seem inconsequential under ordinary circumstances, but in my case, they constituted a significant achievement.

Furthermore, I successfully remained off the ventilator for a continuous period of eighteen hours, bringing me one step closer to complete independence from it. This, coupled with the transition to a smaller tracheostomy tube, signaled the impending move to the step-down unit.

The following day's physical therapy session proved even more promising, affirming that my recovery was undeniably progressing in the right direction.

Friday, June 5, 10:14 AM

John: I just watched Lana do her PT this morning, and she continues to make progress. Today she was able to do several things that she was not able to do yesterday. For her, these things seem small, but her physical therapist said she is light years ahead of just a couple of days ago. Before we started today, she was very nauseous. The nurse gave her some kind of magic drug and cured her nausea within just a couple of minutes.

Today she is on a 24-hour trach trial. If she does well, they will likely leave her off the ventilator. That would mean she's just a couple of days from leaving the ICU and moving to a step-down room. They also removed a couple of her chest tubes yesterday. There were a total of nine; now, there are only four.

The removal of my chest tubes brought an immense sense of relief. Being wrapped in bandages that enveloped my entire torso was incredibly uncomfortable. Despite the cool room temperature and a fan blowing directly on me, I was constantly hot. As the bandages began to come off, I finally experienced some relief. But the adhesive, oh my word! Every dressing change was excruciatingly painful, leaving my skin raw and resulting in prominent scarring.

Yet, amidst the whirlwind of medical activities, there were glimpses of the future the Lord had in store for me. On this particular day, God instilled in me the desire to write this book. While I knew there was a story to be shared about His boundless grace and mercy, I had never considered myself a writer. Allowing the words to flow onto these pages required me to step aside and let God take the reins. Yet, my tendency to intervene and slow the process has become an obstacle. Perhaps that's why it has taken me so long to complete it. Even now, I find myself getting distracted. So, let me refocus and return to the story at hand.

Three significant hurdles were triumphantly cleared on June 6.

Firstly, I achieved the remarkable feat of brushing my own teeth with the aid of an electric toothbrush. It was a truly incredible experience. No one warns you that dental hygiene tends to be neglected during a coma. My dental hygienist had a field day scraping off the accumulated plaque during my initial post-transplant visit. Once she finished, it looked as though my shirt had been showered in dandruff. Plaque was absolutely everywhere. I know, it's rather gross!

Secondly, I mustered the strength to take six steps, relying on the assistance of a machine solely for balance, and found myself able to sit with reduced support. Ken, my dedicated physical therapist, offered words of encouragement, emphasizing how immensely proud I should be of my progress. And indeed, I was, even though I yearned for a swifter pace of improvement. I had grown accustomed to my body responding instantaneously, but I came to realize that recovery entailed not only a physical battle but a mental one as well.

And lastly, as the clock struck noon, I had successfully remained off the ventilator for an impressive thirty consecutive hours and was still holding strong.

John's final daily update went out later that evening.

9:02 PM

John: Lana is now approaching almost 40 hours without the ventilator. Unless something really odd happens, I think she is done with it.

On Monday, she will do a swallow test where they film with a camera inside of her throat to see how her muscles are working. This is an important step in her getting out of the ICU.

CHAPTER FORTY-ONE

FAILED FEES AND STEP DOWN

The Week of June 7

Oh, that blessed swallow test!

The last meal I had was on April 29. After that, my nourishment was delivered exclusively by a tube that traveled through my nose to my stomach. My family humorously referred to this process as "receiving tube juice through my nose hose," which, to be honest, captures it quite accurately.

Swallow tests, like the fiberoptic endoscopic evaluation of swallowing (FEES), are conducted to evaluate a patient's swallowing ability. Given the prolonged period I spent intubated, my throat suffered significant damage, making me vulnerable to the possibility of aspiration—when food or liquid finds its way into the lungs. Therefore, it was crucial to check for any potential issues with my swallowing and understand the nature and severity of any potential issues.

During the procedure, a slender and flexible scope is gently inserted through the nose, making its way back to look down at the throat. Who could have imagined that the nose would serve as an access portal to the intricate workings of our insides? Nevertheless, this endoscope enables the speech-language pathologist to observe the intricacies of the swallowing process in real-time.

If the test showed no problems and I successfully passed, I could cautiously resume eating. This pivotal milestone was yet another prerequisite toward saying goodbye to the confines of the hospital.

On the day of my first swallow test, I experienced a mix of anxiety and confidence. I believed passing the test would be easy–after all, how hard could it be to swallow a few bites of food? I soon realized it's actually much harder than we think, especially with damaged vocal folds.

Once the scope was in position, a buffet of green food was placed in front of me–green pudding, green gelatin, green cookies, and green milk. The speech-language pathologist (SLP) explained that the green food dye would make each bite visible as it traveled from the mouth to the esophagus. The process began with me taking a tiny sip of milk, then another, and another. Then, I was given a container of gelatin and instructed to swallow each small bite carefully. Throughout the test, the SLP attentively studied the screen displaying the inner workings of my throat.

"Let's try the pudding now," she suggested, her expression revealing a hint of concern as she examined the screen.

Moving the pudding closer to me, she instructed, "Try another small bite, but this time, tilt your chin down as you swallow."

Finally, I was asked to take another sip of milk. At this point, it became apparent that the test wasn't going as she would have liked. The SLP explained her observations to me.

"That's all we'll do today. It appears that your vocal folds aren't closing completely when you swallow, which is not what we want to see. We need to give your throat a little more time to heal. I'll schedule another test for you in a week or so."

Once again, disappointment struck. Not only was I denied permission to eat, but it also meant the nose hose would have to stay.

Before leaving the room, I half-jokingly asked the SLP if I could at least finish the pudding under her supervision. Her response, of course, was negative. I would have done almost anything to savor the rest of that pudding—even though I don't typically like it. The sight of those delectable treats being taken away from my room was excruciating, knowing that it would be at least another week before I could indulge again.

As the days progressed, The Tribe occupied my thoughts more and more. I had been reading their messages over the past several weeks. Yet, it dawned on me that they hadn't received a message from me in quite some time. It was time to change that and reconnect with them.

Monday, June 8, 5:09 PM - The Tribe

Me: Hi, girls! I will keep this brief because it's been a busy, tiring day. I just wanted you to know that I miss you and think of you often. When I need that extra kick in the seat to keep going (daily), I look at your smiling faces in the pictures on my wall and draw strength from you. I can't wait to be able to see you in person.

Needless to say, I'm a Durham girl for quite a while longer, but I hope when I finally am able to leave the hospital, you'll consider coming to see me. I would never have imagined what a challenge this is. Learning to walk, sit, talk, swallow, etc., again. It's crazy. But this, too, shall pass.

Looking forward to hearing back from you and texting with you more very soon!!

Diana: Lana, I saw your name come up for the first time since April, and I am so overwhelmed with happiness and goosebumps!! You are a warrior, my friend. We will come see you as soon as you are ready for us. You have been through a whirlwind, and yet you still remain positive and kept your faith. You are unbelievable!

Donna: Holy crappers!!!! This is the best text of the year!!!!! We love and miss you, crazy lady. I hear you're doing amazing things, as usual. Text when you can. No need to jump to respond to us. You are one heck of a warrior. I have no good advice, but I have tons of love for you.

Rosy: I think my birthday present came early this year (tomorrow is my 55 birthday). Lana, you can't imagine my tears of joy that reading your text gave me. I couldn't believe it when I read your name again. I'm thinking and praying for you every day. I miss you so much and you can be sure that the whole Tribe will go to Durham to see you as soon is possible. We love you so much, and we can't wait to see you again.

Dawn: Omg, I am speechless!! And we know that doesn't happen often!! We have been waiting for this day, Lana!! You have continued to inspire us, and we have followed your amazing journey every step of the way. Your faith and strength have been incredible to witness. We cannot wait to see you again, dear friend!!

These incredible ladies truly possess the magic touch when it comes to lifting my spirits. But, while the accolades were undoubtedly uplifting, it was the heartfelt conversations with my closest friends that truly touched my soul and gave me the extra boost I needed to keep going. Their unwavering presence and support filled my heart, making the following days even better.

On June 9, after a lengthy forty-day stay in the ICU, I was transferred to the step-down unit. Before leaving the ICU, I successfully walked 100 feet—a stark contrast to the days when even swaying my hips seemed like an insurmountable challenge. I could feel my strength steadily returning to my now ninety-pound frame (a notable improvement from the previous weight of seventy-five pounds).

My first room in the step-down unit was barely big enough to accommodate a bed, me, and a nurse. The lightweight curtain, suspended from the ceiling to ensure privacy, brushed against the foot of the bed whenever it was drawn shut. Drew, the nurse assigned to my care during the initial two days, had perfected the art of moving in sync with the curtain. Together, they danced gracefully, gliding and twirling, ensuring that all my needs were attentively met.

Thankfully, my stay in the cozy little room lasted only a few days. Soon enough, I was relocated to a much larger corner room, a presidential suite in comparison.

By Friday, June 12, all of my chest tubes had been removed, and my tracheostomy tube was capped. The anticipation of having the trach completely removed at the beginning of the week soon gave way to a disappointing reality. A cautious doctor, weighing the slim one percent chance of needing it again, opted to keep the tracheostomy as a precaution, extending its unwelcome presence in my neck for a couple more weeks.

After being transferred to the step-down unit, the way my physical therapy was approached needed some re-evaluation. Luckily, my background as a corrective exercise specialist and personal trainer came in handy during my recovery. I understood the importance of laying a solid foundation before jumping into walking exercises, so I shared my concerns with the therapy team. Thankfully, my new physical and occupational therapists, who were also athletes, understood where I was coming from and agreed to adjust the focus of my therapy.

We started with targeted leg exercises that could be done while lying in bed or sitting on the side. It was all about building up strength and stability. Slowly but surely, I progressed to squat-like movements—standing up and sitting down—with the bed as a safety net. It was a great way to build my confidence and ensure I had a safety cushion if I got wobbly.

The process was humbling and sometimes frustrating for me. As someone who had always emphasized the human body's potential and witnessed others unlock their physical capabilities, it was disheartening to face my own limitations. There were times when it was all I could to keep my feet under me.

At times, I couldn't help but feel discouraged, wondering when I would reach that turning point where movement would become a source of joy and empowerment for me once again. I had to remind myself that healing and progress are unique to each individual and that patience and persistence are essential.

During those challenging moments, my background in fitness played a significant role in keeping me focused and motivated. I drew from my knowledge of the body's resilience and its capacity to adapt and improve. I knew that the path to recovery wouldn't be easy, but I trusted in the process and relied on the expertise of my healthcare team.

With each exercise session, I felt myself getting stronger and more self-assured. And then came the big moment—I took my first steps without relying on a walker! It was a huge milestone for me. I made my way from the bed to the chair, around five feet away. I can't even put into words how much of a turning point that was for my recovery.

As I diligently followed my personalized therapy program, gradually pushing my boundaries and surpassing small milestones, I began to experience glimmers of that joy in movement I had been missing. Admittedly, it might not have been as immediate or profound as I had hoped. Still, each small victory brought a renewed sense of optimism and a reminder that progress was worth celebrating, no matter how incremental.

The adjustments my therapists and I made to my rehabilitation plan did, however, slow my progress initially in increasing my daily step count. But even though the doctors expressed concerns about the number of laps I was completing, I remained confident that our personalized rehabilitation approach would have positive results. And so, with newfound stability, I ventured back into the halls, tirelessly completing step after step, day after day.

In the days that followed, our rehab approach worked like magic because my lap count started soaring (relative to where they were, that is). The doctors were actually impressed with how my recovery was progressing. Within a week, John received three separate confirmations that my recovery was nothing short of spectacular.

And yet, even with the positive feedback, I couldn't help but crave faster results.

CHAPTER FORTY-TWO

PAMPERED

The Week of June 14

Throughout the week, I pushed myself and built enough stamina to conquer two laps, covering a distance of 620 feet. It was an undeniable accomplishment, but despite my progress, discouragement remained. I was completely aware of the long journey that still lay ahead. In order to be discharged from the hospital, I had to conquer an intimidating eighteen laps, equivalent to a mile. There were days when that distance seemed insurmountable, causing me to collapse onto my bed, overwhelmed with tears of frustration. The road seemed daunting, tempting me to surrender and make Duke my permanent residence. But I clung to my unwavering belief that God had brought me this far, and with His guidance, failure was simply not an option.

And the Lord blessed me with plenty of others to help me through the process. The staff in the step-down unit was great. They displayed remarkable patience, kindness, and genuine care, always ready to come to my aid when I needed a hand. Whether it was diligently managing my medications day and night, aiding me with bathing and changing hospital gowns, retrieving items I clumsily dropped (which occurred all too frequently), or adjusting the fan to regulate my body temperature, they went above and beyond the call of duty.

In fact, a few of these extraordinary individuals even devoted their time to pampering me with what they called a "beautification day." Granted, it lasted twenty minutes instead of an entire day, but the duration didn't matter to me. In that brief timeframe, they succeeded in restoring my self-confidence. First, they assisted me in shaving my legs, followed by a dry shampoo session that resulted in a stylishly messy bun. Then, upon completing their work, they stepped back to admire their masterpiece.

"Oh, you look so pretty, Ms. Lana," one said with a smile.

At that moment, it didn't matter that I wore no makeup, had a feeding tube secured to my nose by tape, and donned a fashionable blue and white hospital gown. I felt a genuine sense of beauty.

However, it later dawned on me just how thoughtful that nurse's statement had been. After spending nearly two months confined to a hospital bed, my only glimpse of myself came through the lens of my phone's camera. Consequently, I had been unable to inspect the back of my head for quite some time. Thus, I remained oblivious that a substantial portion of my hair had fallen out, leaving a three-inch-wide bald spot on the crown of my head. Fortunately, the nurses spared my feelings and didn't tell me.

Another remarkable milestone during that week was my newfound ability to transition independently to an upright position. I maneuvered myself to the edge of the bed and confidently planted my feet on the ground, all without requiring assistance. Sam, my occupational therapist, was thrilled when she saw my achievement.

She rewarded me with a round of applause, then promptly presented me with a new challenge. "Let's see if you can stand up without my help. Don't worry; I won't let you fall," she assured me.

In the realm of fitness, there's a well-known saying: "Trainers are why I have trust issues." Thanks to Sam's relentless dedication, I was beginning to grasp the essence of that statement. She was an exceptional therapist who consistently pushed me to my limits daily, reminding me to "embrace the suck."

On June 17, I underwent a procedure where hyaluronic acid was injected into my vocal folds. These injections aimed to plump up the tissue and enhance the closure of the vocal folds, reducing the risk of aspiration. There was also potential that they could improve my voice quality, which I had been struggling to regain. After the procedure, I was placed on voice rest for two days.

The injection helped a little but didn't provide a complete resolution to the issue. Following my second swallow test, I was permitted to consume fluids with a nectar consistency, but solid food was still off-limits. While the nectar drink quenched my thirst to a certain extent, it left much to be desired in terms of taste. Another swallow test was scheduled for the upcoming week, and I hoped with all my might that I would pass, granting me the freedom to indulge in actual food again.

Over the following 48 hours, my feeding tube seemed just as eager as I was for its departure. Somehow, it managed to work its way out of my stomach and had to be replaced... twice. I missed a few liquid meals during that ordeal, leaving me with little energy to complete my laps.

Yet, even with this setback, I continued to praise God for His abundant blessings upon me. Sharing His goodness with others had become part of my daily routine.

Saturday, June 20, 9:25 PM - The Tribe

Me: I'm feeling much stronger today. Standing up is getting better. Of course, I still need assistance, but I'm able to do more of the work myself. Things we take for granted are slowly returning. Like brushing my teeth, taking my own socks off, bathing myself, and controlling my breath during exertion. There are too many things to list. But I'm blessed to be here doing it, as hard as it is.

Every day I see God work miracles, and I give Him all the glory for the gift of life.

I'm making serious changes to how I spend my time when I finally get home. Hug your families tight, and be sure you're enjoying each day. Live life to the fullest, girls!!!

Donna: Your entire experience has brought us all to our knees trying to understand the grand plan, but now we know that we don't need to understand it. We need to embrace it, trust it, and listen for it. It's called FAITH for a reason.

I couldn't have said it more perfectly. Rather than striving to comprehend the intricacies of God's magnificent plan, our focus should rest on wholeheartedly trusting that He possesses the understanding and guidance we seek. This period of my life was serving as a reminder that by faithfully following God to the best of my ability, I was aligning myself with His divine purpose. He used this time to reinforce the profound truth that unwavering trust was important to His greater plan.

Trusting may seem simple in theory, but it isn't always easy to put into practice. Nevertheless, I had no choice but to walk in unwavering faith and trust throughout this challenge. Trusting my surgeon and doctors came naturally; they were renowned experts in transplant procedures, handling their cases with precision every day. Likewise, my physical therapists were well-versed in guiding individuals through recovery, having supported countless others in reclaiming their strength. With my family and friends, I had complete confidence that they would never abandon me, given their unwavering support throughout my life. And although I couldn't fathom how these pieces fit together in the grand "plan," God possessed the wisdom I lacked. Simply knowing that the Lord understood the purpose behind my pain provided me with the strength I needed to persevere.

CHAPTER FORTY-THREE

BEST ANNIVERSARY GIFT EVER

The week of June 21

To my surprise, the hospital staff began inquiring about exercise and nutrition, catching me off guard. They were intrigued by my knowledge of how the body responds to food and exercise and asked for advice on ways to improve their diets and, ultimately, their health.

One particular incident shed light on my expertise. Due to the medication, my blood sugar levels were a wreck, and my body struggled to keep up. To address this, the nurses would administer insulin, causing my blood sugar to plummet. Consequently, I would be instructed to consume sugar-laden foods, such as applesauce, to counteract the drop. Predictably, my blood sugar would then skyrocket, requiring another dose of insulin. This cycle continued, leaving me bewildered as to why we were trapped on this erratic blood sugar rollercoaster.

I shared my thoughts with one of the nurses, expressing, "I think we might be contributing to the problem. If I keep eating foods and juices high in sugar, my blood sugar will keep rising. Doesn't the hospital offer diabetic-friendly options, like unsweetened applesauce?"

"Yes, I'm sure we have some alternatives," she replied.

"Can we give that a try?" I proposed. It seemed like a straightforward solution to me, leaving me baffled as to why no one else had considered it.

Ding, ding, ding! I could see her thoughts racing as the lightbulb flickered to life in her mind. I smiled, acknowledging her newfound realization. From that moment forward, the floodgates of nutrition questions opened.

My sister-in-law suggested it might be a glimpse into God's future for me. The prospect of returning to my fitness career filled me with excitement, but I had made the conscious decision to approach it with open hands and an open heart, ready to embrace whatever plans the Lord had waiting. I surrendered my journey to His guidance.

In the meantime, I continued my daily walks around the hospital hallways, hoping my days inside would soon end.

Much to our delight, John received news from my care team that Duke Hospital was easing its Covid restrictions, permitting one visitor per patient starting Wednesday, June 24. Remarkably (or perhaps divinely orchestrated), June 24 also marked our 14th wedding anniversary.

It had been sixty-four arduous days since I first entered the respiratory clinic. Now, after a grueling journey and a life-saving double-lung transplant, the time had finally arrived for me to reunite with my beloved husband. Though he had been faithfully by my side throughout my coma, I had no recollection of his presence during that time. The anniversary gift of 2020 undoubtedly surpassed any we had exchanged in the past and likely any yet to come.

John urgently searched for a place to stay in Durham. His plan involved securing a hotel room as a temporary solution while continuing the hunt for a suitable long-term rental unit. According to Dr. Reynolds, the anticipated duration of my rehabilitation in Durham post-discharge would likely span at least two to three months. However, as was often the case, I had different plans for the length of my stay. It's worth noting that my personal training background helped me use my hard-earned knowledge and confidence to push my body safely. And I planned to use them to accelerate my recovery.

Surprisingly, searching for a rental house proved less time-consuming than expected. John stumbled upon an appealing home online, conveniently located near Duke, so he reserved it immediately. Shortly after that, we discovered that the house was owned by a doctor from Duke Hospital who also had experience with the transplant process. John reached out to the homeowner to inquire about our stay. In an incredible twist of fate, she revealed that another family had canceled their reservation a mere thirty minutes before John finalized ours. Astonishingly, that very family contacted her just thirty minutes after our deposit was sent, requesting the reinstatement of their reservation. The sheer serendipity of John being on the computer, visiting that website, at that precise moment, seemed truly remarkable. Evidence of God's hand once again.

John arrived in Durham the night before his first visit to the hospital. He had thoughtfully packed every essential item, including our trusty Nutribullet for protein shakes. Before unloading his Jeep, he took a quick self-guided tour of the house, acquainting himself with the layout. The main bedroom and bathroom were conveniently accessible from the open living room, connected to the kitchen and breakfast nook. It was perfect. As he returned to the car to begin unpacking, he surveyed the nine wooden stairs leading inside from the garage. He thought about how apprehensive I would be when I arrived. However, he reassured himself, knowing my competitive nature would kick in when I stood at the bottom and gazed upward. With that confidence, he bounded down the stairs to gather our belongings.

After settling in, he reached out to me, and we discussed the schedule for the upcoming day, carefully considering the timing of the medical staff's rounds. He planned to arrive at 9:00 AM and stay until visiting hours were over. Our time apart was drawing to an end, and we eagerly anticipated having the entire day together.

He woke the next morning anxious to get to the hospital. As soon as it was time, he navigated his way to the parking deck, then through the maze of tunnels and checkpoints to my room. I heard him talking to the nurse outside my door, but he couldn't enter immediately. He had to first put on the required protective gear. It felt to me like it was taking forever. But in reality, it was probably only a few minutes. Then, I heard the door to my room open.

Our reunion was nothing short of incredible. We were as excited as kids on Christmas morning. Despite John having to don a hospital gown and mask, it didn't deter us from immediately embracing each other when he entered my room. It was the best hug I'd ever received. Tears of joy streamed down my cheeks as I felt the weight of the medical trauma I had endured begin to lift. John and I have always drawn strength from one another, and this time was no exception. With his unwavering support, I could finally let my guard down and find solace in knowing that everything would become more manageable. Gone were the days of relying on the nurses' station for every task requiring assistance. My partner, my other half, stood beside me once again.

Warm anniversary wishes poured in through GroupMe, and John took the time to respond later that evening.

Wednesday, June 24, 7:36 PM

John: Let me begin by saying it feels amazing to be in the room with Lana for our anniversary today! I got to walk with her twice this afternoon. The first time she did four laps; the second time, she did three. When you combine that with the laps she did this morning, she did a total of ten laps today! Because she is doing so well with her physical therapy and her lungs have cleared up so nicely, her doctors are talking about removing her tracheostomy much sooner than anticipated if she completely passes the swallow test on Friday. In fact, her lungs are doing so well that they did not do the scheduled bronchoscopy on her this week because she didn't need it.

Thank you for all the anniversary wishes! God continues to put people into our lives at just the right time for just the right reasons.

John dedicated the following day to being by my side before heading home to pack for our indefinite move to Durham.

Though my walking distance was slightly diminished compared to the previous day, John and I did some resistance exercises aimed at strengthening my legs and arms. He also provided a much-needed shoulder massage. Surprisingly, of all the pain one might expect me to experience, my shoulder caused the most discomfort. My "cranky" shoulder, which had troubled me for years, grew increasingly aggravated from lying in a hospital bed for such an extended period. I'd been cut in half, and someone else's lungs had been placed into my chest cavity, but it was my shoulder that brought me to tears. How strange.

The next day, another swallow test awaited me, and once again, I was anxious to pass. Failure would potentially require the placement of a feeding tube directly into my abdomen, while success might result in an earlier removal of my tracheostomy tube. Regrettably, I didn't pass the test completely, but I fared well enough to advance to a soft diet, sparing me the need for a stomach tube.

Sh-woo! Now bring on the food!

Saturday, June 27, 6:27 PM

John: Today has been a good day for Lana. She has been eating all day… literally. She still has to eat very slowly, so when they bring her a meal, it takes a while. Today she's had eggs, apple sauce, tuna salad, and various vegetables, and is now having a grilled cheese sandwich for dinner. She also had a brownie and a muffin. To be clear, she hasn't eaten much of any of it except for the brownie and the muffin!

She also set a personal record today for laps with 11. She did that on a Rollator (a walker with wheels), which is the type of walker she will leave the hospital with. According to the physical therapist, it's almost twice as much work as the one she did ten laps on. She is also now standing up from a sitting position without assistance.

She still weighs 90 pounds, which is 30 pounds of muscle gone. That means she has a long way to go to get as strong as she was, and it will take quite a while, but we're confident that she'll get there at some point.

The delivery of my shiny new red Rollator caught me off guard. I'm not entirely sure why, but I had this notion that I would walk out of the hospital unaided, effortlessly shouldering my bags. Perhaps my mind still held onto the image of the strong woman I once was, failing to acknowledge the reality of my current state: weakened and broken. I allowed my imagination to wander, picturing myself back in the gym, lifting weights and leaping into tuck jumps. Visualizing myself in that empowering setting fueled my determination to keep pushing and improving.

The week drew to a close on yet another positive note. John and I received news that we would attend discharge training on Monday or Tuesday. It's remarkable to think that right after the surgery, everyone anticipated a recovery period spanning months, not weeks.

Once again, our prayers had been answered by the grace of God.

CHAPTER FORTY-FOUR

TWO STEPS AND TWENTY-THREE LAPS

The week of June 28

On June 28, after a long wait of sixteen days, my trach was finally removed, about twelve to thirteen days later than I had anticipated.

A few days earlier, I had taken the initiative to research the removal process to educate myself and make sure I was prepared. It turned out to be a relatively simple procedure. First, they would remove the tracheostomy tube and then ask me to cough to help clear any secretions that may have accumulated around it. What surprised me was that after the tracheostomy tube is out, they cover the stoma (the hole in the neck) with a bandage and let it heal naturally. The wound around the stoma starts healing from the inside, and new tissue grows to fill the hole. The wound heals so quickly that the decreasing size of the opening is visible each day. The human body is incredibly resilient.

So after days and days of waiting, I finally sat in my bed trach-free, albeit wearing a necklace of bandages.

My appetite kept growing, and along with it, my calorie intake. I was successfully consuming 1200 calories per day, the minimum recommended caloric intake for women in order to maintain a healthy body. And as I continued to build my strength, I also increased the number of laps I walked around the step-down unit, strolling to the beat of songs by John's daughter, Jessica, from her recording days. By the way, the nurses absolutely loved it! It was evident from their rhythmic movements every time I passed their stations.

I had my sights set on not just conquering the halls but also tackling the challenge of ascending stairs. It was necessary since the house John rented had stairs leading to every entrance, and I didn't want to rely on being carried in and out once I was discharged. Unfortunately, my first attempt turned out to be a complete failure.

Now, here's where things got interesting. My physical therapist that day was in her third trimester of pregnancy and was nearly the same size as me. But that didn't faze her one bit. When she found out about our rental house, she declared, "We better start working on stairs."

So off we went to the emergency exit stairs, where she laid out the game plan. "Turn sideways and grab that handrail with both hands," she instructed. "Put one foot on the step and give it your all to bring the other foot up on the same step. As you step up, use your arms to pull yourself up. I'll be right behind you, ready to lend a hand. Don't worry; I won't let you fall."

Concerned, I asked her, "Are you sure this will work?" I knew how weak I still was, and I didn't want her to risk getting hurt while trying to rescue me if I stumbled.

Confidently, she reassured me, "I'm positive. You can do this!"

I positioned myself as she had instructed, took a deep breath, and mustered all my strength to hoist myself up the first step. But guess what? It didn't work! Somehow, I ended up plopping right into the physical therapist's lap. I'm sure it was quite a site. There she was, squatting down, juggling her pregnant belly, me, and the situation. And if that wasn't enough, tears started streaming down my face. The little strength I had left seemed to escape along with those tears.

My petite physical therapist swiftly got me back on my feet without skipping a beat. She kindly accepted my apology and, believe it or not, encouraged me to give it another shot. Luckily, the second attempt went much smoother, and I managed to conquer two steps. I walked away from that session with a newfound sense of confidence. So, I continued to work on mastering the stairs.

Meanwhile, John and I completed our discharge training. As he learned how to handle my medications, I watched in awe. The sheer number of pill bottles sprawled out before him was overwhelming, a visual reminder of the new way of life ahead. He listened attentively to the pharmacist's instructions, eager to grasp the best process to avoid any missteps.

He carefully counted the pills, methodically filling the seven-day medication container with four daily doses, thirty-eight pills in total. I had complete faith in his capabilities, yet I couldn't help but feel apprehensive about ingesting such a substantial amount of medication. Before my illness, I had always been cautious about taking medications, opting for a more natural approach whenever possible.

Once John was confident that he understood the instructions, the multicolored bottles were placed in a large bag and entrusted to his care. It was now our shared responsibility to ensure that not a single dose of medication was missed.

On Tuesday, June 30th, I completed my mile's-worth of laps and met the walking discharge criteria. The only challenge left before I could finally leave the hospital was successfully passing a swallow test, which I tackled the following day.

Excitedly, I shared my achievement of eighteen laps with The Tribe, and Donna, just like she used to at the gym before all of this began, responded in her usual fashion, "That's great, but I think you can do 21."

With Donna's words echoing in my mind, I headed back to the halls for another round of walking.

Thursday, July 2, 6:00 PM - The Tribe

Me: Challenge accepted and raised! 23 laps!!

Donna: I knew you could do it!!! We are laughing with joy!!

Rosy: I knew it!! Never challenge Lana unless you want to lose.

Diane: I can't wait for 25!

Me: I won't be here long enough for 25 laps. Next up... outpatient physical therapy.

On Friday, July 3rd, a day etched in my memory, my medications were delivered by the pharmacy, my IV was removed, and the moment arrived to bid farewell to the hospital that had become my temporary home. I boarded my wheelchair chariot and was escorted from my room. As I passed the nurses' station, I offered a wave of gratitude and said my goodbyes to the caring staff I had come to know so well.

The hallways that had been my familiar path for weeks unfolded before me as I was wheeled toward the hospital exit, where John eagerly awaited my arrival. Being outside once again, even for a brief moment, felt glorious. It was a moment of freedom and the promise of new beginnings. Understanding the significance of the occasion, John reached for his phone, ready to capture the milestone.

Determined, I brushed off John's outstretched hand and carefully made my way from the wheelchair to the car. As I settled into the passenger seat, triumph washed over me. Behind my mask, a beaming smile lit up my face, and I waved to the camera. Then, peering back through the rearview mirror, John and I bid farewell to Duke Hospital and headed to our temporary home, where our next adventure awaited us.

CHAPTER FORTY-FIVE

LIFE ON THE OUTSIDE

The week of July 5

The first week out of the hospital was hectic. John and I had to learn how to manage everything the nurses had been handling–dressing wounds, monitoring and preparing medications, organizing meals, and bathing. In addition, he was my driver to and from outpatient physical therapy. In the afternoons, we also had to work in time for me to walk.

It was challenging for John to keep up with his added duties, but he did great.

Mackenzie and Lauren came to spend a few days with us. Their visit was very good for my soul. I had missed Mother's Day and Mackenzie's birthday, plus Lauren had completed college while I was in the ICU. Unfortunately, due to the pandemic, there was no commencement ceremony–not that I would have been able to attend anyway. So having them with me was exactly what I needed.

We also had a Zoom call with John's girls and their families while Mackenzie and Lauren were with us. We were able to enjoy brunch during the call. It was a "do-over" for our Easter brunch–the call that ended early at the onset of my illness. Ali made brunch special by preparing baked French toast and quiche for Mackenzie to bring to Durham.

Our time together was proof that life would return to normal someday. Although, for now, it was still off-kilter.

As I monitored my vitals the day after our family brunch call, just three days post-discharge, I noticed my heart rate had skyrocketed to an abnormal 173 beats per minute, despite sitting calmly on the sofa and feeling perfectly fine. John urgently called my coordinator, who instructed us to go to the emergency department immediately. Deep down, I understood it was the necessary course of action, but returning to the hospital was the last thing I wanted to do.

We arrived at the emergency department around 7:45 AM, where I was immediately given an IV to receive fluids. After an assessment by the doctor, it was determined that I was experiencing AFib, or atrial fibrillation, a condition that affects the upper chambers of the heart. Essentially, in AFib, the electrical impulses that regulate the heartbeat become disorganized, causing a fast and irregular heart rhythm. This can lead to decreased efficiency in pumping blood to the rest of the body and increases the risk of stroke.

I was given medication to help regulate my heart rate and was told to prepare for the possibility of staying overnight if my heart didn't respond quickly.

As Dr. Reynolds slid open the glass door, he greeted me with a mix of concern and disappointment in his voice, like a parent responding to their child's disobedient antics.

"Lana," he said.

"I know. Trust me, I didn't do this on purpose, and I definitely do not want to stay overnight," I replied. "Please, don't make me."

"We'll do all we can, and hopefully, you won't have to. But before you can go home, we have to get your heart regulated. I'll be back to check on you in a little while. Hang in there."

Naturally, I understood the importance of receiving medical supervision while my heart was racing and out of rhythm. I was also fully aware that I had no control over restoring it to its normal state; the outcome relied solely on my body's response to the medications and treatment.

Glancing around, I couldn't help but feel a sense of familiarity with my surroundings. The room was stark white, the bed was just as uncomfortable as the one in the step-down unit, the beeps of the alarms coming from the monitors hooked to my body echoed the same rhythm, and the scent of the sterilizing chemicals took me back to a place I wanted to leave behind.

Leaning my head back, I closed my eyes and began to pray, "Lord, get me out of here."

Several hours passed before Dr. Reynolds returned to my room. Thankfully, my heart had responded positively to the meds and seemed to be back to normal. "Let's continue monitoring you for a little while longer. If there are no changes, I'll get your release paperwork, and you'll be able to leave."

"Oh, thank goodness," I exclaimed with relief. "Thanks, Dr. Reynolds."

Around 1:00 PM, John and I made our way back to our rental home, where I took the opportunity to rest and recharge for the afternoon.

During my routine transplant follow-up appointment at the clinic the following day, Dr. Reynolds delivered some exciting news. He shared that my recovery at Duke was surpassing all expectations, and I was achieving record-breaking progress. As he shared this news, he presented two X-ray images of my lungs side-by-side: one taken the day before my transplant and one taken earlier this day. I was amazed by the dramatic difference. The pre-transplant X-ray revealed extensive damage, with a hauntingly cloudy appearance signifying a lack of air, in stark contrast to the healthy darkness of the current image. As I stared at the images, I realized just how dire my situation had been. Although I knew my lungs were bad enough to require a transplant, seeing the extent of the damage was sobering. I've since searched for images of other damaged lungs online but have yet to find any that compare to the severity of mine.

Dr. Reynolds attributed my AFib to a potential deficiency in magnesium and slight dehydration. He believed the previously prescribed amount of magnesium was correct, but my body needed time to respond. He also encouraged me to stay hydrated, which I hadn't been doing well because I still struggled to swallow. During my healthy years, I was diligent about drinking a gallon of water a day, so I promised to work on increasing my fluid intake.

As physical therapy went on, I continued to see improvements in my mobility. I could walk faster and longer each day, and my ability to climb stairs had increased from two steps just two weeks earlier to forty. In rehab, I was instructed to use the exercise bike, something I'd never been a fan of. Although pedaling to nowhere seemed monotonous, it was a mandatory part of my routine. So each day, I pushed myself to pedal as long as possible. The therapists also added leg presses, curls, and extensions to my exercise regimen. Being on the workout equipment made me feel excited and eager to return to my career at Snap Fitness with renewed strength and energy. My body was responding to the familiar strain of exercise that I had so often savored over the past years. I was moving and tending to my well-being in a way that aligned with the passion for fitness that the Lord had put on my heart so long ago. I didn't know then that he was preparing me for this experience, but in His abounding grace, he set me on the path that would sustain me before I ever knew that I would need it. And although I still had a long way to go, I could feel my body striving to reclaim the vitality it once had.

My goal was to eat 1800-2000 calories each day to gain weight. I had jumped up to a whopping 93.8 pounds, but that was still twenty pounds less than where I needed to be. After being fed through a tube for seven weeks, reintroducing solid food back into my diet would take a little time. Even though my stomach was still adjusting, my appetite was increasing, and my taste buds were ready to take on the culinary world. Because I had restricted myself to only healthy food (remember that orthorexia thing I mentioned), I hadn't treated myself to pizza in four years. FOUR. WHOLE. YEARS. You can imagine the shock on John's face when I turned to him and asked, "Hey, could we order some pizza from Domino's?"

John was blown away and questioned me, "Did you say you wanted pizza? Are you serious?"

I said, "I'm very serious. I've decided that life is too short to avoid pizza."

And it didn't stop at pizza. We became regulars at a local Mexican restaurant, and I had overcome my fear of having a slice of cake.

Lauren and Mackenzie returned for another visit on the weekend of Lauren's birthday, July 10.

Celebrating special occasions had always been a joy for me, but those celebrations were even sweeter now. And so was the cake!

CHAPTER FORTY-SIX

THE FINAL COUNTDOWN

July 13 - August 5

John and I were settling into a routine. There was a lot to accomplish throughout the day, so having structure made things easier to manage. I had physical therapy every day, and I was determined to reach every goal set in front of me in record time.

There were days that I would push myself too hard. That and the side effects from my medications made me tire quickly. But I didn't let it stop me. Instead, I pushed even harder. I began using my heart rate monitor again during my physical therapy sessions. That device has always given me the desire to go the extra mile. Or in this case, the extra few feet.

Just like milestones had to be accomplished to leave the hospital, there were specific goals to reach to be released from physical therapy. Those goals included walking a mile around the indoor track, using the recumbent stationary bike for twenty minutes at a particular pace, and getting up from the ground without assistance. Slowly but surely, I got closer and closer to each of those goals.

John and I were introduced to my post-transplant coordinator. She would take the reins from my pre-transplant coordinator and be my first point of contact when I needed anything transplant health-related. Her role included organizing all my medication changes, scheduling appointments for post-transplant visits, and answering any questions or concerns John or I might have. Because she was my lifeline, she needed to be someone we trusted completely. John and I recognized what big shoes she'd be filling by following my pre-transplant coordinator, so we were both very prayerful that she'd be a good fit for us. Only time would tell.

On July 16, the staples were removed from my clamshell incision, leaving scars resembling stitching on a baseball. I was finally foreign-object-free, and we began discussing dates that we may be able to return home to Charlotte. Although Dr. Reynolds initially thought we would be in Durham until September or October, he now felt comfortable saying August could be a realistic expectation. He didn't give a specific date, but my ears heard otherwise, and my mind was officially set–I would be home on August 7.

I had my last swallow test on July 17. The good news is I got the green light to drink fluids without needing that thickening gel anymore. However, because I still have a minor case of dysphagia, I will always need to be mindful when I swallow liquids so I don't choke.

The weekends settled into a peaceful rhythm in our temporary Durham home. Then, the moment I had been eagerly awaiting finally arrived–I was granted permission to make a weekend trip back home.

On the precious day of July 23, after what felt like an eternity, I stepped foot into the sanctuary of our home. The sheer joy of being surrounded by familiar sights, sounds, and scents was indescribable. The feeling of sinking into the embrace of my beloved bed was pure bliss. But that wasn't all. I needed some pampering, so I made a beeline for the hair salon. My once-healthy hair had thinned dramatically, but what was left had grown to impressive lengths. As my stylist worked her magic, several inches of my hair tumbled to the floor, rejuvenating my spirit. It was a transformative moment, and my morale soared to new heights.

That same weekend, two months after my transplant, John and I decided to head to Snap Fitness for a workout. It felt amazing to be back in our gym and challenge myself beyond the limits set during physical therapy. As I pushed my body, I realized that I could rebuild it to its former strength with time. It was a moment of empowerment, knowing that I had the potential to regain what I had lost. However, there were days (and still are) when it was hard to come to terms with all that happened to my body. I won't deny that this journey has caused a lot of emotional strain, but I strive to remain faithful, knowing that God's purpose far surpasses my desire to regain the previous version of my body.

Our brief visit home marked the beginning of our countdown to the day we would finally return for good. The following week, I had my first post-discharge bronchoscopy. The doctors sent tiny samples of each lung to the lab, where they were examined under a microscope for about a week. A bronchoscopy aims to identify any abnormalities or signs of rejection and are routine procedures that lung transplant patients undergo regularly. Thankfully, on August 3, I received the results, and everything looked great. My new lungs were healthy and happy.

In addition to the bronchoscopy, I had to undergo a 24-hour test to check the pH balance in my stomach and assess any potential adverse effects caused by the medications. This involved inserting a tube through my nose and into my stomach. I wasn't thrilled about having another "nose hose," but I did it without complaint because it was part of the checklist that had to be completed before being cleared to go home.

As the days passed, our anticipation grew. If everything went as expected, we would soon leave Durham behind and start a new, slightly more challenging life chapter in Wesley Chapel.

CHAPTER FORTY-SEVEN

THE COMFORTS OF HOME

Thursday, August 6

At 3:20 PM, with a surge of joy and pride, I completed my final lap around the physical therapy track. Gathering around me, the rehab team shared in my anticipation. Then, in a moment of pure excitement, I was handed a mallet and directed to strike a gong my therapist held. Its resounding clang echoed through the room, marking the significant moment of my graduation from rehab. Applause erupted, blending with heartfelt congratulations that echoed in the air, celebrating this incredible milestone in my journey.

After saying my final goodbyes to the dedicated team who had supported me throughout my recovery, I walked out of the rehab clinic; my head held high and a sense of accomplishment running through my body. It was a moment I had longed for - the freedom to return home.

Initially, John and I had planned to spend one final night in our rental home, but he made a suggestion that I couldn't decline, "Would you like to go home tonight?"

A smile instantly spread across my face, and without a moment's hesitation, I eagerly replied, "Yes! I would absolutely love that."

In a flurry, we quickly packed our belongings and loaded the car, one day ahead of the goal date I had shared with Dr. Reynolds weeks earlier. As we backed out of the driveway, I couldn't contain my happiness, sending a message and sharing the news of our departure with our family.

5:06 PM

Me: Released and headed back to Wesley Chapel!!!

Ali: Freeeeeeedddddooooooommmmmmmmmmmm!!!!!!!

Jessica: BEST NEWS EVER! Fun fact: we had surprise yard letters being delivered tomorrow, but you one-upped us on the surprise and got released early. We canceled; I didn't think you'd react well to strangers in your front yard at 6:30 AM. So... "WELCOME HOME, LANA!"... please pretend these are giant yard letters.

We caught up with phone calls to my mom, Mackenzie, Lauren, and Ali during our two-and-a-half-hour drive home. I also sent a text message to The Tribe, expressing my excitement to see them all in person. At that moment, life felt wonderfully normal, full of love and connection.

We arrived home at 7:40 PM, greeted by the familiar surroundings we had missed dearly. Mackenzie joined us for a quiet celebratory dinner. Then, we unpacked and settled on our sofa, basking in the comfort of our home.

As we sat side by side, I savored the simple joys that had been absent from my life for over three months. Overwhelmed with gratitude, I realized the profound significance of this opportunity—to be embraced by the warmth of my friends, family, and above all, the precious gift of life itself. And on that evening, I vowed never to take any of it for granted again.

CHAPTER FORTY-EIGHT

NOT ANOTHER ONE

Life after a transplant is more complex than you might imagine. It entails a multitude of doctor appointments, regular blood draws, daily monitoring of vitals, and a hefty medication regimen. The side effects of these potent medications are too many to mention and certainly not a pleasant topic to dwell upon.

Nevertheless, my lungs grew stronger, and my body gradually regained its familiar appearance. I envisioned returning to the gym and resuming my career right where I had left off. However, as the weeks went by, I realized I had a long way to go before being able to endure the demanding hours the job entailed. Moreover, I lacked the physical strength to demonstrate the exercises my clients would need to perform during their training sessions.

Unfortunately, these were not the sole reasons hindering my comeback. The government had implemented a phased reopening plan for non-essential businesses, and gyms fell under the "non-essential" category (don't get me started on how I felt about that). The reopening process demanded significant modifications within the gym to adhere to the imposed restrictions, which would require a substantial amount of our time. Given that my recovery had to be our primary focus, John and I reluctantly decided to sell our gym. On

October 1, 2020, my career as a gym owner officially came to an end as we handed over our keys to new management.

Even though we no longer own a gym, my drive to empower women and enhance their overall well-being hasn't waned. While figuring out how to tackle my physical and mental health, I stumbled upon a newfound passion for coaching women's wellness as a whole package. Motivated by this revelation, I dove headfirst into the realms of mindset, goal setting, and self-care, expanding my knowledge and expertise. Today, I proudly embrace the role of a women's wellness and life coach, equipped with the tools and insights to guide and support women on their own transformative journeys.

But during my career transformation, while discovering what my new coaching role would involve, my body secretly began fighting my precious new lungs. For months, I had witnessed my lung function improving, a promising sign that everything was on track. I even went hiking with Donna and Rosy in the North Carolina mountains, tackled some of my pre-transplant workouts (with necessary modifications, of course), and got genuinely excited about the possibility of scaling back my visits to Duke to just once a year. But then, in April 2021, I couldn't help but notice a slight dip in the readings on my home spirometer (a device used to test lung function). It was a tiny drop, but deep down, I had this gut feeling that something wasn't right.

I immediately reached out to my coordinator. She encouraged me not to panic but to keep a close eye on it, which I did. I watched as my function continued to drop day after day until I returned to Duke for an appointment with Dr. Reynolds on May 26, 2021, the day following the first anniversary of my transplant.

As Dr. Reynolds entered the room, in the same tone as the day I experienced AFib, he wasted no time addressing the issue at hand, "Lana. What's going on? Your PFTs are declining." I immediately sensed a validation of my concerns.

I was scheduled for a routine bronchoscopy later that day. Based on the dramatic drop in my PFTs, rather than expecting to discover no signs of rejection, we hoped the results would return with indications of acute rejection.

You see, acute rejection held the promise of treatment, whereas the absence of it would imply the dreadful presence of chronic rejection.

Let me explain. Chronic rejection is a long-term process that occurs gradually over time. Despite an initially successful transplantation, it is characterized by a progressive decline in organ function. Chronic rejection can develop months or years after the transplant. The exact cause of chronic rejection is not fully understood, but it is thought to involve a complex interplay of immune responses, inflammation, and damage to the transplanted organ. In the context of lung transplantation, chronic rejection is known as chronic lung allograft dysfunction (CLAD). The symptoms of CLAD may include shortness of breath, coughing, wheezing, decreased exercise tolerance, and fatigue. All of which I was experiencing.

Regrettably, it turns out I was indeed dealing with CLAD. Despite numerous attempts to manage my decline through medication, Dr. Reynolds suggested a treatment called extracorporeal photopheresis (ECP). This medical procedure involves extracting my blood, isolating specific components, and subjecting them to ultraviolet A (UVA) light after applying a photosensitizing agent called psoralen.

He explained that the procedure would be carried out twice a week over a minimum of three months. Once my lung function exhibited signs of stabilization, the treatment frequency would be reduced to every other week and eventually scaled down to once a month. Provided my lung capacity remained stable, I would continue receiving monthly treatments indefinitely. However, he emphasized that a second transplant would be necessary if my lungs failed to stabilize.

My heart sank, and tears welled uncontrollably. I had just been through the unimaginable trauma of an unforeseen transplant and was finally beginning to get my life back, and suddenly I may have to do it again. The idea was overwhelming, and I struggled to find words.

Offering the only solace available, Dr. Reynolds reassured me, "I'm truly sorry. We're going to take excellent care of you. Dr. Haney has already agreed to perform the retransplantation if it becomes necessary. And we're both confident you'll do great. But let's see if we can kick this can down the road for a while first."

On the morning of June 14, 2021, a port was surgically inserted in the right side of my chest, and later that afternoon, I began my ECP treatments. It took six months for my lungs to display any response and another six months to show signs of stabilization. Because of the slower-than-usual response time, in October, I underwent an extensive five-day evaluation for a potential second transplant. I won't go into all the details, but I assure you it wasn't an enjoyable experience.

As part of the evaluation, I had a meeting with Dr. Haney. Surprisingly, I had only interacted with him a few times during my stay at Duke. On one of those occasions, he candidly remarked, "You look much better than when I first met you when you were a little swollen marshmallow who was almost dead."

I appreciated his straightforwardness. His honest, direct, but never rude demeanor was refreshing. Sometimes you need to hear the truth without any sugarcoating. And our conversation during the evaluation was no different.

He didn't beat around the bush, saying, "I'll be honest with you. I'm fully prepared and willing to perform a second transplant for you. However, you have an extremely aggressive autoimmune disease. There's no guarantee that you won't find yourself back here within another year for a third transplant, which we will do. I have no doubt that you could handle it, but I wanted to make sure you were aware of the possibility. I also have to tell you a second transplant typically carries more risks than the first. Your case, though, is not typical. Normally, the second transplant bridge is narrower compared to the first. However, when you arrived, you were hanging on the edge of the bridge, and we managed to pull you back. So, you've already experienced most of the risks associated with a second transplant. With that being said, the decision is yours. Nobody would blame or criticize you if you choose not to do it."

I sat silently, absorbing everything Dr. Haney had conveyed while John asked several questions. I listened attentively, contemplating the choices before me.

The room fell silent, then Dr. Haney turned to me, asking, "Do you have any questions, Lana?"

"No, I don't think so," I replied.

"Okay then. Take all the time you need to think it over."

I interjected before he could say anything else, "I don't need to think about it. I'll do whatever it takes to stay alive."

He chuckled, gave me a reassuring pat on the knee, and said, "I wouldn't have expected anything less from you. Just let me know when you've reached your limit and are ready; I'll be there."

The confidence Dr. Haney exudes in his abilities is encouraging. When you're entrusting someone to open your chest and replace your lungs, he's the person you want. He saved my life once, and I have complete trust in him to do it again.

CHAPTER FORTY-NINE

HOTELS AND CHICKEN BISCUITS

Dr. Reynolds had initially anticipated that I would undergo a second transplant by March 2022. However, as it often happens, God had different plans for me.

I'm writing this final chapter on May 25, 2023, my three-year lungaversary. Despite my ongoing chronic rejection, the lungs I received in 2020 are still putting up a good fight.

Shortly after receiving the news of being in chronic rejection, I was introduced to a new transplant coordinator, and I can't express enough how grateful I am for her. From the moment I met her, it felt like we had an instant connection, as if we had known each other for a lifetime. Whenever I reach out to her, she's always there, ready to spring into action. What makes her even more remarkable is that she has personally gone through the journey of a double-lung transplant with her father. This firsthand experience has given her an unparalleled understanding of what both the recipient and their caregiver go through. She has felt the same fears and uncertainties and carries a special compassion for those of us navigating the unpredictable waters of transplantation. Her genuine care and concern for her patients make her an extraordinary human being, and I consider myself incredibly fortunate to have her by my side on this journey.

John and I continue to travel to Duke every four weeks. It took some time to arrange appointments in a way that requires only one night in a hotel, but we managed to figure it out. We leave our house around 10:30 AM on Tuesdays, arriving at Duke before my 1:00 PM PFT appointment in department 2F/2G of the pulmonary department, located at the far end of the hospital. I've often wondered why they make patients with pulmonary issues walk such a distance, but I suppose it's beneficial exercise for the lungs.

Following my PFTs, we go to the Blood Cancer Center for my first round of ECP. The procedure takes approximately two and a half hours and tends to be uneventful. A line gets inserted into the port in my chest, and then we wait. Once the treatment is complete, we head to our hotel for the evening. We leave the hotel the next morning around 8:00 AM to return for my second treatment.

There are a few restrictions I must adhere to during ECP. Firstly, I am not allowed to expose my skin to the sun for at least 48 hours after the treatment, as it becomes highly sensitive to UV rays, significantly increasing the risk of skin cancer. The second restriction is more challenging for me; starting 24 hours before the treatment and throughout the process, I must consume no more than 4g of fat per meal, which means three days without cheese! In my world, that's a significant request. So, as a treat, on our way home each month, John and I stop at Biscuitville to indulge in the most delicious chicken biscuits in the world. And no, I don't feel guilty about it.

In addition to the chicken biscuit, I've also managed to let go of any guilt associated with taco Tuesdays, birthday cakes, or the occasional pizza. As a result, I can confidently say that I have overcome orthorexia.

However, there are still battles I must confront. I'm gradually accepting the changes that have come after my illness. Fewer activities among large crowds, less intense workouts, and more rest, to name a few. Some days are more challenging than others in this regard, but I'm discovering ways to keep life exciting despite all the necessary changes.

I still experience occasional bouts of sorrow. However, with the help of the Lord, I am working through my grief. I also recognize that some of these emotions may be side effects of my medications. And let me assure you that I'm not constantly consumed by sadness; I have many good days and never let a day pass without expressing gratitude to the Lord for every breath I take.

Regrettably, I haven't had the opportunity to meet my donor's family. Six months after my transplant, I wrote them a letter expressing my gratitude and promising to do all I could to care for these precious lungs. Although I held a glimmer of hope for a response, I certainly didn't expect it. I fully comprehend the depth of grief, and I understand that each person navigates it in their own unique way. Initially, I had planned to write a second letter, but when I experienced rejection, I couldn't gather the courage to do so. While I acknowledge that the rejection is beyond my control, I didn't want to disappoint them. I sincerely hope they understand the depth of my eternal gratitude for their extraordinary act of kindness. Their selfless gift has granted me three bonus years and counting.

Knowing how precious life is and how quickly it can end, I've learned to place priority on relationships. Family and friends have taken center stage, surpassing any tasks or obligations on my to-do list. There is nothing in this world more valuable than the time spent with loved ones. We make it a point to come together for as many holidays and birthdays as we can, cherishing these moments of togetherness.

As for The Tribe, we maintain our strong bond through regular lunches and occasional neighborhood walks. These simple yet meaningful activities help us stay connected and nurture our relationships.

To borrow the wise words my dear friend recently shared with me, "If someone holds true significance in our lives, we will always find a way to carve out time for them. When our busy schedules prevent us from finding even a single moment, it speaks volumes about our priorities."

This journey has also served as a poignant reminder that our bodies require our care and attention. I advocated for this before my illness and will continue to do so until my last day on this earth. If I hadn't cared for my body, that last day would have already passed. So, I implore you to be mindful of your spiritual, mental, and physical needs. Our bodies are nothing short of miracles; we must treat them as such.

Lastly, and perhaps most significantly, I encountered the love of God in a way I had never experienced before. While I have known Him since I was 14, my relationship with Him has reached depths that were once unimaginable. I found myself in the presence of Jesus, so near that I could almost reach out and touch Him, and He surpasses all my expectations and more. His love is profound, His plans for us are good, He carries us through the most challenging circumstances, and He will never forsake us. My faith has flourished since my brush with death, and I've finally learned to trust Him completely.

Is my life at the age of 53 what I initially envisioned it to be? No, it's not. However, I have yet to encounter many individuals whose lives have unfolded precisely as they had imagined. There are days when I question, "Why me?" Yet, I'm often reminded we were never guaranteed a smooth journey through life or promised that all our desires would be fulfilled. Regardless, one thing we can be assured of is that if we give our lives to Jesus, He will always be by our side, unwavering in His presence and support no matter what happens. So the answer will always be, "Why not?"

A note my friend Wendy Pope placed
on her praise board, after hearing I had
received my new lungs

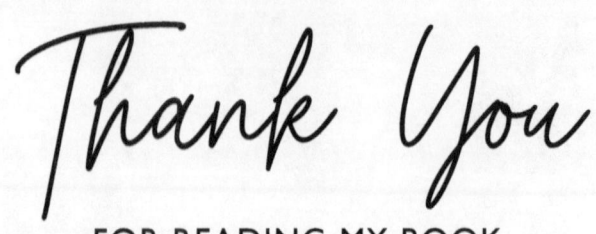

FOR READING MY BOOK

If you enjoyed my story, I'd appreciate your help spreading the word about this memoir on social media or by word of mouth.

I would also be grateful for a review.
Exposure is important, and reviews are extremely helpful.

If you would like an opportunity to invite me to speak at your function, work with me as a coach, or follow my blog, visit my website at:

lanalamkin.com

I love communicating with people!
To contact me directly, my email address is:

lana@livingwellwithlana.com

ALSO BY LANA LAMKIN:

Praise Him Through the Tough Stuff: A 7-day Devotional

FROM THE AUTHOR

Dear Readers,

As I reach the end of my memoir, "Breathing in the Unexpected", I am filled with deep gratitude for each one of you who has embarked on this incredible journey with me. Your investment of time into my story has touched my heart in ways I cannot adequately express. Thank you for walking with me through the trials and triumphs, the tears and the laughter, and for allowing me to share the transformative experience of my double-lung transplant.

Writing this memoir has been a cathartic process, allowing me to revisit moments that were both painful and miraculous. It has given me the opportunity to reflect on the fragility and resilience of the human spirit and the power of hope. But more than that, it has reminded me of the incredible strength we possess when we lean on the Lord during life's most challenging circumstances.

Throughout my journey, my faith has been an anchor, guiding me through the darkest storms. It is my earnest desire that through my story, you too have glimpsed the unwavering support and love that God extends to each one of us. In the face of seemingly insurmountable odds, I hope you have witnessed the profound truth that we are never alone in our struggles.

Life has a remarkable way of surprising us, often when we least expect it. It teaches us to navigate the unexpected, to find solace in the midst of chaos, and to embrace the gift of each new day. While our trials may differ, I am certain that every one of us has faced adversity at some point, and I encourage you to draw strength from your own experiences.

May my memoir serve as a testament to the spirit within each one of us. When obstacles arise, remember that you possess the resilience to overcome them. Have faith in your ability to rise above the challenges, for there is a wellspring of strength deep within you waiting to be tapped. Lean on the Lord, trust in His guidance, and allow His love to carry you through.

For those who may not yet have a personal relationship with the Lord, I humbly encourage you to embrace a path of spiritual exploration and discovery. In the pages of my memoir, I have shared how my faith has been a source of solace, strength, and hope during the most trying times of my life. It is my heartfelt wish that my story serves as an invitation for you to seek a deeper understanding of the Lord and to open your heart to the possibility of a relationship with Jesus. May you find comfort and inspiration in knowing that you are never alone and that there is immeasurable grace awaiting you.

To those who already have a personal relationship with our Savior, my hope is that reading this book has been an opportunity for you to grow your faith deeper and stronger. Life's challenges often test our convictions, and it is during these moments that our relationship with our Father can truly flourish. As you have walked alongside me through the pages of my memoir, I pray that you have found a connection in the experiences and that they have reinforced your trust in God's unwavering love and guidance. May your faith continue to be an unshakable foundation, bringing you peace, strength, and the assurance that you can withstand any trial with the Lord by your side.

I sincerely hope that my words have touched your heart and encouraged you to embrace the unexpected moments in life with renewed hope and unwavering faith. Thank you once again for joining me. Your support and presence have meant more to me than words can convey.

May you always breathe in the unexpected and find beauty in the journey.

With heartfelt gratitude,

Lana Lamkin

Author, Breathing in the Unexpected
Duke Hospital Lung Transplant Recipient #2115 (May 25, 2020)

www.ingramcontent.com/pod-product-compliance
Lightning Source LLC
Chambersburg PA
CBHW030357130626
46549CB00004B/1533